SAVE TOMORROW FOR THE CHILDREN

E. Paul Torrance • Deborah Weiner • Jack H. Presbury • Morgan Henderson

with the assistance of over
5,000 children in 16 countries

bearly limited

Hal English, the cover artist, is a member of the *Pastel Society of America.* He is the recipient of more than ninety awards for his pastel paintings, many from national exhibitions. Represented by eastern, central, and southwestern galleries, his works are hung nationwide.

Copyrights & Permissions

Page 195   From *The Dragons of Eden: Speculations on the Evolution of Human Intelligence* by C. Sagan. Copyright © 1977 by Carl Sagan. All rights reserved. Reprinted by permission of the author.

Contents

Scenarios & Authors

Save Tomorrow For The Children

by Jack Presbury and Morgan Henderson

If today were tomorrow
Then I'd know who I'll be
Finally someone
Would listen to me;
And they'd all see the truth
When I sang out my song
But this time, they'd all sing along . . . .

CHORUS: Save tomorrow for the children
Take good care of today;
Leave this old world
Just as you found it;
We will make our own way.
Just save tomorrow for the children.

I once had a dream
That the sun went away;
People could not tell
The night from the day,
And the earth was a Tin Man
In search of a heart.
Please, stop it, before it can start . . . .

CHORUS . . . .

Will the crystal-clear raindrops
Still fall from on high,
Beckoning roses
To reach for the sky?
Will there still be a place
Where the wild things go free?
Please, tend the garden for me . . . .

CHORUS . . . .

> If today were tomorrow
> Then I'd know who I'll be
> Finally someone
> Would listen to me;
> And they'd all see the truth
> When I sang out my song
> But this time, they'd all sing along . . . .

CHORUS . . . .

CHAPTER ONE

Introduction

Children develop a sense of the future very early. We are convinced that this occurs much earlier than educators have generally thought. In conceptualizing the practical abilities lying within the realm of the "future reaches of creative potential," Torrance and Hall wrote in 1980 (pp. 10-11):

> Another important practical ability that seems to lie within the realm of the further reaches of creative potential is a sense of the future – having a strong, rich, and accurate image of the future. Toffler (1974), Singer (1974), Polak (1971, 1973), and others have contended that images of the future are powerful determinants of behavior, both among individuals and among nations. Polak (1971) believes that creative future thinking involves intuition and fantasy. He maintains that, without fantasy, there is no vision and, without vision, there is no future thinking. We predict that this ability will become increasingly important in years to come.

Thus, when the organizers of the Fifth World Conference on Gifted and Talented Children invited Torrance to conduct and report an international study of the characteristics of gifted children around the world, his immediate reaction was that the most important characteristic delegates to this conference needed to know of gifted and talented children is their image of the future.

During the previous ten years Torrance had experienced considerable success in eliciting images of the future through having children write scenarios of their anticipated careers (Torrance, 1977). So, he thought, "Why not an international scenario writing contest?" It was his desire to involve youth from ages 9 to 18. The announcement of the project states the rationale and the general instructions given the scenario writers:

You are there! You are the hero/heroine! The year 2010!

Have you ever thought about what you want to be doing in the year 2010? What are your dreams? What do you want to achieve?

What do you want to do for your family, your country, the world?

You have such imagination! This is a challenge to it.

The driving force behind your future success is your image of the future – your dreams. A positive image of the future will inspire you, energize you, and give you the courage and determination to move forward to new solutions and achievements. To dream, to plan, to be curious about the future, and to wonder how much you can influence it by your efforts are important aspects of your being human. All of us need a new image of the future, one that is exciting and compelling to the imagination.

Try to express your image of the future through a scenario of not over 1,500 words. Make yourself the hero/heroine of your story. You can write either in the first or third person. The story you are to tell is about what you expect to accomplish by the year 2010 and how you solved the problem and challenges of those years between now and 2010. Then go ahead and describe what else you would like to accomplish in your lifetime.

Why Scenarios?

Even in the adult world scenarios play important roles. The late Herman Kahn, one of our foremost futurists, explained in an interview shortly before his death in 1983 (Reston, 1983), "We draw scenarios and try to cope with history before it happens." Frequently, scenarios attempt to show in dramatic ways what is likely to happen if certain trends continue with no interference.

As a result, action may be taken to avoid the consequences predicted in the scenario. Many businesses, professions, and agencies prepare and are guided by alternative scenarios. We believe that positive images of the future are powerful and magnetic forces. They give us the energy, courage, and will to take important actions. They motivate what we learn and achieve.

Polak (1971) argued that societies have always had to rely upon a creative minority for their images of the future. Barbara Clark (1983), in *Growing up Gifted,* also maintains that throughout history there have been individuals and moments that have brought dramatic change. She also asserts that it is now becoming increasingly evident that such moments are occurring more frequently and that there is a great need for gifted people to bring their vision to these times. The children who wrote scenarios in this international project seem to have this vision and their scenarios express it elegantly.

Edward Cornish (1977) of the World Future society has set forty-nine reasons why it is important to study the future. The scenarios submitted in the International Scenario Writing Project seem to respond to the reasons and make them come alive:

1. Forecast crises so that they may be averted;
2. Assist in deciding the future we want;
3. Prepare us for living in a changing world;
4. Discover a format for working together cooperatively;
5. Contribute to, and further, science and thought;
6. Encourage more creativity;
7. Increase the motivation to learn;
8. Develop a well-balanced and integrated personal value structure and philosophy of life; and
9. Provide a means for recreation and fun.

These are indeed difficult tasks. However, a willingness to attempt difficult tasks comes through as the most persistent characteristic of the heroes and heroines of the scenarios from every country participating in the International Scenario Writing Project. The reader will see this characteristic clearly and artfully portrayed in most scenarios in this book.

The Theme: Save Tomorrow For The Children

The theme of the 5,000 scenarios and that of this book is: *Save Tomorrow For The Children*. After Jack Presbury and Morgan Henderson had read over 300 of the international scenarios and had evaluated, discussed, and thought about them, Torrance suggested they create a song to capture the essence of the scenarios — the message the children of the world are trying to communicate. *Save Tomorrow For The Children* resulted:

> If today were tomorrow
> Then I'd know who I'll be
> Finally someone
> Would listen to me;
> And they'd all see the truth
> When I sang out my song
> But this time, they'd all sing along . . . .

CHORUS: Save tomorrow for the children
> Take good care of today;
> Leave this old world
> Just as you found it;
> We will make our own way.
> Just save tomorrow for the children.

> I once had a dream
> That the sun went away;
> People could not tell
> The night from the day,
> And the earth was a Tin Man
> In search of a heart.
> Please, stop it, before it can start . . . .

CHORUS . . . .

> Will the crystal-clear raindrops
> Still fall from on high,
> Beckoning roses

To reach for the sky?
Will there still be a place
Where the wild things go free?
Please, tend the garden for me . . . .

CHORUS . . . .

Torrance and Weiner each read nearly all the over 5,000 scenarios – many of them dozens of times. Immediately, they sensed that Presbury and Henderson had caught and distilled the essence of the children's message. It is clear that the scenario writers are concerned – yes, worried, even afraid – about many of the things happening in their world – THEIR TOMORROW. They desperately want someone to listen to them. They want to communicate with one another. They want to take responsibility, and they believe they can "make it on their own," if given a chance.

We thus decided to treat the words of the song as hypotheses and the scenarios as the raw data against which these hypotheses can be qualitatively tested. Thus, the main lines of the song become chapter titles and the main contents of the chapters are scenarios selected from the over 5,000 submitted.

CHAPTER TWO

If Today Were Tomorrow, I'd Know Who I'll Be

When Hamlet asserted that the Question was, "to be or not to be," he was probably oversimplifying the situation. The issues of being and becoming are very complex, and children of the world between the ages of 12 and 18 perhaps know this most acutely. These children experience a period of emotional development which Erickson (1950, 1964) characterized as, "the search for identity." The task which the children must face is to answer the question, "Who am I and where do I belong in life?" (Bigner, 1983). Moreover, they must deal with the issue of, "What can I become in the world as I envision it in my adulthood?" In the quest for identity, children come to know themselves and their values, and enter the path that leads to future careers. They must become themselves, separate from others and, at the same time, begin to recognize where they will fit with others and what skills they have to give. They must "free themselves from the expectations of others and play their own game" (Torrance, 1983a).

As children struggle to know who they'll be, they meet resistance from family and friends, who often invite them to stay as they are. They also perceive the world as changing in such a way as to prize conformity over individuality, inaction over action. To successfully complete this developmental task, the children must remain hopeful and believe in themselves. However, even such optimistic an adult as Rollo May (1969) has suggested that:

> *Studies have shown that the persons who survive most effectively in space ships, and who can adjust to the sensory deprivation necessary for such a life – <u>our comrades of the twenty-first century</u> (ruling ours) – are those who can detach and withdraw into themselves (p.33).*

Many fear that such detachment could lead to apathy and the withdrawal of will and love.

In scenario writing, the children can practice seeing themselves as fully grown and influential in a world made better by their contributions. The scenarios of the world's children do not show signs of apathy. They do show evidence that the children are eager to understand their own development, and that they believe the world can become a place where diversity is respected and individual talents prized as useful for improving the human condition.

The scenarios which follow display a vivid picture of children with an already good sense of who they are and an eager longing to know who they'll be.

– The Reunion –

Peter Carl (Age 15)
Newton High School, Newton, IA, USA

Everyone climb up on my lap, and I'll tell you a story about the old times in our family. Everyone settled? Good! Well, the first real family reunion we ever had was back in '67. At that time the family was pretty well scattered over the universe. My grandfather, Arthur Carl, had turned 100 that year and decided it was high time to call the brood together.

Grandfather had three good-looking red headed girls who were all married to hardworking, rugged individualists. Each son-in-law was convinced that he had found the way to live the perfect life. And since they all had completely different life styles, when they got together there was enough fussing and bickering to wake up the entire East Coast City – so it had been a while since they had seen each other.

. . . What's that? You want to know about Grandfather . . . Well he was a strong, shrewd farmer, and he owned 3,000 hectares of rich black land in the middle of the state of Heartland. He was so old he could remember when there had been 50 states in the Union instead of six . . . Yes, I know we have seven now, but that's another story.

Grandfather's land was 57 kilometers east of Des Moines City, and almost all of it was planted in sunflowers. It was out of character, for he was not a sentimental man, but he still raised 5 hectares of corn just for old time's sake.

Well, he farmed all that land alone, although he did have a good many computer-operated robots that did the actual work. He had a guaranteed harvest contract with the Food Division of Pepsi-Cola International, and I think he was pretty well-to-do. So he sent money to the daughters to bring their families back to Heartland for a reunion . . . but I'm getting ahead of the story . . .

Grandfather lived by himself in the house that his father, John, had built before him. He'd seen many changes – the little towns bulldozed to make more farmland, and the inhabitants scattered to the industrial states, Great York along the east coast, or Dixie or Pacifica. His nearest neighbors lived six kilometers to the north which didn't bother Grandfather in the least. He had everything he needed, and his '65 Ford Copter could easily make the Des Moines landing pad in eight minutes.

Don't think he was old fashioned! True, he lived in kind of an archaic old house that still had solar panels for heating and cooling, and his television had only a 49-inch screen, but he was about as up and coming a modern man for his time as you could find.

. . . Well, to get back to the reunion . . . after Grandfather sent the ticket money, the families all agreed to come and decided that Christmas would be as good a time as any to meet. The daughter from Great York thought the families should meet on neutral ground – suggested the Outer-Mongolian Marriott but was overruled by the other two girls who really wanted to come back to the old homestead.

The oldest daughter was Lisa, and she was married to a naturalist named Walter Kieth . . . . You don't know about naturalists? Well, long ago, even before the beginning of the twenty-first century, there were some Americans who believed nuclear war was inevitable, and so they moved to isolated wild areas of the country where they hoped they would be safe. They called themselves survivalists and they believed in complete self-sufficiency, including guns. Well, the nuclear war never came, but the survivalists found their way of living very satisfactory, and so they and their descendants remained in the wild areas, except they started to call themselves naturalists and they forgot about needing guns – except to kill a wild animal now and then.

Lisa and her husband were typical naturalists. They lived on 18 hectares of woody, wild land in the Ozark hills. Ozark was sandwiched between the great states of Heartland and Dixie and was a protectorate of the federal government because of all the different species of plants and animals that grew naturally there. The inhabitants of Ozark always refused any government aid and had as little to do with the outside as possible. Once in a while a bold tourist from Dixie would detach his vehicle from the cable interstateway and manually drive along the rock trails of Ozark, but the naturalists tended to keep their distance even from friendly tourists.

As I said, the Kieths were typical. They all worked hard, mostly just to get their food – they grew it, they caught it, and they preserved it – they even built their own electric generator. And, true to form, on the day of the reunion, they came puffing to Grandfather's place in a steam-powered car that Walter Kieth had made himself. It was wood-fueled and altogether pretty strange – but it got them there. Half a dozen red haired children were crowded in the car. The oldest was a boy named Carl (after Grandfather) but nicknamed Carli. The other five were younger and all girls. Never mind their names – they were look-alike stairsteps – rosy cheeked, robust, happy little kids. This was their first trip out of the hills in six years, and they were excited!

Next a long black town car drove quietly up the long lane to the house. It was Leni and her husband. They were from Great York, the megalopolis state that stretched from the north Atlantic coast 1,792 kilometers to the south. Great York, even then, was the cosmopolitan and cultural vanguard of the States – and Leni's husband, a computer crime specialist, never let anyone forget it.

The car doors slid open, and their son Carl, also named after Grandfather, was first to get out. He cautiously shook hands with the naturalist relatives and looked rather blankly at the kilometer after kilometer of empty brown fields that surrounded Grandfather's house. Grandfather liked Carl; he enjoyed his conversation, but privately thought Carl was overly timid and not a very helpful boy because he didn't seem to understand how the most basic of things worked. It wasn't a matter of intelligence – it was just that the boy had been brought up with total conveniences which made him seem a little stupid in any ambience away from the city.

They all watched as a Blue Taxi-copter made a noisy landing on Grandfather's pad port. It was Jennifer, her husband, and their teenage son – the family that had left Earth sixteen years before to pioneer a mining colony on the moon. Three thin, tall dignified people climbed stiffly out of the taxi. They walked cautiously on the rough ground, and, though they had purchased quantities of winter clothing at the spaceport in Des Moines, they shivered in the sharp December air.

Their son, so often lovingly described in letters sent from the colony, was also named after Grandfather, but his parents always called him Carleton. Life was still stark and plain on the moon, and consequently, colonists tended to call people and things by fanciful names – they were big on poetry and words in general.

The boy, Carleton, looked joyously around him, then lifted out the luggage, set it down, snapped his fingers in a strange little rhythm, and the luggage cheerfully lumbered toward the front door. Grandfather swooped Jennifer and Carleton in his arms – shook hands with his son-in-law and hustled everyone toward the back door and into the house. Everyone hugged and kissed everyone else.

. . . What's that? Oh, you want to know about dinner . . . . Well, Grandfather, like most people back then, hardly ever cooked. And so he had bought the "Extra-Deluxe Christmas Dinner Kit for Fifteen, Plus Leftovers – PRAIRIE HERITAGE STYLE" with two kinds of red meat and 19 side dishes. Personally, he would have preferred "Chinese," but he thought his daughters would expect traditional fare, and he was right. The daughters were very pleased with the kit and immediately got busy with it – heating some of it – cooling other parts, cutting it, and making all kinds of approving bustling noises.

The sons-in-law, after trading perfunctory remarks about their occupations, settled down in front of the old television set to watch the International Football playoffs.

As cousins often do, the children stared somewhat suspiciously at each other. Copying their fathers, they traded a little information about schools. The naturalist children said they studied reading, arithmetic, agriculture, and social studies in a one-room school four miles from home – but most of their education happened right at home. By the time they were six, they understood the specifics of the electric generator, how to nurse a sick horse, how to plant, to harvest, to hunt, and on and on.

Carl, the Great York relative, did not actually go to school. His parents subscribed to a private educational computer service which he worked with every morning, studying mathematics, law and citizenship, and word processing. In the afternoons, like most urban young people, he took private lessons – ballet, painting, martial arts, computer tech., and parenting.

Carleton's moon school had afternoon classes which emphasized literature, math and particularly earth history for the colonists did not want to forget their heritage. In the mornings, Carleton worked in the apprentice program. Although he hoped to become a mining engineer he had to qualify first as a maintenance trainee.

Carl couldn't imagine anyone as young as Carleton actually having an apprentice job – but Carleton said the job was very real, and also very hard – and that he often worried about making a mistake that would cost a life and mean that he might be sent away from the colony forever.

Carl was appalled that any society would put so much responsibility on a student and decided he didn't want to hear any more about Carleton's strange education.

Carleton was oblivious to his cousin's disinterest – he was far too busy examining his surroundings. Wood furniture – none of it automated – and STEPS going to the upper level of the house! Carleton thought steps must be quite fun and wondered why there were none on the colony.

The daughters called "DINNERTIME!" and the family gathered around the table, but were interrupted by a steady knocking, bumping sound outside. Grandfather opened the front door and found the luggage futilely attempting to climb the front steps. He picked up the struggling luggage and carried it inside. A little embarrassed, Carleton took the luggage from Grandfather – snapped his fingers in the odd little rhythm to stop it, and then happily carried it up the staircase; he had been hoping for a reason to climb those steps!

The "Extra Deluxe Prairie Heritage Christmas Dinner" was everything it promised to be. The table overflowed, and the daughters were glad they had put their own contributions away until later. The mother of the family from Ozark had a momentary qualm about the nasty preservatives and additives that were undoubtedly lurking in the food, but shrugged and thought, "Well, it's only for one day . . . . "

It was a meal that met all of the adults' childhood recollections of what a Christmas feast should be! The children, mostly disliked almost everything and wished for more familiar food. Adults and children conversed genteely throughout the meal. Grandfather said that it was a very proper party, but privately he wished they would all relax.

After the table was cleared, everyone settled around the little pine tree that the naturalists had brought. The tree was decorated with baubles proclaiming the year in which they were acquired – the oldest dated 1982. Grandfather had asked everyone to wrap their presents in paper, and so the tree and the packages looked very traditional.

The children eagerly opened their presents, but then a murmur of dismay was heard about the room. Each child had given what he liked best to the others. Carl gave immense semi-automated scio-rockstar posters. Carli and his sisters presented everyone with the finest pocket knives that could be found, and Carleton's gifts were micro chips which analyzed the landscape of the moon.

Well sir, everybody just sat there feeling (to use an old twentieth century word) BLAH which meant they were about as cheerful as a medium sized black hole. But, Grandfather came to the rescue! He said the presents were magnificent, and that the true spirit of Christmas was to give what you would most like yourself to someone else – but, in this family, that just didn't work, so each person was to keep the presents he had brought.

So Carl returned Carli's knife with relief, for knives were illegal in the city, and he retrieved his animated posters with delight. Carli happily fondled the best knife in the world, and Carleton contentedly held his computer chips describing the topography of the moon. Then Grandfather gave little platinum pins in the shape of the sunflowers to the children and credit slips to the adults.

At two o'clock a wet sparkling snow began to fall, and all of the children piled on the warmest clothes they could find and headed outside. Carleton reveled in the snow, scooping up handfuls and forming it into balls. Carli, mistaking his intentions, immediately made a very firm snowball and hurled it at Carleton who was knocked flat in the snow. Carl, although he didn't much like Carleton, thought Carli was being deliberately mean and retaliated with an even bigger snowball which hit Carli in the nose. At this point the two youngest girls grabbed Carl by each ankle and he went down in a snowbank – face first!

Carl's mother seeing this from the window, dashed coatless from the house, and emphatically told Carli what she thought of his behavior. At this point, all the mothers got into it. Fortunately, Grandfather interceded, herding the grownups back to the house and leaving the children to settle things for themselves. Whereupon Carl abjectly apologized to Carli for his mother's weird behavior, explaining that his parents were up for parent license renewal in January, and that every two years when it was renewal time, his parents always acted peculiar for fear he'd catch a cold or get a bruise and then the license authorities would not approve them as parents. Carli had never heard of parent licenses, but he understood that mothers sometimes do some pretty strange things and so he wasn't upset at all.

Meanwhile Carleton was just enjoying floundering in the snow where he had fallen. He spent a few minutes practicing the art of snowball manufacture and thought he had the hang of it. He suggested that they have a snow battle, and they did. A marvelous, sticky, wet, cold snowball fight! And then they built a fort. And had another battle! And then they made a snow person and another and another. A glorious afternoon!

When it started to get dark, Grandfather waved all his snowy grandchildren back into the house. The grownups were settled happily around the old fireplace. Grandfather had a good fire going with pressed sunflower stalks. And suddenly there was *everything* to talk about – the old times, funny things the daughters had done when they were children, politics, the weather, high prices, space ghosts – hopes and fears and dreams.

The daughters produced the food they had held back from the opulent dinner. There was honey from Ozark wild bees, drizzled on home-baked wheat bread; strawberries as big as baseballs, grown in the hydroponic gardens of the moon; and, from the city, red plastic liters of Cokes and a giant size Hostess Twinkie big enough for 20 people which Carli was allowed to cut with his wonderful knife.

And as the orange flames of the sunflower fire died down, we sang an old song, " . . . all is calm, all is bright . . . . " It was truly Christmas.

. . . And that, little ones, is the story of our first real family reunion . . . . Oh, you want to know what happened to the children . . . .

Well, the little girls grew up to be striking red-headed ladies – just as headstrong as their mother and aunts. They left the Ozark country one by one as soon as they were 18 and headed for Washington. They all went into politics, and some people say they were responsible for getting the old ERA Amendment finally ratified. Eventually the youngest girl retired to Grandfather Carl's farm. She lives there now and raises 2,995 hectares of teocinte, and, just for old time's sake, five hectares of sunflowers.

Carl, the boy from Great York, visited Carleton up on the moon colony. He fell in love with the landscape and the certainty of life up there – became a mining engineer and lives there yet in his own bubble – covered crater.

After the reunion, Carli returned to Ozark and spent years trying to build a steam-powered copter. But, he never got it off the ground. Finally he gave up, went to college, played football, and eventually became one of the biggest advertising experts in Great York – famous for his natural approach to media sales.

And Carleton, well, you probably guessed that I'm Carleton. In a way my life stayed in the same direction. I did become a mining engineer, but I did not stay on the moon colony. I was always fond of water, and it was mighty scarce on the moon, so I was a natural for pioneering this underwater colony here in the Indian Ocean. And, yes, I know you've always wondered why I have the only split-level compartment in the colony . . . although I am not a sentimental man, it is because of old Grandfather Carl's stairway.

. . . And, that, dear children, brings us up-to-date and to the end of this story. Now, if you will all get off my knee, I will venture up the kitchen steps and see how our octopus fricassee is coming.

– Newsdate 2010 –

Barbara Ellen Petzen (Age 17)
East Coweta High School, Senoia, GA, USA

I couldn't sleep. Even the Magic Fingers on the hotel bed only seemed to taughten my jangled nerves instead of soothing them. Braving the chill air of the room, I threw aside the thermo-blanket and padded across the plush gray carpet to my newscase. I studied the thick briefing manual for awhile, making some oral notes on my voice recorder. Finally I gave up with a sigh. It was no use – my mind wasn't on my work.

I walked out onto the glass-enclosed balcony and flipped the switch to activate the NatureSeem, choosing "Wild Meadow" incense and birdsong. I lay on my back and gazed at the tiny pin-pricks of light immeasurably distant, nearly obscured by the haze. And I dreamed, dreamed of soaring among those stars, drifting euphorically in the heavens.

I awoke to the sweet sound of birdsong and stretched luxuri-ously . . . and gasped at the breathtaking crimson-orange of the sunrise. Brilliant streaks of warm rose colored the sky, setting fire to scattered clouds of violet flame. A single gull cast a black silhouette against the rising blood-red orb, mirrored in the glassy incarnadine ocean.

My reverie was interrupted by the insistent clamor of the alarm clock. "Please get up. It's six thirty-two, please awaken. You're going to be late again. Come on now, up and at 'em, the early bird gets – " Slightly irritated, I switched the clock off and stepped into the shower with a last, longing glance at the sunrise. The next one I saw would be very different.

The perfuming spray served to alert my fuzzy senses and I emerged fresh and eager for the day's extraordinary events. I pulled on a brightly colored papercloth coversuit and quickly dusted my face with the fashionable mica-sheen. Pleased with my appearance in the mirror, I gathered my equipment and ran down to the monorail terminal outside the hotel's red-mirrored entrance, surprising passersby with an excited grin as I settled in my seat. One young man returned my smile; the rest hurried back to their morning *World Times* videocasts. How could they know where this day would take them?

My euphoria swiftly bottomed out as I stepped out at Space Bay Six. At the end of the runway, Venture IV crouched like a panther ready to spring upward into orbit. I searched the sky, but there was no far-off gleam against the robin's-egg blue to indicate her destination – the orbiting lab-colony Utopia.

A growing disbelief mingled with my gnawing apprehension. Could it really be that I, who watched the first shuttle launched in my teens, was to be one of the first passengers to ride into space to the first supra-terrestrial colony? I mentally shook myself and resolutely shouldered my newscase, following the squaking metallic summons to the briefing room.

After several last minute orientations, the press corps was finally escorted to the waiting ship. We'd already affectionately dubbed ourselves the Space Cadets, and we joked nervously about "tourist class – already!" as we trudged behind the sleek limousines bearing the United World Council dignitaries. Finally we were on the ship itself, safely triple-buckled in super-padded seats. Dozens of news cameras a safe distance from the blast-off zone scanned the ports. I smiled and waved impishly before imitating the other press members, all busily recording the scene on hand-held audio-video-corders.

It seemed only a few minutes before the warning lights came on. The cabin lights dimmed, and as the huge engines ignited, I could have sworn I heard my heart thudding above the thundering roar.

The Venture lurched as the whine grew to a high-pitched scream. My facial muscles were pulled painfully downward and I bit my lip and closed my eyes, hands clutching the edge of the seat. When I gathered the courage to open my eyes, the earth was already far below. My gasp joined a chorus of ooh's and aah's. The pushy, super-macho anchorman in the next seat, however, looked slightly green. "Serves the chauvinist right!" I thought vindictively before my attention was drawn back to the window.

The earth spread below us in panoramic splendor.

Face pressed against the glass, I peered at the unfolding scene. "There! There on the northern end of the American isthmus, I was born. And moved," my fingers tracing a line across a thick glass and the distant turquoise Atlantic to a tiny island, "there, to Suffolk. And then back to the States, to Florida and then Georgia." My mind slipped back over the intervening years to pick up the thread of my youth. Leaving high school at a frustrated 17, I'd fled to New York, now a great megalopolis whose lights were just visible (even from here!) as they glided into the twilight zone between day and night. There, through luck and persistence, I'd acquired an internship at the *Times,* working through college. Graduating with a double major in journalism and psychology, I left the States to see the world before I settled down to my career – and there Dame Fortune smiled on me. Riding back to my motel after a London play, I saw a headline in a cast-off newssheet about a new world-wide news organization–WorldComm Enterprises. I was at the offices at promptly nine o'clock the next morning and joined the staff.

The next years flew by. WorldComm expanded and my assignments grew more complex and carried more responsibility.

Then, in 1993, disaster struck. The United Nations Building was bombed, obliterating blocks of Metropolitan New York. Shock waves stunned the world. Accusations flew, escalating into threats of annihilation. Unstable governments toppled, and the U.S., Soviet Union, and many other countries maintained military alert. Months dragged by, the tension exacerbated by international power play and the mysterious destruction of historic monuments world-wide. Then, in November of 1994, the unspeakable occurred. In panic, one of the superpowers fired a small nuclear missile. The drive mechanism miraculously failed and the deadly warhead fell into the Pacific, contaminating hundreds of square miles of water.

The people of the world stopped dead in their tracks and there arose from the silence a unanimous public clamor for a new world accord. The relocated United Nations suddenly became the focus of world attention and hope and it took new powers, new goals, and new authority along with a new name – United World Council. The American Peace Corps was adopted by the Council and expanded into a combination police and service force.

Throughout this shakeup and reforming of the world's political, economic, and social jigsaw puzzle, the Council channeled all their efforts into using the earth's resources wisely, repairing damage, and scientific research; and I traveled the globe, reporting on various aspects of the world situation and how they affected the earth as a whole. I audio-video-recorded stories on the use of the polar regions as huge ice-boxes for emergency food and on the subsequent colonization of both northern and southern regions to relieve overcrowding and famine in Asia, actually living in Arctic Colony Ptarmigan for six months with the colonists.

I earned a master's degree in oceanography to report on the progress of the sea mining and farming efforts. Huge beds of kelp were cultivated on the continental shelves, both for human consumption and for "grazing grounds" for the huge fish farms. Scientific progress grew at a phenomenal rate — greater even than that of the industrial revolution of the early twentieth century. Endangered species were carefully protected and natural resources were used with maximum efficiency and replaced where possible. New energy sources were explored and exploited. Advances were made so quickly it was difficult to keep up. That's where my job came in. The world was changing before our eyes, and as a reporter I was at the threshold of it all, reporting to the world's ever-lasting masses the triumphs and setbacks of society.

It was a thrilling feeling. Each morning I awoke excited, eager to begin the day's work. I felt that as a newsperson I had a heavy obligation to be sure that my stories were accurate, thorough and easily understandable so that everyone could know how their world was changing.

Nor in this time of scientific achievement was culture neglected. Nations had not lost their identities when the Council came to power, and patriotism was channelled into pride in heritage rather than hostility — for the most part. There were, of course, exceptions, because it was impossible to erase centuries of prejudice and hatred in a few astounding decades.

Public education became universal and progressive. The arts were encouraged and greatly respected and huge CultureFests were held annually. Infant international trade guilds sprang up, equalizing standards and promoting advancement.

In 2004, I published a book, *The New Renaissance,* written largely in journal form during plane flights and travel between assignments. In it, I outlined society's progress since the disaster and analyzed the events and situations leading up to it. In one chapter, I tried to extrapolate what would have happened had not the disaster occurred; if civilization had continued its headlong course of war, prejudice, and overpopulation. Finally, I wrote of the future, even predicting the success of the project I was now a part of.

I compared humankind to a single man: I traced our progress through our mysterious birth a million years ago, our long, complex childhood, and a trying, tantrum-filled adolescence. "And now," I wrote, "Now we've passed the test. We've grown up. There will be more problems, maybe bigger ones that will make our petty wars look like schoolchild spats. But we've done all right so far – and the new dawn is rosy, bright, and promising," I concluded.

The New Renaissance was a best-seller, and I was surprised and pleased by its success. I've been asked whether I'll write another book. It's a distinct possibility, but for now I'll keep reporting.

That announcement that the Venture was docking with Utopia brought me abruptly out of my reverie. Excitement coursed through my veins like electric-hot blood. Of all the stories I've covered – all the events that have made billions tremble, laugh, marvel, and cry – this could be the most momentuous. It was definitely the most thrilling personally.

I pushed my way into the aisle with the others, watching the huge air-lock door. Beyond was the processing bay of the orbiting colony. My voice shook as I described the atmosphere into my audio-video-recorder. "Here I stand, on the threshold of the first permanent, self-sufficient colony in space; on the threshold of the last and greatest frontier for human pioneers." The doors *whissssed* open. Wryly, I thought, "One small step for me, a giant step for mankind," took a deep breath, and stepped firmly into the bay of the Utopia.

– The Year 2010 –

Chantal Botha (Age 12)
Ellerton Primary School, Three Anchors Bay, RSA

I woke up with a start one early morning at the sound of my computer alarm clock, already busy making me my usual cup of coffee. At first I didn't know where I was, but I came to reality with a click remembering it was the year 2010. I propped my head against the pillows which were supported by the perspex headboard. I pondered over the dream I had during the night. When I dreamed it, it all made sense but as I thought about it, it seemed as if my mind was running haywire! One thing I was able to make out was that my dream was in the year 1982. 1982! It came to me as a shock. Twenty-eight years ago seemed like a lifetime. Had it really been so long ago? I reflected my thoughts back to that year. Everything seemed so different compared to now. It wasn't so modern then. You had to do everything yourself. OKAY! There were computers but not a fraction as many as today. In those days, cars needed petrol, there was a very different way of educating young citizens, always political affairs for the headlines, we read our news on paper sheets then and worst of all, there were riots and wars, all because of the racist and nationalistic feelings.

I smiled as I looked at my husband with pride. He was sound asleep, silk sheets covered right up to his chin. I was so proud of his ingenuity, being able to invent computers and robots useful in our everyday life. My mind switched to my teenage children, Shelley, who was 14 and just beginning her puberty, and Gary, who was 17. They were always jostling for the privilege of doing more than their share of organizing the household computers.

I pushed back the bedclothes and swung my legs out of bed, ready to start a new day. I programmed a breakfast on the "MEALS" computer. While that computer was busy, I studied the daily news events, global and local on another computer. It was all so simple, all I did was press the news button. The computer keeps a running record of date, tides, weather conditions, in any case. This whole procedure of absorbing the day's events took about five minutes. The best thing about it was that after we had requested printouts of special articles we wanted to store, we just put them in a computer which reduced the pieces of paper down to tiny photographic plates and if we wanted to read them again or find information, we just programmed it back to a readable size.

The sounder went off, meaning the breakfast was ready. I switched it off quickly, then pressed the buzzer which sounded in my kids' and Roy's rooms. Useful things, I thought, as I heard running staccato steps on the spiral, carpeted staircase. Roy sat down to have his breakfast but Shelley and Gary just grabbed a sandwich, yelled goodbye and were off to their clubs and centres which is the education system. School, in those days was where we had to learn and work hard. I remembered studying feverishly, the day before an exam, trying hard to memorize everything. Math was my worst. I could never remember how to do the different forms of percentages or ratios. The EDUCATION SYSTEM now is more fun and interesting for youngsters. For instance, if you wanted to do modern dancing on a specific number of days, you would alternate practical work with research. The same applies to rollerskating or any other interest. There are many clubs as well as choir, religious clubs, photography, dance, exercise, meditation, swimming, etc. If you wanted to you could do an academic course and quite a few people do, so my daughter, Shelley told me.

After breakfast and programming several computers and robots, I did my usual morning "ritual," meditating and relaxing with plants and exercises. I always looked forward to these little sessions of mine and I was grateful to the tribes whose ancient lifestyles had given us the knowledge of lots of different and rare plants, none of which science had yet discovered. Scientists took great care to propagate them. They have been on the market for about two years now and are "naturally" in great demand. There are so many kinds – some just for their beauty; some plants from which wisdom and knowledge can be obtained from older, wiser people when inhaled; for health; for peace; plants which soothe one if unhappy or upset; ones for keeping awake and alert and there are those which put one into a dream world. I sat down in a comfortable position, closed my eyes and just took quite deep breaths. After that I felt so much better, more peaceful and quite jovial. I looked around in admiration at my greenhouse, which was a sort of a meditation and relaxation room as well. I always took a great deal of pride and care in my plants, giving them a lot of attention when needed. I knew full well what would happen if I neglected them. I knew that without those plants, all the misery and unhappiness would be "planted" inside the world and root their way into our souls again.

Curiosity got the better of me so I took our electric car for a pleasure cruise to see how the things have changed since my teenage days. It was, of course, complete with computers, programmed to transmit only helpful, courteous communications. For instance, to warn people who aren't aware of the danger ahead, or to tell them if an old or handicapped person is about to cross a street or if an accident has just occurred nearby, the ambulance and hospital can be contacted via the computer telephone in the car. I compared them to my dream of the previous night. Everybody was friendly and there was a peaceful atmosphere.

There was no pollution around, no smoke pouring out of chimneys. I thought of the good solution we had invented for these two problems. For the pollution, computers were invented with large, plastic bags. All you have to do is put the rubbish inside, where each type of recyclable material is sorted out and reduced to pulp or grain by a shredder or a grinder machine. These are deposited in homes as well as in streets. If anyone litters, he has to pay an astronomical fine. All the food is distributed according to need. Every day a computerized buggy comes around to collect unwanted food for the poorer section of the globe by jet. It's not the cost of redistribution that is important but that no one is hungry. Now that there is no greed or war, everybody helps each other and not one bit of food is wasted.

The other problem was the hatred and the jealousy that went on between the blacks, whites, and coloureds. The president of South Africa was assassinated in 1988, as well as other presidents who thought whites superior to blacks. New presidents had been elected. They were so different from the former presidents. Instead of leaving problems to become worse, they all got together with the new governments and they discussed and experimented with solutions until they found the right one for everybody, especially the mass of black population. For instance, a better education, therefore more schools, more books and teachers, better living conditions, and more homes. All the new presidents believed in equal rights and they demanded it too.

I looked around at the buildings and the flats which stretched up high into the clouds. Tall and modern looking, all of the windows are tinted glass with aluminum frames. The houses are in bubble shapes and are made of perspex bricks with tinted glass in the shape of portholes. Lots of palm trees and exotic plants surround these BUBBLE houses making it seem tropical and modern at the same time. The flats are like condominiums with a cinema, a library stacked with lots of books for those who still wish to handle information and literature, a swimming pool with cubicles, a gym to do exercises as well as relaxation and meditation rooms. There is also a restaurant if you don't want to cook your own food. If you are bored there is also handcraft and many other kinds of activities. The flats are also made of perspex bricks with tinted glass windows and balconies for safety use. Driving leisurely past the shop windows, I noted how the fashions had changed since the 1980s. The fashion is now more elegant and sophisticated. The material is different too. Plant material is the in-thing for the time being as well as pure silk and silver plastic, which people enjoy wearing when going on a Space journey, to Space HOTELS or Space Restaurants. That is where people go on holidays or to dine "up and out." To get into space, one can either hire a Space Buggy or go on the space ships or Space Shuttle. I remembered that in my younger days aeroplanes, trains, or ships were used to get to a faraway place at a very expensive price too. It's amazing, I thought to myself, here we are in the present time but how many more such radical changes will take place in the future?

CHAPTER THREE

Would Someone Please Listen To Me

The theme of this chapter is the anguish experienced by those who believe they foresee tragedy in the future, but feel powerless to make themselves heard. Like the Trojan prophetess Cassandra, the characters in these stories are visionaries: They see that Man's self-serving ways are leading the world toward annihilation, and each experiences the loneliness of being a single voice crying unheard in a technological wilderness. They know the pain of trying to warn the world to change, and of being rejected, labelled, or punished. This, of course, has often been the fate of gifted young people who are ahead of their times.

As adults, we like to think of the development of a person as hierarchical; older is wiser. We say to the teenager who protests, "I used to be idealistic, just like you; but when you get to be my age, you'll see it's not so important." We like to think of ourselves as more sophisticated than adolescents, and alas, this may be true. The dictionary defines "sophistication" as, "adulteration, the act or art of quibbling" (Webster, 1978). Indeed, we adults sometimes are reduced to tired quibbling, because we feel powerless to change things. We have been proved wrong often enough to realize how much we do not know. We feel overwhelmed by the logic of both sides of every argument, and sink into a swamp of confusion and ambiguity. Adolescents, on the other hand, live in a black-and-white world of right and wrong, good and evil. A teenager has not yet perfected logical argument, and thus relies on intuition and feeling as the basis for judgment.

Adolescents can energize the world, pushing us to make decisions, take action, and change our ways before it is too late.

But, children have great difficulty getting adults to listen to them and take their proposed solutions seriously. Torrance

(1963, 1965) has for many years identified this as one of the most serious deterrents to the development of creative thinking abilities in children, and to their willingness to use creative thinking skills in solving problems. In workshops developed for teachers between 1958 and 1962, a central theme was: "Be respectful of the unusual ideas and questions of children."

Children are rarely granted a listening audience. As this book was being assembled, two exceptions appeared in the news, and the public reactions to both of them were interesting.

On August 23, 1983, *The Atlanta Constitution* featured a story about Ariela Gross, the 1983 Presidential Scholar from Princeton, New Jersey, who dared to speak out in favor of a nuclear freeze. The Director of the Commission on Presidential Scholars warned her mother that, should Ms. Gross speak out, she could have "her name marred as a radical," and her $1,000 scholarship revoked. Although many of her fellow scholars apparently agreed with her, only 14 of them were willing to sign a petition against nuclear arms. One of them told her, "Don't you understand, as Presidential Scholars, we give up some of our rights?"

The second news item concerned Samantha Smith, an 11-year old Maine girl who wrote Soviet leader Yuri Andropov about her concern over a nuclear war between the United States and Russia. Andropov invited her to visit Russia as his guest. When she talked to the U.S. press about her favorable impressions of the Russian people, a typical reaction was, "But, remember, it all boils down to the fact that Samantha Smith is still just an 11-year-old girl."

Many of the problems concerning the young scenario writers are essentially the same problems that are cited in *Global 2000* (1980), a report commissioned by President Jimmy Carter during his last year in office. James J. Kilpatrick, in an article in *Nation's Business* (February, 1981), commented on the lack of attention given to this important report. While Kilpatrick admits it is a gloom-and-doom report, he feels it is not without hope. The message of the report, he points out, is that impending catastrophe may indeed be averted – or at least minimized – if sensible policies are initiated now. Kilpatrick sees as necessary to avoid catastrophe the very things our scenario writers promise they will invent, discover, or initiate, if given a voice.

– Noah II –

Clint Bryan (Age 15)
Newton High School, Newton, IA, USA

Suddenly the room was filled with light, as if a hundred suns were rising. Noah, watching from the window, saw the mushroom cloud rise into the sky. On the ground there was chaos – women screaming in the streets – naked, charred children – grown men fighting for entrance to the tiny fallout shelters. And out of the dust and rubble and horror boomed a voice, "NOAH, NOAH!"

. . . "No-ah, wake up," his wife, Marian, scolded. "You're going to be late again for work – honestly, Noah, I don't see how you can just lie in bed in the morning!"

Noah Watson sleepily opened an eye and acknowledged his wife. She continued to fuss, "I've made your coffee, and breakfast is ready. Hurry!"

Groaning, Noah lifted his 50-year-old body from the bed. He stumbled to the stainless steel personal room and caught a glimpse of himself in the mirror – balding, six o'clock shadow, and that 'spare tire' that had become more noticeable than ever this year.

He showered and shaved, and, then, dressed in a drab copper suit, sat down to his usual breakfast of tofu, peaches, and coffee. He ate quickly and then moved to the kitchen computer, murmured a few words to it and immediately received a print-out of the *New York Times*.

He poured another cup of coffee and began to read the happenings of the past eight hours. The orange headlines read, "Russians Develop Massive K-Bomb; Top U.S. Experts Fearful!" Noah felt a vague twinge of something once known or yet to happen, as if someone had sat on his burial crypt. Sighing, he turned to the business section.

Later, at the office, Noah reached for the intercom and asked his secretary to summon Prescott. While Noah waited, he studied the Prescott file. Business had been unusually frantic recently – amalgamated was up 13.8% and now Brian K. Prescott was efficiently attempting to squeeze every last aluminum nickel out of the Company. Noah gritted his teeth and closed his eyes.

"NOAH," a voice called.

Opening his yes, Noah snapped, "Prescott, is that you? Let's get to the – – – " Then he realized that he was still alone in the office.

"NOAH, ARE YOU LISTENING? I HAVE A TASK FOR YOU."

Noah Watson demanded, "What is this? A prank? Believe me, I've heard all the 'Noah' jokes already!"

"NOAH," the great voice boomed, "I HAVE SHOWN YOU A VISION OF THE COMING HOLOCAUST. *I CAN SPARE YOU* AND YOUR FAMILY TO PROPAGATE A NEW AND BETTER PLANET."

"Sure, and I suppose you want me to build an ark and take two of every species aboard, snapped Noah.

"YOU'RE CATCHING ON, NOAH! A TRADITIONAL ARK IS CLEARLY IMPOSSIBLE. YOU WILL NEED A CRAFT THAT CAN TRANSPORT YOU OUT OF THE EARTH ZONE. JUST FOR OLD TIME'S SAKE WE'LL CALL IT THE SPACEARK. AS FOR THE ANIMALS, YOU WON'T HAVE TO WORRY ABOUT AS MANY SPECIES AS YOUR PREDECESSOR. SINCE I GAVE YOU ALL FREE WILL, YOU PEOPLE HAVE MANAGED TO DRIVE A GOOD MANY OF MY CREATIONS INTO EXTINCTION. ANY-WAY, SPACE WON'T BE A PROBLEM BECAUSE YOU CAN JUST PACK FRESH FROZEN CHROMOZONES FOR THE LARGER SPECIES."

Noah laughed, "Okay, guys, joke's over. Where's the camera?"

The large voice announced somewhat petulantly, "WHY MUST HUMANS ALWAYS DEMAND PROOF OF MY EXIS-TENCE? WELL, NOAH, IF YOU WANT SENSATIONALISM, HOW ABOUT THIS . . . . "

And Noah Watson involuntarily rose up, first on his toes, and finally off the floor. It is difficult to maintain any dignity while levitating six feet above the carpet, and Noah demanded that the voice release him. Then he pleaded.

"OH, ALRIGHT, NOAH! REALLY YOU OUGHT TO DO SOMETHING ABOUT YOUR WEIGHT – I HAD AN EASIER TIME LEVITATING A WATER BUFFALO IN INDIA YESTERDAY."

With that, Noah was lowered very gently into his chair. "I-ah-well, um . . . . "

"NOAH, THINK ABOUT WHAT I ASK. BUT TAKE CARE YOU DO NOT WAIT TOO LONG TO ACCEPT MY ASSIGNMENT . . . . " The voice faded away, and Noah Watson was alone.

With trembling fingers Noah pressed the intercom and told his secretary to cancel *everything* for the rest of the day. "I'm just not feeling well at all."

"Yes, Sir," responded the calm, liquid voice of his secretary robot, "Have a nice day."

". . . Well, Noah, it looks like you've got the old chronic exec. syndrome – hypertension, ulcers, and general stress. You work too hard, and as your doctor, I'm prescribing a good, long vacation." Noah huddled in the skimpy hospital gown and waited for Nurse Kool to detach the wrist wires leading to the computer. Naturally, he had not told the good doctor about the visions and the Voice – he might be losing touch with reality, but he wasn't that crazy yet!

Dr. Van Elswyk, in a tone not unlike that of God (or whoever that Voice had been) announced, "Take six of these elevator pills every day, and stay away from your office for at least a week. The pills should give you some temporary help, Noah, but you're also going to need to help yourself. Stop working so hard and start thinking pleasant things for a change, Noah."

When Noah arrived home earlier than usual, Marian was alarmed, "Noah, are you ill – you look so pale. Come here, do you have a fever?"

"Marian, I've been to see Doc Van Elswyk. She says I'm just tired, and it's time for a change of scenery. I'm going to bed. You go on and finish your hologram program."

"Can't I fix you some hot sunflower soup?"

"No, I just feel like sleeping now. Thanks, Hon."

Noah slept deeply and dreamed he was on a vast spaceship traveling at incredible speed away from earth. Marian was with him as were his three sons and their families. They watched the view screen and saw the beautiful green earth grow smaller and smaller; suddenly it burst into white flames — and then there was nothing. Earth was gone.

Noah woke. He knew then that eventually he would agree to leave earth with his family and take the chromozones of every living thing. But, he had much to do before he said "goodbye" to earth.

First, he phoned the office and said he would not be returning. Then for three days he huddled in his tiny den making lists of what to do and what to take. Often he was dissatisfied with his lists. The carpet was littered with wads of discarded strategies. "Crap!" he muttered under his breath. This wasn't the Christmas pageant in sixth grade where he wrapped up in a sheet and followed a tinfoil star across the school stage. It wasn't finals at MIT — or even the Prescott case. God was entrusting him to faultlessly execute a plan to save the living things of earth.

Marian entered the room. She watched him cautiously for a moment and then asked, "Noah, why didn't you leave that work at the office? The doctor said not to work until you were feeling better."

Noah said carefully, "This isn't office work. Come sit here with me, Marian, I have something very important to tell you. Now try not to think I am joking or that I have lost my mind. I have never been more serious or more sane . . . . Marian, I have had a vision, a vision from God. There will soon be a nuclear holocaust — the ultimate holocaust, and then there will be no more earth. God wants us, you and me, Marian, and the children, to get two of every small life form and frozen chromozones for the bigger ones and get aboard a spaceark and travel far from earth to a new planet. Marian, what are you thinking? Marian???"

Marian wept. She repeated over and over, "Oh, you poor man — you poor dear soul . . . . "

There was no reasoning with her, and finally Noah sadly walked away. He would convince her later. At the moment he had other things to do. For something deep within him was quietly insisting that the 'deadline' (bad pun, he thought) was being moved up.

. . . Officer Carl sat in the dim, deserted squad room of Police Precinct 83. Legs comfortably propped on the desk, he was telephoning his immediate superior. "Sorry to bother you at home, Sarge. What's that, I woke you – well, I'm double sorry about that, Sarge, but I thought you should know about the arrest that Patrolperson Mellick made tonight. Seems this guy was sneaking around MCBE . . . . What? You know, that scientific place. Anyway, Mellick asked what he was doing out in the dead of winter without a coat, carrying a cage of white mice and leading two chimpanzees, and he babbled something about an ark and Noah and K-Bombs. Yeah, I know, I know, lots of nuts running loose this time of year. We have this particular nut cooling in Cell Nine . . . . He keeps yelling that he's Noah and he has to catch an ark . . . . We have him in the strait jacket. Yes, he's under control . . . . Right! We'll hold him till morning and then give him a psychiatric scan. See you in the morning, Sarge."

Officer Carl clicked the phone to off, made the proper notation on the night computer, and walked to the window. There was a bright glow from the light of the sunrise. "That's funny," thought Carl, "I must have dozed off. I could have sworn that it was just past midnight."

– No One Wants To Know –

Tom Eggett (Age 15)
Crestwood High School, Atlanta, GA, USA

Prence looked out over the desolate and forgotten city. Its absence of life reverberated throughout the top floor of the Hilton Hotel he occupied, sending spasms of grief and wonderment scintillating through him. The grief from its dead radiance, the wonderment from the thought of mankind's desertion of such high technology. Its buildings still gleamed with newness, the flora continued to exude a liveable atmosphere. It looked like a toy model conceived back in the late 1980's when man was still doing the preliminary testing of the underwater dome. He retreated back down the stairway, his footsteps echoing the emptiness of the still elegant Hilton.

He drifted through the streets, his eyes searching for one of the openings down to the security of Level A. The faint hum of the still operative atomic generators reached his ears. Prence had always wondered how the huge dome continued to stay lit. The empty buildings frowned at him with bare insides as he stumbled past them. The abnormal pressure started to affect his movements. He sighted the unused computer building and instantaneously proceeded toward it, before the cumulative pressure could overtake him. Prence fought open the door; "should have left it open," he thought. The waiting comfort of the open airlock greeted him once inside. He plunged through it, succumbing to its absorbing thrust that threw him down to the dome interaction room on Level A. As he was collecting his thoughts, the airlock guard of the Level arrived to assist him with the formalities concerned with returning to the underground world again.

"Find anything helpful this time up, Prence? You really shouldn't time it so close each time you go up, you know. One time the pressure will get you and it'll be one less for the farmers on Level H to provide for."

"I think I may have been able to finally determine with all the evidence I've gathered, why our forefathers retreated to this basement world and left the beautiful city to lie useless and lifeless. I found that . . . . "

"That's O.K., I'll read it in the annual report Prence," the guard said, giving Prence a humorless smile as if he were still a small child. "Now back down to that Level of yours before it becomes too late and the axe, um . . . excuse me, security, won't let you."

Prence felt a surge of rage gathering in him. Why was it that nobody cared? Didn't anyone believe that it was important to find out why the dome and communication with the outside world was abandoned for mole tunnels and frightened silence? Why didn't anyone realize that there were other people in this world? Just because he was a professor of history for the dome's underground inhabitants and was always eager to find out about the past.... "I could go on forever," he thought. "They don't care."

"Let's go," Prence acquiesed.

They passed through the various security functions of Level A: fingerprint, mindscan, voiceprint – they were all familiar to him now. At first he hadn't understood them, but eventually they became clear, after more study he'd found why The Administrators, the present-day governing body, had thought them necessary. If an outsider were to infiltrate their society, the problems which would arise would be insurmountable. Finally, the security procedures culminated, Prence was able to return to Level M and his home.

He entered the express tube and punched in directions. It began its descent downward. He passed through the no admission Levels B and C, called the "implement" levels by most. These levels were only for The Administration. Levels D through G, the manufacturing centers of the colony were called "Bee Hive," "I think," Prence surmised. A few workers joined his tube. Then came Level H, the most important level of all – food production. It was really something the way those scientists converted that phosphorescent material into sunlight for the plants. He quickly whisked through Levels I through L, the mining facilities; the "mole" levels were rich in materials necessary for the colony's survival. Then the tube stopped: Level M, the seldom used Education Level. The tube continued to the lower levels, all living quarters below his level now. He disembarked from the tube and navigated the maze of corridors to his home cubicle. The eye computer at his door acknowledged him and he entered. Sleep came easily.

He awoke groggily, his body still not totally adjusted to the new pressure. He thought about getting up, but apparently his body didn't. As his eyes focused on his surroundings, he remembered where he was – back under – in his room on the Education Level of the colony. It wasn't much, but he really didn't need all those elaborate furnishings like the ones he saw up top yesterday. It was basically carved rock; the bed, nightstand, and chairs, melted and carved from bedrock, with cushioning on top of course. There was a bathroom and naturally a computer with a VID-Screen. Most importantly, though, was his small collection of books passed down to him from his parents, ex-dome occupants. He wondered how it must have been like with them, when the dome was still functioning . . . all those luxuries. "Well," he thought, "I might as well do something before my classes start." He gathered together all his notes and a recorder and began to dictate his conclusion on why man retreated underground.

"The threat of a nuclear holocaust appears to have been the predominant factor in man's underground movement. The U.S.S.R. and the U.S. were on the edge of the cliff, both ready to jump off when the officials first approved the tunneling under the city and into the ocean floor. Security was set up tight and communication with the outside world was diminished. Slowly, the government moved the people underground, bribing them with the omen of a nuclear holocaust ready to beseige the earth. At first it was only tentative, but then the people began to realize the pressure was beginning to increase because of the greater amount of space – the dome plus the underground expansion area. An airlock was set up between the dome and tunnels, but many still died from prolonged pressure exposure. Within five years the entire city had reverted to the underground and has existed for 15 years up until now." Prence paused for a long breath, here was his startling discovery, "The nuclear situation had been cured! Secret communications three years ago confirmed this and now we all could return to the city!"

Four security men lasered through the door. Prence glanced up with a knowing look in his eyes. He knew the end when he saw it! The security officers didn't hesitate with their task; they had a job to do. Prence's death wasn't painful; only satisfying to those who relished his death to keep their power. There was no sign of the tape or recorder (or Prence), when the four security officers exited.

– Dum Vivimus Vivimus –

Estelle Fritz (Age 15)
Salolburg High School, Salolburg, RSA

You know Man, you are a strange one. You want to be enslaved by a god and master which you call a computer. Oh, and further, you tell me that you are human. But, your computer god tells you about making artificial Cumulus Clouds in the skies and putting bullet holes into little children, the plastic product of your test tubes and faceless geniuses who only exist as numbers in a sperm bank. Do you really think these bullet holes will be filled with salvation? No, Man, I suppose you just shrug your shoulders, take up your gun, and swim through this river of worn-out life, just to walk out and kill more on the other side. Or, did you think these bullet wounds were going to be filled with candy?

You Man, have promised yourself a life on the mountain tops since time began. And you wanted to climb this, the highest peak with a rope platted with strands of strive and study. But, first it frayed and then broke, making you fall and fall and fall and you rolled down in the deepest of valleys because of your so-called ingenuity.

Where man, where did your politicians go wrong? Did they go wrong when they decided that community farms and work places were to be erected, or when they decided mankind should be made into academic ticky-tacky, or when they raped individuality and identity? Where did they take our being, our suffering? Did they perhaps hide the other self in us in a safe?

Are our eyes only fascinated by the wrath of warriors and are we only delighted by inimical bombs which burn out the eyes of our brothers, or seeing friends being choked to death? Are our brothers the only source of macabre playthings? Do they not mean more to you than a single thrill?

It is wonderful to be able to push a button and tune into a world library and read anything you like, or to push another and listen to all the music you want to hear, or to push yet another and you can be transported to wherever you wish.

But, why has this button stopped us from thinking? Is it because the politicians do not want to be exposed as mediocre, and, therefore, fathom the secret that they are not the leaders which they pretend to be. But anti-intellectuals who rule the world by advertisement.

But, what has happened to the philosophers? Why do they not lead mankind anymore? Why no more Plato, Aristotle, and no more Dante? Has the egg that hatched in the 70's and 80's now become a fully fledged monster which breathes fire and brimstone at any soul who tries to think for himself?

Oh, God in heaven, I pray to you that the year 2010 may bring us individuality and the ability to suffer, and please God, may Saint George be re-born and slay this monster. Let us live to wonder in Cosmos-fields. Let us see the birds fly in great swaths across blue skies. Please let us see our cumulus clouds made natural again. Please, let us see the year 2010 bring back the reign of the individual . . . .

CHAPTER FOUR

And They'd All See The Truth

The impelling motivation behind children's creativity is their desire to discover the truth. When children find the truth, they naturally want to share their excitement with others. Soon, however, they learn that some adults do not want to see the truth, will not listen to it; or will not believe the truth when confronted with it. This phenomenon is a common expereince among gifted and talented children, and is dramatically symbolized in a fascinating story, "In Hiding," by Wilmar H. Shiras (1974). Timothy Paul, an exceedingly gifted boy, learned to read when he was barely three years old. However, his grandmother, who was raising him, refused to believe the child could read, and punished him for lying and trying to fool others. Timothy experienced the same reaction to other discoveries of truth. In self-defense, he taught himself to write by the time he was four, so he could record his discoveries, even though he had to keep his writings secret. Later, he published his truths in popular and professional journals, under a series of assumed names, while still contriving to appear "normal" by earning only average grades in school.

Truth takes many forms; two of these may be characterized as "truth for all" and "truth for one." "Truth for all" has emerged throughout history in the shape of major shifts in how we think about our physical universe. Nicolaus Copernicus suggested that the earth was not the center of the universe; Charles Darwin proposed that all of life's species have adapted and evolved; and Sigmund Freud asserted that some thoughts are beyond our conscious control. Each of these new "truths" met with heavy resistance, because each challenged the conventional wisdom of the times, and each held far-ranging implications. It has been argued that such truths are only working hypotheses or theories, and that they are continually being deposited by newer, more useable truths. What seems to be a constant in this process is that new ideas will always be resisted by the establishment.

"Truth for one" is a personal truth. It is the experience of each individual and is, therefore, always true. Instead of stating, "This is the way things are," personal truth communicates, "This is the way I see it." There are as many personal truths as there are people, and so it is logical to assume that each of us has a truth which, if said out loud, would challenge the conventional wisdom. To do so would be to risk the ridicule and wrath which has been the fate of truthsayers throughout history. So most of us keep silent or, worse yet, deceive ourselves into thinking we must have been mistaken — that what we thought was truth, was not. We ourselves then turn into the establishment, intolerant of the speaking of truth. We put truth itself, and its messengers, at risk.

The scenarios in this chapter reveal the depth and wisdom of these young writers, and their understanding of the importance of communicating truths. The fictional heroes and heroines share their hard-earned knowledge so others may profit from the mistakes of those who have preceded them. They reflect the joys and benefits which might result from communication of their discovered truths. Yet, they also reflect an awareness that truth, and its dissemination, are often regarded as dangerous. In spite of this, the protagonists display courage in the service of truth, even against overwhelming odds.

Observations of children and adults during creative activities, the personal accounts of eminent creative people, and experimental studies (Torrance, 1976) leave little doubt that the need to communicate is a strong and complex force. Although the desire for recognition may be one motivation for sharing a creative invention or discovery, other basic human needs are also involved. One of the most pervasive motivations for sharing one's creation may simply be the need to discharge the excitement and energy built up during the creative process; the creator cannot relax until he or she has found an open-minded listener with whom the creation can be shared. We have repeatedly observed this phenomenon in both children and adults; once they have made a creative leap to a new truth, they feel an urgent need to communicate it to someone. This is not simply "showing off," but the final step which provides necessary closure to the act of creation.

Perhaps one of mankind's most fundamental needs is to maintain contact with reality. Since the creative person places great importance upon inner realities (personal truths, truth for one), and since the production of an original idea makes the person who produces it a minority of one, at least for a time, there is a strong need to "check out" this new reality by sharing it with others.

Yet, most of us can recall our frustration as children at not being able to make adults understand, because we had no words to do so. It seems that very young children understand the meaning of what is said to them long before they master the use of language, and they suffer frequent humiliation from being unable to communicate their insights. As a result, they need and develop an inner fantasy world as a survival strategy. Even older children such as our scenario writers can communicate their truths more fluently in the form of fictionalized stories than through other means.

Before presenting scenarios depicting the children's perceptions of the problem of communicating truth, we would like to suggest some ways to help children cope with the inevitable tentions arising from social pressures against such communication.

1. Deliberately arrange a time, place, and environment that encourages rather than discourages communication of creative discoveries. Teachers can create such situations through devices such as the class meetings, described by William Glasser (1969), or sociodrama (Torrance, 1975).

2. Find a mentor, or some other adult or peer of high integrity with whom it is safe to communicate. Teachers and counselors, as well as parents, may help highly creative children and young people find such a mentor, sponsor, or patron.

3. Seek opportunities for collaboration in pairs or small

groups when creative goals exist. In a number of experiments (Torrance, 1971), it has been demonstrated that children and young people seem more willing to attempt difficult tasks, produce more original ideas, appreciate the quality of their ideas more, and enjoy the creative experience more in smaller groups.

4. Seek to develop communication skills through authorship. Teachers and parents may deliberately encourage this and create opportunities. Even kindergarteners and first graders can dictate their stories, poems, songs, and ideas to a recorder (human or electronic). As children and adults become authors, they develop an identity and a role which facilitates their creativity and makes their personal truths public events.

Truth, like creativity, seeks the light. "Truth for one" is not always "truth for all," but it is certain that truth in any form always needs to be communicated. As a prisoner in Virginia, struggling to write songs, told one of the authors of this book, "There is no such thing as a creative act in isolation. Everybody needs an audience."

– Mission –

Mandy Carter (Age 17)
Collegiate High School for Girls, Port Elizabeth, RSA

The woman walked with an air of caution, as if carefully testing each step before bestowing it on the barren, rocky path. Her face and figure were that of a woman in middle age, the slight stoop to the shoulders suggesting the weight of many burdens. Although possessed of generally unremarkable features, her eyes, a clear grey, gave strength and purpose to her face. The air was crisp, the sky a gathering dark, and the distant hills clothed in shadows. She pulled an ill-fitting coat closer about her shoulders.

She reached the small community a breath away from nightfall. She gazed up at the high walls and was startled when a voice floated down, abruptly demanding her name and business. She received no answer to her subsequent reply and was made to wait outside the gates for two hours. At one time, she saw the face of a young boy peer inquisitively through the gap between the gates. She smiled, and after a moment's hesitation was rewarded with a tentative half-smile. Then he disappeared. Shortly after that the gates opened and a large, stocky man peered sullenly through the dark at her, suspicion coloring his voice. He offered her a bed for the night, at a price, and checked to see that she had no forbidden literature with her. His hostile face warned her to forget meals, food was scarce enough.

Inside the tall gates was a gathering of primitive log cabins. The fields they cultivated were probably outside, she thought. The bed was a straw pallet, most likely lice-ridden, but this did not bother her. She sat in her doorway, watching the people about their evening meal. It was high summer, and they are outside around an open fire. Ignoring her own hunger, she gazed around at the people themselves. Her agile mind was already noting words spoken and the reactions to them. The children, particularly, came under close scrutiny. She smiled in anticipation. Now all that was necessary was permission to stay the summer. It was a busy time in the fields, helping hands were sure to be appreciated.

The work was back-breaking and the hours were long, but the woman was strong and possessed nimble fingers. As the others in the community saw her good work, they slowly began to soften towards her. At times this took the form of an extra helping of food, a small snippet of conversation or even a smile. But, contact with the children was still frowned upon and she had to wait patiently for the right moment to occur.

Then, one day as she was picking strawberries to be preserved for the long harsh winter she came upon the young boy whom she had seen at the gate. He was sitting quietly in the shelter of dense bramble bushes, his body turned so it hid from her the object of his concentration. She came closer, and peering over his shoulder, saw it was a book. At her gentle touch on his shoulder he sprange up abruptly, ashen-faced and already stuttering half-formed excuses. She smiled at him reassuringly and asked quietly what he was reading. He handed it to her silently. She glanced at the title and felt an odd quirk of nostalgia at the familiar words, "Physics is Fun" by J. Harvey. The copy was very old, literally coming apart at the seams, and she handled it with reverent care. "It's a very good book," she said. Once again she was favoured with what appeared to be a characteristic fleeting half-smile. "Do you understand it?" she asked. The boy shook his head. She settled herself on the grass and began to talk quietly once he had sat down next to her. The evening bell recalled them to the present and both sprang hurriedly to their feet. "Tomorrow?" she asked. The boy nodded and turning on his heels, disappeared into the bushes.

Often, in later years, when she thought back on that long, hot summer, bramble bushes appeared before her mental eyes. They spent every spare moment there in discussing and reading his meager supply of books and in answering his questions. He was thirsty for knowledge of any kind and she was glad to teach him. One day, while in the middle of a discussion, he suddenly looked up at her and asked, "What was the world like when these books were written?" She considered a moment, frowning, and then asked, "What do your parents tell you?" "They say it was evil and corrupt," he said, "filled with evil men, greedy and covetous, seeking to become gods, and destroying our refuge, earth, to fulfill their selfish and eternal desire for knowledge which only god rightfully possesses."

"Do you believe them?" she asked. He shrugged, confused. "Do you know why they believe that?" He shrugged again. She smiled. "Let me tell you – " She began her story with herself, a young woman, 25 years old and working as a teacher in the small town of Hartford, Kansas, USA. She had come from a tight-knit family, something that was rare in that year of 1990. She had already been teaching for three years and had been on the verge of marriage, a step that was regarded as unbearably old-fashioned by her friends. But, her respect for her parent's wishes had totally precluded any other suggestion, although, child of the modern world that she was, the more common alternative of living together had appealed to her.

She had actually been visiting her parents the evening that the news of the first earthquakes came in from Southeast Asia. She remembered the blase reactions of the rest of her family to the terrible suffering that was seen. Only her father had shown any genuine concern. But, then the earthquakes had begun to occur more regularly and violently over widespread areas to the bafflement of the scientists. People had begun to worry. Another familiar sight in those early days had been the Reverend Jackson, religious fanatic whose philosophies had been given wide coverage throughout the country. He had believed that all of man's evil had resulted from seeking knowledge that was not meant to be his. To know how to read the Bible was sufficient, beyond that man merely had to know how to till the earth. He had declared that the earthquakes were a sign of God's righteous anger and not surprisingly, he had gained a large number of converts, most of which had gone to live in his communes.

But then the world's attention had focused on a more important event. World peace talks had finally been arranged and every leader in the world had been gathered on that historic day of June 15, 1990, under a single roof, that of the United Nations Building in Brussels. The meeting had just been called to order and the President of the United States had risen to begin his welcoming speech, when the first shock waves struck. Within 20 minutes, the entire building had been reduced to pitiful rubble. There had been no survivors. The world had gone into a state of shock. Still the Reverend had ranted. He had been gaining converts daily. But the worst had not yet been over. The earthquakes had still been occurring regularly, even in previously stable zones and had slowly destroyed almost all the major cities in the world, causing the breakdown of communications, roads, sanitary facilities, and cutting off supplies of food and water.

On the seventeenth of October, 1990, a mild tremor hit Moscow and within two weeks almost its entire population had died of a mysterious, virulent disease. It was never revealed that the tremor had caused considerable damage to the main research laboratories of the KGB. The disease had spread with incredible speed and a bare two months later had devastated the entire European Continent; from whence it spread to Africa, via a fishing boat which somehow had managed to safely navigate the straits of Gibraltar. For a while, due to stringent bans on immigration, it had seemed as though America might be saved, but soon the disease flared up in Boston. Its source was never traced.

Her parents, her two brothers, and her fiance had all died within weeks of each other. She had survived, along with others who had seemingly also been possessed of some kind of built-in immunity; and the colonies of the Reverend Jackson's followers who had been protected by their extreme isolation. Most of the city dwellers who had not succumbed to the disease had gone to live in these communes. There had simply been nothing else left. Scavengers, many of them criminals, had made life in the deserted cities a danger. She, too, had attempted to live in one of the communes and had been threatened with expulsion for attempting to teach the children basic arithmetic. She gazed at the elders of the commune in amazement, unable to accept what they had been telling her. These simple people, shocked by what they had seen happening around them, had taken the Reverend's word to heart. Their children were taught to read and write, but more than that would be sure to bring down the wrath of God upon them. She had left the commune shocked into a startled realization of what was happening. She had had a mental vision of the world sinking back into a second dark ages, all the learning and technology now available to man dying out completely, the dream of living in space, which had seemed so near to realization, once again as distant as the stars themselves, merely because of one man and a series of unprecedented natural disasters. Then, however, she had caught herself up, remembering that the present situation, as far as she knew, prevailed only in the United States. But still she had thought of all the years, all the young potential they could lose before trans-Atlantic communication was restored. Someone would have to attempt to instill the desire for knowledge in these people again. The adults were lost to her, she had decided. It would be the children whom it would be her mission to teach.

Now, in this year of 2010, she had already been fulfilling her mission for 20 years. It had been a hard, lonely life, requiring constant deception and myriads of lies. At times, the temptation to settle in a commune had almost been irresistible, but always her duty had called her onward, to the next community, the next child.

The boy's horrified gasp brought her out of her reverie. Framed by the bramble bushes was the face of one of the older women of the commune. She was staring horrified at the open books at their feet. Then, she disappeared and the woman listened to her heavy footfalls with sadness. She looked at the boy, "I'll have to leave," she said quietly, "immediately, I think. Will you be all right?" He nodded, his eyes fixed to the ground.

The woman walked with an air of caution, as if carefully testing each step before bestowing it on the barren rocky path. Her shoulders drooped miserably and her grey eyes were cloudy with unshed tears. She stopped suddenly to consult a crudely drawn map. She had more than six kilometers to go before nightfall. Straightening her back, she quickened her step, her eyes fixed on the far-off horizon.

– The Writing On The Wall –

Carl J. Horn III (Age 13)
Conway Junior High School, Orlando, FL, USA

Tap! Tap! Tap! . . . the noise from my hammer and chisel combines and swells with the tappings of my colleagues. The noise reverberates throughout our soon-to-be tomb. The sardonicism of the situation makes me want to laugh, though all morning I've been struggling to hold back the tears.

Here we are in the year 2010, a handful of the top minds in Western Civilization, reduced to working with makeshift implements. Our final mission now: To carve out a legacy for future generations.

As I look around the small, dismal chamber that remains, I find myself visualizing the subterranean laboratory which existed until today. Our lab was built, equipped, and staffed to survive a nuclear disaster so we, in turn, could assist the above-ground survivors face their future. The lab was actually a small self-contained city. Our "city" had its own greenhouse for growing food and a water and air recycling-purification system. Carved out of a stone layer and lined with Thallead, the densest material known to man, we were 17 kilometers underground.

Our research center, a scientist's dream, was comprised of technological equipment containing trillions of data. There were neutron microscopes that could view a billionth of a millimeter, scanners that could zoom in on any part of the earth's surface, transport rocket tubes that conveyed us to any part of our city in a matter of seconds, micro-dot libraries, and moles (vehicles that were able to burrow underground).

I was especially proud of my humanoid computer which was programmed with the gamut of human emotions. This computer enabled me to advance my research on human emotions and how external forces react with them. As a psychophysicist, my work involved a combination of mind control and behavior modification which would aid survivors in accepting and coping with their fragmented world.

However, the beginning of the end started two days ago, when man's inhumanity to man reached its climax. We watched in awe and despair as the world's cities succumbed to their nuclear deaths. As the Telstar satellite sent its pictures to our monitors, I was humbled by the appalling devastation man had brought upon himself.

The conflict which started between two nations grew into a chain reaction encompassing the globe. Lifetimes of knowledge and accomplishments were destroyed by the greedy and power-hungry humans who lived among us. Can the need for domination of one man over another ever be controlled?

Our prognosis on the outcome of a nuclear war envisioned many areas being annihilated, while other sections would come through unscathed. However, there was a flaw in our doomsday forecast – something so mundane that we completely overlooked its effect – Mother Nature!

This morning, two days after the initial explosions, nature revolted at this final outrageous assault committed against her by man. She mustered her forces and retaliated with her troops of earthquakes, hurricanes, erupting volcanoes, tornadoes, tidal waves, and meteor showers. No land mass was spared her fury!

It was during an earthquake that our "invincible" city was all but demolished. A few of us managed to escape to this storage room, a cave-like chamber, which is all that remains. A small niche in our underground dwelling, it is dark, and the stone walls now added to the chill we had already experienced.

We soon learned that we were trapped and had only a limited amount of oxygen and water to sustain us. Therefore, we decided we must spend our remaining hours inscribing the highlights of our technology for future man.

Fortunately, the storeroom had an ample supply of flashlights, hammers, screwdrivers, and even a few chisels. We assembled our tools, and it was decided that each of us would choose a vital area of knowledge to convey.

I was amazed at how quickly my companions determined the information they would leave for posterity. I felt rather inept, as I could think of everything – and nothing – at the same time. What a decision! My final imprint on the world . . . what should it be?

Suddenly it dawned on me. What good were all of these scientific breakthroughs when we still destroyed each other? It was then that I knew what my inscription would be.

I began chipping on the wall at the far end of the room. No one has bothered to ask what I am going to write. They're all too busy with their complex formulas to care about my choice. My message is a simple one, something we've forgotten or possibly never really knew:

"LOVE ONE ANOTHER"

As I carve the words, a sense of deja vu comes over me. Perhaps the present is merely history relived, and we've all been through this before. Maybe man has destroyed his world in the past and has struggled to come back and rebuild it. I feel heartened by this thought, for I know the survivors of this calamity will pull together and rebuild toward a better and more peaceful world. As they strive toward their future, so they will delve into their past and one day unearth this tomb.

Hopefully, those who have endured, will use their hearts, along with their heads, and read the writing on the wall.

– The Peace Fighters –

Cathy-Ann Ferguson (Age 12)
Ellerton Primary School, Three Anchor Bay, RSA

It is the year 2010. I am 42. I have been working for 22 years as a peace fighter. I am a qualified scientist but I don't use my qualifications. Looking back to my childhood I have realized how much the world has changed. We have food, clothes, and houses growing in our back garden! We have developed two plants which taste fine, one you cook and the other you convert to drink. There are also clothes and houses "growing" because we have two fibrous plants. One, when turned to pulp, then put out to dry, makes clothing material and the other gets woven into mats which make lightweight, sweet smelling walls. These houses are warm and can stand up to any weather and bend to any conditions. The earth's cities have also changed. Instead of overpopulation, we are a little underpopulated. People all have a comfortable home and a big garden. They also have a good job which pays them a fair sum of money, but my main worry about the world has always been and still is – war. More than half the world's population has been killed by war.

So, that is my reason for joining the group of peace fighters to help them discover different things which will turn everyone into a peacefighter.

When I joined the group I was immediately assigned to work with the Leader, who was an excellent scientist. He was working on a new machine which will remove the thought of war from people. One day a humanoid smuggled himself to our midst. He was an exact duplicate of our head but we knew straight away it couldn't be our leader because he told us to build this invention at all costs, now this duplicate was telling us to destroy whatever we were working on. We realized that the scientists must have been replaced by the authorities. We arranged for a spy to follow "the thing" to its flat and destroy it. The government thought they had demolished our group but they were wrong.

When our head died we had to find another leader. I was the only other scientist, so they said I had to take over because I was excellent at keeping order. I accepted the offer because if I did not there probably would not have been any peacefighters left. We worked night and day for over a month on our invention. Finally, it was done. We had to try it out to see if it worked. We designed a new, comfortable chair and fitted our gadget into the chair perfectly. We took the chair to a furniture shop where a buyer tried it out and put the built-in earphones on. As the first bars of the rich, relaxing music penetrated his ears, he took the earphones off and said that he would buy 20 to see if it sold well and if it did he wanted a hundred more. He went on to tell us how he hated the planet's pointless wars. We realized that our invention was a total success. We celebrated all night.

We decided that a chair wasn't enough. We would have to develop something like a house spray. We would develop a new spray so sweet-smelling that whoever smelled it would be against war. It was the only way. We spent the next few weeks figuring out the unique formula which would have this effect. I didn't think it would but we took it to a supermarket and sure enough, it worked. We did a survey on behaviors and discovered that even the most warlike families had changed. The chairs and the sprays were selling like hot cakes. Even prisoners got their cells sprayed with our disinfectant adaption of our sprays. I was sure that at this rate we would have an atmosphere of peace.

We went on to invent what we called "Peace Gas" and put it in the policemen's spray guns instead of tear gas. There were many reasons for the governments of the world not to want peace. If there was peace, they would lose their power and their profits.

In all the excitement about the success of our experiments, one of us must have slipped. Somehow the government knew. Probably the cleaning ladies were caught in the process of secretly slipping the Peace Capsules into the Dictator's rooms. Because, one evening when I was returning home, I was seized by one of the Governor's guards. I was marched straight to prison.

I've written this whole story down in the hope that one day someone would find it. I am waiting for the guards to call me. I am to be shot for trying to make peace! I hope that whoever reads my story will start another group of Peace Fighters and survive to bring peace to the world.

CHAPTER FIVE

When I Sang Out My Song

Why a book of children's scenarios anyway? Why not simply present a content analysis – a list – of the concerns expressed by the world's children, and let it go at that? Surely there are better writers in the world, authors at once more poetic, and more scientifically sophisticated than children?

As we have said, the children have much to teach us. Beyond that, they are developing their art, exploring their present and future through creative expression. A work of art tells more than its creator can say any other way. A dance, a song, a scenario, recreates an experience of the inner life of its creator and transmits it to us whole, as a finished product. Even its creator cannot fully explain its message. It is necessary that adults understand not only the thoughts of the young people – our futures – but their dreams as well, dreams best communicated through art forms.

Art provides a direct link between creator and audience – here, the children of the world and the grownups; both learn something new as a result. When poet Allen Tate (1952) was asked to write about the process he goes through to create a poem, he replied that such an essay would produce only theories, useful only to critics who do not like his poetry. He continued,

> I say this because it seems to me that my verse or anybody else's is merely a way of knowing something; if the poem is a real creation, it is a kind of knowledge that we did not possess before. It is not knowledge 'about' something else; the poem is the fullness of that knowledge. We know the particular poem, not what it says that we can restate . . . . And an experience of it is not quite the same as a philosophical statement about it (p. 136).

Thus, we give you the scenarios themselves.

Tate is talking about the importance of art in the world. The scenarios offer us direct experience of the songs inside children, songs that will bring us new awarenesses if we only listen. In writing scenarios, the children perhaps tell us more than they can say in any other way — perhaps, indeed, more than they can know in any other way, because the scenarios themselves become, in Tate's words, "a way of knowing," and allow the children to reach beyond themselves through fiction.

In our first scenario, "Don't Be Afraid to Think for Yourself," 15-year-old John Davis writes of his hero going to see the film, THE ROCKY HORROR PICTURE SHOW, and discovering for the first time the importance of being true to himself. Now, no logical analysis could explain how a child can learn from a movie, a fanciful work of the creative imagination, something all the "back to basic" lessons of the schools have not been able to teach him. And, analytical methods will never be able to teach what art teaches us, for art reaches beyond thought to the wisdom of intuition and emotion.

The scenario writers in this chapter realize the difficulties and conflicts they face in pursuing the creative arts, for it is most often in the arts that young people encounter the strongest opposition from parents, teachers, counselors, and the system. The children know they will need courage to realize their dreams, sing out their songs. Not only must they fight for the right to be unique, to have control over their lives, but they must also in some measure withdraw from the community of their peers to resist conforming, to make their own way, create newness, and the community will inevitably resent such withdrawal. These children may experience the pain of being labelled "workaholics" as they enter fully into the all-consuming discipline required of one who would attain mastery in an artform.

Art is a lonely pursuit, and falling in love with art is the only thing that makes the loneliness bearable. Indeed, biographies and autobiographies of people who have produced the ideas or taken the initiatives which have changed the world for the better reveal that the source of their creative energy was the act of falling in love with something at an early age, and pursuing it throughout their lives. Falling in love with an image, a vision of a possible future, is one of the most powerful wellsprings of creative energy, outstanding accomplishment, and self-fulfillment available to humankind. Strong evidence for this conclusion emerged from a 22-year longitudinal study conducted by Torrance (1981), in which he asked children in the third, fourth, fifth, and sixth grades to name what they were in love with, what they wanted to do when they grew up. Some of the children consistently said, "I don't know." Others changed their future career images from year to year. But about half of the children were unwavering in their career choices, and, as adults, ended up in careers consistent with the future careers they had chosen as children.

These childhood career images proved to be a significant factor of adult creative achievement. Such achievement was measured using five different sets of criteria, ranging from the number of publicly recognized and acknowledged creative achievements of the adult, to the adult's number of unrecognized creative lifestyle attainments. As a matter of fact, this indicator (having or not having a future career image they were in love with as children) was a better predictor of adult creative achievement than indices of scholarly promise and attainment.

Many gifted young people, however, find it hard to pursue their own dreams. Frequently parents, teachers, and peers have strong expectations of gifted youngsters – expectations that are wrong for them. But, because they do not want to disappoint those who love them most, many children find it hard to resist playing the games others expect them to play. It is a great tragedy when a child gives up doing the thing he or she loves most, to satisfy someone else's dream.

If children are to have the opportunity to fall in love with something and to achieve whatever they can do best and love most, we must teach them to value themselves and to follow all paths open to them, including the arts, for art brings certain kinds of knowing not accessible in any other way. Several years ago, Torrance (1983a) wrote "A Manifesto for Children," to encourage them to sing out their own songs:

1. Don't be afraid to fall in love with something and pursue it with intensity.

2. Know, take pride in, practice, develop, use, exploit, and enjoy your greatest strengths.

3. Learn to free yourself from the expectations of others, and to walk away from the games they try to impose on you. Free yourself to play your own game.

4. Search out and cultivate a great teacher or mentor who will help you play your own game.

5. Don't waste a lot of expensive energy trying to be well-rounded. Do what you love and can do well.

6. Learn the skills of interdependence, giving freely of the infinity of your greatest strengths and most intense loves.

– Don't Be Afraid To Think For Yourself –

John Davis (Age 15)
Mainland Regional High School, Linwood, NJ, USA

To all you individualists, I have decided to write the tale of my life from 1980-81 until now, 2010.

In the years before eighth grade, I was caught up in a programmed society where you had the right to think for yourself until you decided to do so.

When eighth grade came I was exposed to "The Rocky Horror Picture Show" which changed my entire outlook on life. I decided things didn't have to be what everyone else said they were. I took some advice from Dr. Frank-n-Furter who said "Don't dream it, be it." This helped me considerably, instead of just thinking of different things to do, I did the unusual things and didn't care if others in the society thought there was something wrong with me because they were programmed in society to think that way. The movie gave me a reason to deprogram myself. In this way I would have a mind for myself.

When I arrived in high school the teachers were expected to get 375 society programmed kids, kids who would accept anything a teacher said without even saying why; instead they

got about 350 society programmed kids and about 25 deprog-
rammed kids, kids that thought for themselves and asked why?
when a teacher initiated a new theory. The teachers were in-
furiated that some kids would not accept what the teacher said
just because they said it. There were a few teachers that saw that
we, the kids that weren't society programmed, wouldn't make it
through the school system in the classes we had. These teachers
took it upon themselves to group us together and they formed
special classes for us. These teachers had been similar to us in
their younger years at school. These students became my closest
friends, and although we haven't kept in close touch we are still
close friends.

Most of us went to colleges where logic was readily
employed. I took many philosophical courses; from these
courses, and my past experiences, I formed my own philosophy
dealing with getting more people to realize that they are caught
in a set pattern of life that they didn't decide on and to make
them think for themselves. The first thing I told them to do is to
let loose and creatively explore their environments, doing what
they want to do within reason, without fear of what anyone thinks.
Second, find an example of what I told them to do first, such as
"The Rocky Horror Picture Show" in my case, and study it and
allow it to influence the way you think. I didn't publish my
philosophy until five years ago. After I had it published the same
government that gave me freedom of the press seized the book.
They banished the book and they threw me into a solitary con-
finement cell obviously thinking it would hurt me. I suppose I
had freedom of the press until I decided to use it. The stated
reason I was thrown in jail was "for corrupting the traditions of
society."

Throwing me in this cell did not hurt me because I was
given a guitar, and in the time I have been in here I have mastered
it to what I consider a standard of excellence, and also paper
and pens which I am writing this with. The rest of my time I
spend in meditation and/or sleeping.

Back to my story. Directly after college, before publishing
my book, I had gone into independent research on the govern-

ment's impact on the actions of society. Society fears the government so they do anything the government tells them to do without asking why? I decided this must be the influence that acted upon the other students while I was in high school. At this point I published my book including this information.

That caught you up to today so I'll be going off to play guitar. Don't worry about me, I'll be fine. Just some last minute advice to whomever reads this. First, don't be afraid to think for yourself, even if you are the only one who thinks that way. You're unique! If you think for yourself and you feel you can't tell anyone, keep it in your mind and don't forget it. Don't go against your beliefs. Remember you are you and don't let anyone bring you down. Great ideas are often years before their time.

– A Bouquet Of Flowers –

Hilary Lyn Barnes (Age 12)
Rustenburg Junior School, Rondebosch, RSA

I had my usual nervousness as I sat in the corner of the room at the back of the stage. In half an hour I would be on stage playing the "Emperor," Beethoven's fifth piano concerto. As I sat, anxiously exercising my fingers, my mind drifted back to the first time I had played this concerto. My nervousness tonight, although intense, could not be compared with what I had felt then. That night had become the opening bar to my life as a concert pianist – the night that I had won the International Pianoforte Competition at the age of 19, the year 1991!

My love of music had started as a baby. My mother told me that even before I could walk, I would bounce up and down in time to any music that reached my ears. This love had grown within me, and by the age of 11 I had known that my life would be one filled with music as the ambition to become a concert pianist had taken a firm grip on me.

I remembered how my family told me that the competition in the music world was very strong and that one had to be outstanding to be recognized at all. Simply being good was not sufficient to achieve the goal on which I had set my sights. I often wondered whether they had thought I really was not good enough. I had wanted to be like Vladimir Ashkenazy. A very determined child I had been, and my practicing matched my determination with the result that I had spent hours and hours and hours at the piano. That determination that I experienced then has never left me in all these years!

At the age of 13 I had won my first cup in the concerto section of the Cape Town eisteddfod. I had played the first movement of Beethoven's first piano concerto. How I had loved learning that work and will I ever forget the excitement when the adjudicator announced that I had won the cup. My excitement had been shared by my family and friends and had led to a great deal of celebrating.

As the winner of the concerto group, I had then been asked to play with the Cape Town Symphony Orchestra and that was the first time I had performed on stage with a full orchestra.

I went on to win the International Pianoforte Competition, and from then onwards my career blossomed like a rose. I toured the world playing great works by great composers.

The year 1994 brought a sadness to me such as I had never known. My grandfather, my friend and companion, died. That part of my life had been the deepest, darkest valley I had ever been through. I wondered whether the sun would ever shine again. Although I had loved my parents dearly, my life had centered around my grandfather. It had been at his knee that I had learned and heard many nursery rhymes and stories. From him I had learned the names of flowers, the habits of the birds, and the ways of people. More than all that, he had shared with me my first love – music. He had been a constant source of encouragement and inspiration.

The period following his death had been one of total barrenness. I gave no performances whatsoever. Practicing had brought bitter heartache, the very music that we had loved so much then caused pain and the result had been a temporary turning away from the piano.

Slowly, however, as time had healed, I had learned many other beautiful works including Beethoven's Fourth concerto,

Mandelsshon's First and the pianoforte section of Beethoven's Sonata Number 8 for piano and violin. I had later performed that work with Jonathan Rubinstein, a famous violinist. It had been a great success and the audience had shouted for more which we had gladly given.

But, my family had been right – the competition in the music world had remained intense and during my two years of musical drought, many other outstanding pianists had emerged. It had taken three years of hard practicing and dedication and determination to become recognized once again.

At this time of my life I realized for the first time how wonderful classical music was. Right from the time of its conception, it had remained the type of music that people never tired of. No matter how much electric music they made with synthesizers and computers, classical music would always remain the most beautiful and most well-loved music. Electric music would never have any emotional effect on one, whereas classical music could dissolve one into tears by its sheer beauty, or could make one so radiantly happy one would want to laugh and sing and jump for joy.

I sighed. It had been a hectic afternoon. The piano tuner had come to tune the piano, and after doing so, the computer had registered that three notes were out of pitch by 0,21 of a musipitch. After about one-and-a-half hours the piano tuner had corrected that, but then he still had to tone the piano. Once again the computer registered that a note was not right by 0,18 of a musitone.

After what seemed like hours, I had eventually had a chance to try the piano. It was beautiful, and the tone was absolutely magnificent. As for the acoustics in the hall, they left nothing to be desired! The walls were made out of solid wood, that was about 30cm thick and the ceiling was a high glass dome. Above the glass was a thick layer of metal to protect the glass from falling objects.

Suddenly, the computer buzzed and I was brought back to reality with a start. The thickness of the walls rendered my room completely soundproof and I could, therefore, warm up with some scales on the piano provided for that purpose.

Five minutes later, the computer alerted me once again. It was time for me to go on stage. As I walked onto the platform, I was welcomed by thousands of people, clapping and shouting. Out of the corner of my eye I noticed an old, grey-haired man, sitting in the front row. It was none other than Vladimir Ashkenazy, smiling broadly and clapping loudly!

I sat down at the piano and adjusted the stool to the right height by pressing a button on one side. As the first notes of the orchestra sounded in the hall, I entered my own world – a world of music – and I became unaware of the thousands of people sitting, listening to me.

The applause was deafening! I sighed with relief as I shook hands with the conducter. As I turned to take a bow, the audience rose like one man. I was totally overwhelmed, never before had I received such an ovation. I became aware of a beautiful bouquet of flowers being thrust into my arms, and to my sheer joy I realized that it was being presented by the maestro himself, Vladimir Ashkenazy.

In that bouquet was a lot more than flowers – it said something that words could not say. This master of music had somehow now passed on this title to me.

– The World Of Dance –

Natalie Yvette Shinhoster (Age 12)
Lee Roy Myers Middle School, Savannah, GA, USA

Hello, my name is Jenifer Task. I live on the planet Das. On my planet we dance, act, or sing for a living. Our audience comes from long distances to see us perform. They travel on galaxy grabbers. Galaxy grabbers are similar to trains, however, they have no tracks.

I'm a dancer on Das. I dance ballet on Das. I would like to tell you of one fear everyone dislikes . . . getting old. I didn't avoid it, but proved that old is as good as new.

Today was one of those "always rushing" days. After leaving from a dance class I had an audition for a part in a very old ballet entitled "The Nutcracker."

When I got to the Dome Theater a very tall young lady approached me and said, "What's ya' name, lady?" Very disturbed I answered, "Jen."

"Oh, yea. Jenifer Task. Jenifer Task! Oh! Miss Task I didn't recognize you, I'm sorry!" she exclaimed.

"That's quite alright." I said extremely pleased.

"Mr. Williams will see you now," the girl said shamefully.

As I walked in, all the light panels were off except the spotlight. Like many other auditions the judges didn't want to be seen.

Mr. Williams said, "If you would like, you may warm up in room seven."

As I walked into the room I saw my past. Many beautiful young eager girls ready to make their mark on the world.

"Miss Task, you're to audition in three minutes," the voice on the intercom announced.

Once I handed the pianist my music I danced as though I had only a few seconds left in my life. As sweat bounced off my face and ran down my neck I leaped through the air with tremendous height and speed. In performing my last jet'e and arabesque, my audition was complete. I heard a voice from the audience say, "Thank you, Miss Task. We'll call you soon."

From my past experience I knew that "we'll call you soon" meant the ol' heave'ho. However, I'm proud to say I was wrong. Mr. Williams called to tell me that I got the lead part in the "Nutcracker."

I knew from here on in I was going to be on a tight schedule. I had to go to dance class very early, then get to rehearsal which was all day. The rehearsals lasted almost one month.

The night finally arrived! There were over one million people in the Dome Theater. When we finally began to dance, the time went by extremely fast. The scenery was painted vividly and our costumes were light and feminine. The entire ballet was full of life, warmth, and sensitivity.

At the end of the performance Mr. Williams presented me with one dozen long-stemmed roses – as if 14 curtain calls weren't enough. He also whispered in my ear that I would be in the next ballet.

The next week as I was on my way to the studio I felt as though someone was following me. Suddenly someone grabbed me from my waist. I remembered taking defense classes when I was younger. You should try to jab the person with something pointed such as keys. Keys! I'm holding some! I rammed my keys in his throat.

I ran down the street calling "Police, Police!" When a policeman arrived he grabbed the man. He had escaped from the prison dome.

When I got to the theater, Mr. Williams gave instructions of what time to be at the theater and what days. We practiced different dances until we got the correct steps. Next we put the steps to music, and lastly picked costumes.

The performance began at eight o'clock. As I danced I could feel myself running out of air. Once the ballet was over I was weak and couldn't catch my breath.

I told Mr. Williams; he said I must be dreaming, although I wasn't. As soon as I got home I looked at the Medi-Com or medical computer. There showed only one person in my family who had my symptoms after doing different exercises of some sort. It was called Asthma. However, it is called T.B.T. or The Breath Taker on Das.

When the night of the third recital arrived, I felt very faint. When I got on stage and the spotlight hit me, the sweat ran down my forehead into my eyes. I couldn't see anything and then I fell to the floor.

Once I woke up I was in the hospital. My doctor, Dr. Charles Hayes, was standing over me.

He asked me a few questions. "Has this happened before?"

Very weakly I answered, "No, however, I felt very weak and tired once last week."

"From what you've told us and from the tests we took while you were unconscious we believe you have T.B.T." Dr. Hayes declared.

"I've read up on T.B.T. on my Medi-Com. It could be fatal if not taken care of and usually occurs to people 40 or older," I stated knowledgeably.

"True, and because you are 40 and it's in your family, we are positive you are a victim of T.B.T." Dr. Hayes said.

While in the hospital recovery room I received a letter from Mr. Williams saying, "We of the Das Dancing Committee think that you should be dropped from Das dancing performances." I was furious. Just because I'm 40 and have T.B.T. doesn't mean I'm dying!

When I completely recovered from my illness, I thought for many days at a time. The first thing that I thought of was my career. I wasn't going to let 30 years of dancing slip through my fingers.

I had a very clear picture of what I was going to do. I put a lease on a large dome. I would teach dancing there. When the owner of the dome saw my credits he explained how I would be able to own the dome in four months.

I called the studio The Dome of Dance. In the first few months I made enough money to buy the building and put leases on two other domes.

Soon my studios were all over Das, and soon to be all over the universe.

So, sometimes a fatal problem can become a very prosperous idea!

– Happy Family –

Bridget Burke (Age 12)
Sacred Heart Girl's College, Hamilton, New Zealand

Although this was supposed to be a family resort, there weren't many families there, mine included. I had had to leave my children with my parents until the divorce was fixed up. I couldn't leave them with my husband, who I knew was probably away somewhere drowning his sorrows at that moment. Of course, I could hardly blame him. Boredom had driven many of my friends to much more dangerous past times. The rate of unemployment, the cost of living, the lack of anything worthwhile to do had turned him and others into alcoholics. He literally swam home at night, he was so drunk. Then he began taking the housekeeping money and hitting the kids. He slept in the lock-up as often as he slept at home.

My brother, a lawyer, was organizing the divorce papers. Convenient. The number of people filing for divorce these days slowed things down, so he recommended this beach hotel to me, so I could "pull myself together." I had pulled myself together on the second day of my arrival and now spent my time taking pictures, going for walks, and window shopping in the city.

Funnily enough, books had gone out of fashion. There were only private libraries and the only books now on sale were about hundreds of years in the future or about green men, blasting the earth to pieces. I hated these books because of what they had done to the literature I grew up with. Enid Blyton was unknown, Jules Verne stories considered "kid's stuff." I longed, suddenly, for home and my bookcase. I wished more than ever that my husband would stop drinking, and that I could think of a way to provide him with the money to get help.

"Are you all right, dear?"

I looked up. In front of me, looking at me, was an old lady in a white dress and pink cardigan, who had her handbag hand-cuffed to her wrist. She looked so worried that I realized I must have been crying. I had been.

"Look, love," she said, taking my arm, "come to my house and we'll have a cup of tea and I'll see if I can help you. I'm really a very nice person, you know."

I felt like laughing, but I saw the earnest expression on her face, and so I nodded and started to walk along behind her.

Eventually I found myself telling her everything – all my troubles. I felt deeply grateful for her sympathy, and her cup of tea – real tea. There was also homemade shortbread. I felt so relaxed there that I fell asleep on her sofa.

The next day Molly and I sat and sewed together little rag toys, which she would give away. Then after lunch she said she had a surprise for me.

"I don't normally tell people about my secret, but maybe it will help you." And she took a little key out from behind a clock, which she used to open a little door. She propelled me inside, and I gasped with wonder and delight.

I was in a rather small room, but it was lined from floor to ceiling with shelves of books. Molly sat me down in a well-worn Lazy-Boy armchair, and proceeded to pile my lap with novels, biographies, poetry books, reproductions of Shakespearean plays, and even little children's books. I spent a whole week reading and decided what I would do. I would write.

For the next month I was kept supplied with paper and ink – there were no typewriters in Molly's home – and the end product was the story of a middle-aged woman with a broken marriage, three neglected children, and not much purpose in life. It told of an older woman who helped set her straight again. The story behind the story was mine, and my feelings wrote themselves onto the paper. I was satisfied that my message would get through. If people were more considerate and less selfish, the world would be a better place. I sent the script to a major publisher and waited for a reply.

Three weeks later I received a letter from the publisher asking for an interview. To my surprise, he wanted to buy my script, copyright, and contract. He wanted to know how much it would cost, so I told him to decide and I went back to Molly.

I told her that I was leaving. She looked a bit sad, but told me it was the best thing. She told me to wait where I was and she would be back in a minute.

When she returned, she had a little box. Inside was a duplicate of the library key. "You come back here anytime you like, dear, and remember to bring the kids, won't you?"

I was astounded. "Isn't there anything I can do for you?"

"Yes, you can give me the first copy off the printing press, and take your husband to this doctor. He is highly recommended. Don't forget, you can never get too much of a good thing. Your marriage will be all right now, dear."

And she was right. My marriage was patched back together, slowly but soundly, and the money rolled in. We moved to the country where I was in second heaven. I was sure Molly, who died, would be in heaven, after handing on her happiness to me.

Many, many people read my books and lots of others started to write. Space Invader Parlours came second to book shops and libraries. When I went next to the family resort there were children everywhere and there were no vacancies at all.

– The Choice –

Elizabeth Besen (Age 15)
River Del High School, Oradell, NJ, USA

Elizabeth sat silently in the empty courtroom, the eye of the storm, calm and quiet, while the press and public clustered outside. Soon they would come thundering in to witness a life or death decision. But why should she, an alumna of Yale and Harvard, a senior partner in New York's most prestigious law firm, worry? Today, however, for the first time in her professional life, she was overcome by a new and unnerving feeling: she didn't believe in her client's cause.

Her client was a brilliant young artist, on whom life had played a dirty trick. The purpose and glory of his life, his capacity to create, was threatened. If he continued painting, he would pay with his life. And yet he had insisted on the right to pay that final price.

His lawyer, impeccably chosen by the omniscient computer, was dismayed by his decision. She was almost disturbed enough to regret having specialized in "law and medical ethics."

Soon the courtroom buzzed with the electricity of an anxious crowd. The computer-selected jury of programmers, engineers, business executives, and a lone file clerk, sat silently. The video recorder came to electronic life, and a bland voice asked all present to stand as the judge, also designated by computer on the basis of his training in medical ethics, strode to the bench.

"This court will now come to order."

All witnesses were sworn in advance, and the physician's professional qualifications conceded.

The petitioner's attorney approached the jury box. "Section 3011 of the Unconsolidated Laws, effective September 26, 2008, provides: 'In order to preserve life, medical doctors may appear in court, seeking permission to perform treatment without the patient's consent.' We will prove that if Jean Laurent refuses to submit to surgical amputation of his left arm, he will die. In accord with regulation 3011, Dr. North requests a court order compelling Mr. Laurent to undergo this operation."

Then Elizabeth rose and addressed the jury: "My client, Jean Laurent, recognized as one of the world's most brilliant artists, has been offered a prosthetic replacement for his cancerous left arm. He has declined, because he believes this procedure, in altering his capacity to paint, will take all meaning from his life. We will prove he is mentally competent to make all decisions concerning his personal privacy and quality of existence."

The attorney for the petitioner called Dr. Samuel North to the witness stand. "Dr. North, would you please explain Mr. Laurent's condition?"

"Mr. Laurent has myxosarcoma in his left arm: a cancer which affects bone and connective tissue."

"Have you had previous experience working with myxosarcoma patients?"

"Thirty-one years."

"Is the condition fatal?"

"Yes."

"Can Mr. Laurent be saved?"

"If his arm is surgically removed and replaced by a prosthetic. I must add that such devices have been perfected to a degree inconceivable in the past. Electrodes, attached to shoulder muscles, send and receive brain impulses that allow the patient to manipulate the prosthetic nearly as well as he had controlled his original limb."

"Does this procedure enjoy a high degree of success?"

"Definitely. Through rehabilitation, including bio-feedback, almost all patients regain normal digital function."

"Thank you, Dr. North."

Mr. Caldwell sat down, satisfied.

Elizabeth approached the witness stand, paused, then spoke: "Dr. North, when you were asked to evaluate the success of this procedure, you spoke with great assurance, isn't that right?"

"Yes."

"Isn't the procedure ever unsuccessful?"

"Failure is virtually impossible."

"But there is a chance?"

"Well, one can never . . . . "

"Are there other treatments?"

"Yes, but chemotherapy and radiation have twice the failure rate."

"So you are admitting that even with today's most advanced medical techniques, Mr. Laurent might still die?"

"Yes, but the chan——"

"That will be all."

Elizabeth called her first witness, Dr. Abigail Blackwell.

"Dr. Blackwell, did Jean Laurent undergo psychological testing?"

"Yes."

"Did you find him sane and capable of making decisions?"

"Yes."

"Thank you, Dr. Blackwell; that will be all."

When Elizabeth returned to her seat, her client's eyes gleamed in appreciation. She smiled back, trying to look confident.

Mr. Caldwell sprang up and strode to the witness stand.

"Dr. Blackwell, as an experienced psychiatrist, you must have studied the clinical characteristics of certain groups, correct?"

"Correct."

"Isn't it true that many artists tend to be self-centered and stubborn?"

"*Some* artists have been known to be strong-willed."

"And react hastily when opposed?"

"Yes."

"Then artists can be characterized as intent upon pursuing their own ways, rather than being amenable to suggestions from others?"

"Generalizing to that extent is . . . . "

"No further questions, your Honor."

Elizabeth called Jean Laurent to the witness stand. "Mr. Laurent, please explain why you refuse to have your arm amputated."

For a moment, the artist sat silently, staring down; then he raised his head slowly and began to speak, as though in self-communion: "An artist is not a piece of clay that can be easily molded into a desired shape. An artist is like a diamond, a complex of intricate psychological facets. He perceives the world in a most individual way, and then tries to translate his feelings through colors, textures, and images."

"An artist's works are fruits of freedom, creatures of both his reason and his senses. Without his work an artist's life is nothing: an assembly line, a meaningless gesture. Art is a series of impulses that put significance into the commonplace; a constant re-evaluation of the world. 'How dull it is to pause, to make an end, to rust un-burnished, not to shine in use! As though to breathe were life.'"

The jurors sat riveted to their seats by bolts of shock and confusion. Their eyes indicated they had been moved by the artist's appeal. Their faces blanched as if the blood had drained away old ideas and opinions, leaving them free to consider his words.

*   *   *

The spectators had grown clamorous. Hammering his gavel, the judge demanded silence.

Mr. Caldwell began his closing statements: "Ladies and gentlemen of the jury, the purpose of the medical profession is to save human lives. In the past decade, scientists and researchers have made stunning headway in their pursuit of life-saving practices. Mr. Laurent has refused treatment, condemning himself to almost certain death. Though he has been proved mentally competent, Dr. Blackwell has testified that artists tend to be strong willed, prone to hasty and irrational decisions that are often not in their own best interests. Perhaps Mr. Laurent does not realize that with proper rehabilitation, the prosthetic arm will be almost as supple as his original one. Able jurors, the decision is yours: Will you allow Dr. North and his colleagues to perform surgery offering Mr. Laurent his life, or will you leave Mr. Laurent to deteriorate and die?"

Elizabeth, who had been contemplating her own thoughts, was now convinced that Mr. Laurent must be given the choice. Our dearest possession may be the right to determine the quality of our existence. And those who have lived with the greatest exultation may be unwilling to settle for less. She must act from the heart. Laying aside the prepared speech, Elizabeth clasped her hands and addressed the jurors: "The operation Dr. North wishes to perform may prolong Mr. Laurent's life. But to my client, mere quantity of time is not the issue. He cares deeply about how he fills whatever years are left to him. Life must keep its splendor; his days must count for something. If he loses his capacity to create, the whole world will suffer a loss. We will never see further evidence of his passion. Mr. Laurent is the best judge of his mind and spirit, and he says that *they* will die if he is forced to use an artificial limb, insensitive to the dictates of his creativity. Let him be spared the disgrace of having his body assaulted. If you force this operation upon him, you will be killing an artist while merely keeping his body alive. Without his arm, the bridge from an artist's soul to the canvas that displays his images to the world, Mr. Laurent's life will become only a waiting room for death."

Elizabeth moved, almost without volition, back to her seat. She didn't know if her words had conveyed the full sweep of her feelings, but she had tried. Her eyes on the jurors, Elizabeth reached out for Mr. Laurent's arm.

* * *

"This court will now come to order" boomed the judge. "Ladies and gentlemen of the jury, have you reached a verdict?"

The head juror rose: "Yes, we have, your Honor. In this matter of amputation, the jurors of this court award to the defendant, Jean Laurent, the right to create his own life. We deny Dr. North a court order to perform surgery."

"Court adjourned."

Mr. Laurent smiled radiantly at his attorney – who promptly burst into tears.

CHAPTER SIX

Take Care Of Today

Maybe all this would have to happen, but then again maybe it won't, if we look after our world, our country; if we learn not to litter and be so careless; if we stop fighting and destroying plant and animal life, polluting our air and sea; causing destruction and actually destroying man. If we learn to look after our world and country, maybe, just maybe, we will survive.

(From scenario by Nicola Kent of
East London, Republic of South Africa)

Herman Kahn, who died in 1983, was one of our most influential futurists. "Until his death, Ban-the-Bombers and the whole gloom-and-doom set had felt 'The Wrath of Kahn'" (Reston, 1983). Kahn's last vision was to help educate the children of the world to develop a more optimistic, yet realistic image of the future. Much of his energies were devoted to the creation of pilot programs to attain this vision.

The fact is that the children of the world *are* hopeful, but, like young Nicola Kent, they are also worried – worried about what we are doing to their tomorrow – worried that irreparable damage will be done before they have their chance at leadership. Their concerns are vividly expressed in this Chapter's scenarios.

Herman Kahn (Kahn & Wiener, 1967) used scenarios quite effectively, and some of them resulted in important initiatives that have made critical differences in our "present." In a 1982 interview, he said, "We draw scenarios and try to cope with history before it happens."

It is imperative that we "take care of today," because today contains the seeds of tomorrow. If we look closely, we can see implications for our future in current ways of behaving and conducting affairs. Scenario writing is important because it helps us to "make strange" (Gordon, 1961) our present situation, and see it with a fresh perspective, avoiding the cliches and habitual disregard we often have for the world around us. Forced by the scenarios to focus on today's implications, we begin to see new relationships and to avoid obvious and trite solutions, the "premature closure" of the jaded perspective.

On July 7, 1983, newspapers and television news reports carried a human interest story that speaks to the way we treat one another today. A group of Marines, part of a peacekeeping force stationed in Lebanon, had raised a goat as a pet. They fed it, bathed it, loved it, and named it "Col. Bill E. Goat." The young Marines decided to send Bill E. Goat to the Naval Academy back in the States, as a good luck gesture for the Academy's upcoming Fall football season. All the red tape was cleared; the vet gave the goat a clean bill of health; the Navy Department approved; the State Department approved. Colonel Goat was put aboard a plane en route to the United States.

When the goat arrived at Kennedy Airport, it was summarily slaughtered. The official who gave the order was quoted as saying, "Sentiment [surrounding the killing of the goat] is fine, but foot-and-mouth disease could cost the American people millions of dollars. This is our policy . . . there are no exceptions." Subsequent television interviews with the Marines in Lebanon showed their sorrow and frustration; they could not understand why their goat had to die.

Four months later, the nation was stunned to learn that a Lebanese terrorist driving a truck loaded with explosives had broken through the guard perimeter of U.S. Marines and rammed into a barracks, killing over 200 men as they slept. The same Marine peacekeeping detachment that raised Col. Bill E. Goat now mourned its human losses. This time, the news media ran stories of families attempting to cope with the loss of loved ones, trying to understand why these young men had to die. The nation focused again on the question of why our troops were in Lebanon, and searched for reasons for the seemingly-meaningless deaths, needing to find purpose in the tragedy.

Most people accepted "premature closure," the easy answers: "They died to protect our interests in the Middle East;" "They died for the American way of life;" "They died for the glory of the Corps." And so on.

A closer look at the young men, however, suggests they may not have willingly died for such abstractions. For these were boys who had raised a pet goat, and then been angered and dismayed when someone killed it in the name of "policy." These were individuals living life in a sentimental and caring way in the midst of potential war.

Individuals should come before policy, be they goats or young men. If we could ask the Marines who died in Lebanon, "How can we take care of today so tomorrow will be a better place?" they might tell us of a tomorrow in which feelings will be prized, and humane considerations will allow individual exceptions to every policy rule. Perhaps this is what they died for.

Most of the time we fail to recognize how what we do now sets the stage for what we will be later. It takes a crisis like the Lebanese tragedy to force us to see today as the footprint of tomorrow. A down-home Tennessee philosopher of our acquaintance has a saying, "Before you can know where you're going, you've got to know where you're at."

Edward Cornish (1977), of the World Future Society, believes that scenario writing helps develop the creative potential in children by making them more aware of future problems and possible solutions or precautions. Thus, in scenarios, children are encouraged to crystallize their thoughts about the promise and dangers the future and their adulthood may hold for them. Survival research (Torrance, 1965) indicates that the greatest danger in life-threatening emergencies and extreme conditions is a failure to recognize the seriousness of the situation. Preserving our humanity in the face of war, technology, or dehumanizing policy is very serious business. The children who have written the scenarios in this chapter seem to understand this, and they must be taken seriously.

– The World Of Us –

Yoav Segnier (Age 13)
Haifa, Israel

There were no more names, no more words like "I," "he," "you
. . . ."

The elections of 2008 caused all this. The party that won
the elections decided that society comes before the single (this
word also does not exist anymore) and as the keyword of society
is "we," all other words for people were declared illegal. People
found it quite difficult at the beginning but got used to it.

Children who were born after 2008 grew up speaking only
about "us," "we," "our . . . . " Life became very pleasant . . . .
There were no rules because of the world of "US." *We* don't
have to tell *us* what to do. There were no crimes because there
were no rules and there were no punishments because there
were no crimes.

And then one day an uncivilized creature entered this world.
It was a strange man that lived somewhere far away from civilization and spoke all the time about "I." "He" did only what "he"
wanted. "He" even had a name. The "we" were shocked. This
man was like cancer to them, but they didn't even know that
"he" also didn't understand what was going on. And as things
go on, in every contact between two worlds that don't understand
each other, things were bad, very bad.

A world where there are no rules, crimes, and punishments
can be either a jungle or . . . .

A man can survive in a jungle but this new way of life was
so strange that Robert (that uncivilized man with a name), like
any civilized man, tried to change it and he succeeded. But
changes can be both good and bad. He told them that they are
singles so they all together became *one* single. Now it was a
fight that was one against one, but in no way fair. It was also a
fight that anyway it would end will be the end of the human race.
And Robert knew that, so really there isn't any end to the story,
but that isn't important because no one will ever read it.

(Robert – 2010)

– Our World Is Doomed To Die –

Tracy Lee Field (Age 12)
St. Dominic's School, Boksburg, Transvaal, RSA

I am living in the year 2010. It has been a very difficult year. One of drought, poverty, and sickness. On the 25th of October we had the first summer rainfall. It was a happy occasion. From the year 2009, 19 November, we were living in drought. Because if it didn't rain no one could grow any crops. Therefore, people got sick and many died. It was a great tragedy.

I, Tracy Lee Field, was born on the first of May, 1970. I am now 40 years old. I had taken my degree in medicine, a very sad profession because the earth is drying out. The problem of over-population on the earth is serious and people are pioneering to settle on other planets.

The year 2000 started the year of the Atomic Age owing to the lack of fuel resources. The problem encountered with atomic power is devastating, causing skin and eye cancer; on account of the blowouts and continuous leaks of this deadly energy, they are slowly killing the earth.

When I was a little girl, I can remember a metal called gold. Today this metal is very rare, caused by the overworking of gold mines. Uranium is the most sought after metal in today's era. The trading currency today is based on moon stones.

In 1990 we saw the last of some major plants such as ferns, grape vines, peach trees, and oak trees, now that the air is very polluted. The atmosphere around the earth has become polluted because of the overload of industry and continuous use of insecticides.

We have slowly but surely upset the balance of nature, causing the abundance of flies, mosquitos, bees, ants, bugs, and spiders. Today the word "conservation" and its meaning as regards wild life is extensively used.

There is no such thing as motor cars but now there are flying objects. Airplanes are not often used on international flights but are especially designed for space travel.

The earth is developing into a concrete jungle with life's

essential things being pushed away. If only man saw what was happening to the earth, he could save us, but all he thinks of is the development of science and survival.

Today life is like a big jigsaw puzzle with pieces being lost every day.

So very few of us believe in our saviour God, and now I say a prayer, "Dear Lord, please save us from extinction."

– The Escapees –

Bob DiDia (Age 16)
Middletown South High School, Middletown, NJ, USA

I believe it's around the year 2010. Or possibly, it might even be 2011, depending on whether I've miscalculated the number of winters spent up here in these mountains. Actually, I left the ranks of civilization in 1987 to come here and haven't gone back since.

You might ask why . . . why are you up there? When I graduated from high school in 1984, my mind was a mess. I had no idea what I wanted to do, be, or what college to choose. In the meanwhile, I decided to get myself a job for that summer. It was a pretty good one for a kid just coming out of high school and I made a fair sum of money. Because I couldn't decide on a college, I thought the best thing to do was stick with my job and make as much money and see and meet as many people as possible.

During that fall in '84, I met a lot of people on the job. Some were funny, intellectual, mean, ugly, and peculiar. I really enjoyed meeting people and thought that it would be great to embark upon a trip across the U.S. to see how they differ from place to place. So, I set my mind to take a trip across the U.S. north, south, east, and west to get a good look at America and its people.

That spring in 1985 was super. Never had my mind been so free of trouble and problems. With the money I had saved from work, I bought a van, packed up and set out to see the "real" America. Two years later, I moved to the mountains. It was then, in retrospect, I saw America in a different light. The land was overdeveloped and everywhere I looked pollution prevailed.

People, for the most part, were always putting each other down and confirming themselves to separate peer groups because they were afraid to stand alone in a crowd. Nobody was willing to help anybody else; everybody cared exclusively about themselves. People were afraid to be individuals.

That's why I'm here. Originally, I only planned to go the mountains to find a peace of mind. Instead it became my home, probably forever. My life has been totally simplified. The food I eat I catch or grow myself and the house I live in was built by hand. As for human contact, I'm not alone up here. Every once in a while you get the stragglers from society who are trying to escape what the world offers them. People like me.

– Tomorrow's A Minute Away –

Christina Cotillas (Age 15)
Bishop's Hatfield Girls School, Hatfield, Herts., UK

It's the year 2010 and I am 42 years old. It's only 27 years ago since I was still struggling through my last years at school. When I left school with my exam passes kept tightly under my belt, my family and I moved out of England and back to their home – Spain. That was in 1987, then, it was all the same as I remembered it from my school days. All the buildings, roads, cars, same old people walking their dogs, and going to work by the same old routes. Everything was the same . . . normal.

For the next four years I worked steadily through most of the year until August which was when I took my vacation. It was just the same as always until it happened. The world of total technology was here. First I noticed this gradual change in my job. I was no longer needed. My job was taken over by computers. My companions and I were, as you might say, thrown out – literally. Everywhere we went the same notices loomed out saying "No Vacancies – Computers taken over." It made us feel sick. Our wonderful free life was being taken over by . . . robots and computers.

Little children were being brought up on mini-personalized computers that taught them the essential needs until the age of ten, and then they were passed over to the master "Brain," that taught a hundred children at a time. This was distressing; everything had changed so much.

In the next three months, the last straw finally came. We were no longer allowed to have our own lifestyle. Our houses were to be transformed to match up to the standards of the supreme council. What next? Our cozy flats, houses, rooms, beds, chairs, windows, roofs, everything . . . transformed.

Whereas once you could open a cupboard and take out what you needed, you now had to press a three digit code, of your own choice, and this would open the cupboard for you. If you couldn't remember the code an alarm would go off and alert the guard at the door who would immediately come and release the code for you.

I was upset; looking out of my window, I could see guards standing at the entrance to every door, house, office building, and shop within the radius of five kilometers. Of course the next city would have its own system.

Television monitors were installed in every room of my house, and I was watched morning, noon, and night; every movement was carefully monitored and kept in the computer files. I managed to persuade the security guard to not monitor my movements in the bathroom because I wasn't likely to commit an error that could change the human race. He agreed and I was free from the revolving eye for 15 minutes. If I took longer, I would be monitored for two days non-stop.

Life was beginning to be a living hell, or at least a prison. What I needed was company. I hadn't been out of the house for three months, because I had been told I didn't need to. I was dominated by the "big A" as I called it, what could I do?

It was the 24th December, 1991, in other words, Christmas Eve, and I was alone, so I decided to phone my friends. Although rather difficult to do, I did it.

On Christmas Day I had my cousins, my aunts and uncles, and also my parents and gran round. The total number of people was about 50 eating and drinking. Of course, everything was prepared. The champagne was green, the wine was blue, and our food was contained in tree tables – they were pink, blue, and purple. But, amazingly enough, they did taste of the food we were eating. And the last one even had lumps in it – just like the nutty nougat and marzipan.

On New Year's Eve we had another reunion party – this time it wasn't with my family – but I phoned my English friends from my school days. We had an interesting evening although we were being watched every minute as though we were criminals or something like that.

In April, 1992, I met someone that I was later to marry. We had a wonderful month together because the monitors are turned off when you find yourself a "mate." But, he had to go. He said he would be back, but he wasn't sure when because he had to go where the army sent him to do some kind of secret job – something to do with lasers. His profession normally was a trained physicist, but, of course, he had been taken over by another electronic friend.

My friend came back after three months of waiting for him. So on the 13th of June, 1992, which happened to be on a Saturday, we got married. I was now a married lady, 24 years of age and expecting a child by the man I loved.

In February, 1993, I had a baby boy. Although I was absolutely delighted with him, I knew that when he was five years of age I would lose him. He would be sent to the computer schools and he would learn how to program and then be educated. Then when my little boy was ten he would have to go to the "brain" until he was 16. Twelve years without seeing him – he would be controlled by the state and then dominated like the rest of us. What if he wasn't mentally stable? What if he couldn't cope? These questions revolved in my mind over and over again.

Five years went by and I had another child. Charlie, my son, had been sent to school. It was 1998 and I gave birth to a little girl. Lucy would not be taken away because she was a girl and, therefore, her place is in the home. Alex, my husband, taught her himself to program and read computers.

Lucy is now 12 and Charlie is 17. He has joined the secret army, training to evolve the laser into action. Trying to protect our city against the bad of the world, keeping out enemies. We now have our own laser field reaching across the surrounding countryside to keep them out.

Looking back on these past 27 years, I begin to really think about just how good our natural childhoods were. Walking along a casual road in summer, perhaps eating an ice cream cone, knowing that you are not going to be stopped by a guard and asked for identity papers. Seeing all the variations in cars – some big, some small. Looking forward to summer holidays, Christmas, and things like that. Little old ladies with shopping in their trolleys.

Where have these days gone? Why does technology always, always win . . . it's no fun. It's true – tomorrow is a minute away . . .

CHAPTER SEVEN

We Will Make Our Own Way

In these scenarios, children throughout the world envision their heroes and heroines as changing the future by courageously following their beliefs and dreams. They recognize this will not be easy, but they affirm that they do have such courage, and that "they will make their own way."

This resolve to "make our own way" is particularly evident in attitudes about schools, including college. Many of the authors — including 55% of the American entrants — see themselves as attaining their career competence through self-directed and experiential learning. Further, many of them see present schools and teaching methods as obsolescent.

In 1974, Torrance asked a sample of about 200 gifted elementary and high school students in several states what occupations they thought would become obsolete by the year 2000. Thirty-five percent of them named, "teaching." Early in 1975, he asked this same question of young people in three underdeveloped countries: Thailand, Taiwan, and the Philippines. Thirty percent of them named "teaching" as a likely candidate for obsolescence. Only "laborer" — raw, manual, human labor — was selected more frequently. Torrance collected similar data while in Japan in 1975, with similar results. In the summers of 1976 and 1977, Torrance asked the same question of 400 gifted high school students in the Career Awareness and Futures component of the Georgia Governor's Honors Program. Half listed "teaching" as likely to become obsolete. The closest runner-up (35%) was "farm laborer."

There are reasons why young people today believe they cannot depend on schools and colleges as a resource for attaining the competencies they need for the future. First, many perceive teachers primarily as "dispensers of information" and "correctors of errors." In addition, the most gifted among them find their teachers quite limited and outdated in the information they dispense, and find much error in their "correcting of errors." Frequently, such children are more advanced than their teachers, more willing to cross the new frontiers of knowledge. They realize that dispensing information and correcting errors can be accomplished more easily, accurately, economically, and efficiently by computers and other information systems than by human teachers.

Young people have also learned that teachers and schools (including colleges) are not very responsive to the future needs of students. This has been pointed out by such scholars as Michael W. Apple (1983), who, writing in a well-known educational journal, states that teachers are losing their capacity to respond to student needs. He argues that this is evidenced by movements to standardize curricula. Apple believes textbook publishers will further standardize content, basing it on competency tests, and routinizing it as much as possible so lessons will produce measurable outcomes with little variability to fit cost/control models. He maintains that already, this process is "deskilling" teachers. He acknowledges that while we need better programs, they will be successful only to the extent that students feel school has something to offer – both now and for the future.

There is considerable evidence to suggest that gifted young people in particular feel that the schools they attend have nothing much to offer them. For example, Safter (1983) completed an intensive study of three gifted boys attending three different junior high schools. All three were learning in fantastic ways, with great enthusiasm. All of their learning activities, however, were outside school, and conducted without the aid of their teachers. In fact, there was not much communication between them and their teachers and, in most instances, the teachers were unaware of the boys' learning activities.

Torrance's (1983b) research also reveals that this phenomenon has been occurring for the past 10 to 20 years. In a 22-year longitudinal study, he found that many creatively gifted students entered college, but soon discovered that the curriculum was unresponsive to their future career needs. After frustrating efforts to satisfy these needs, they withdrew from college and attained career expertise through self-directed and experiential learning. Some of them found responsive mentors who guided their efforts to some extent. These mentors were sometimes able to help certify or validate the student's expertise so their careers could progress despite the lack of traditional credentials. As foreseen by our scenario writers, some of the students experienced difficulty in validating their expertise and were forced to resort to irrelevant and sometimes wasteful ways to attain the label of "expert" necessary if one is to be validated in our society. For example, one brilliant and inventive young man in the study had created a series of powerful and effective computer programs. Businesses and corporations refused to even listen to him, however, because he lacked traditional credentials. In frustration, he entered law school, earned a law degree, and gained admission to the bar. Although these achievements were completely irrelevant to his expertise with computers, they gave him credentials. Plowman (1979) has suggested that socially-approved mentors be used to certify such expertise – a service that presumably will be needed by the 55% of scenario writers who anticipate they will have to acquire their expertise through self-directed and experiential learning.

These young writers may be unrealistic to think they can make it on their own, bypassing traditional routes. However, even recognizing that the expectation exists, and that it has already been realized by today's young adults, at least to an extent, presents a challenge. Certainly the larger society must become involved, both in making schools more responsive to student needs, and in validating and certifying expertise or competence, however it has been attained.

The scenarios for this chapter were especially difficult to select, because there was such a variety of candidates. We hope the ones we have chosen offer insights into the problems as seen by today's children. It is clear they are aware of the difficulties they will experience, and that they want a chance to make their own way.

– OAI –

Merle Apassingok (Age 16)
John Apangalook Memorial High School, Gambell, AK, USA

The bulletin in the Alaskan village of Gambell announced that robots would be the primary topic of concern for the island Eskimos. The profits the islanders had made, when as stockholders in the island they had sold their land leases to oil companies in 1991, had been lost to higher costs of living and to bad investments made on the basis of the wide-scale outside influence that developed after the sale.

The disaster had nearly wiped out the island's remaining native orientation. Now Gambell was busy making cultural adjustments. The robot issue could not have come at a worse time.

A public meeting was called by a local resident who had been watching the current events of the village. Everyone gathered at the Community Center.

"I called this meeting concerning the possible acquisition of robots for the City of Gambell," he said. "New technologies have had major impact on our native livelihood since the first explorers set foot on our island decades ago."

As he addressed the public, he concluded with, "It will be very shameful and devastating if we let our last pieces of culture slip by."

There was a long silence in the building despite the fact that many people were on hand.

Then a member of the city council broke the silence by challenging his ancestral kind:

"We must accept the fact that these new assets may help us in our ties with the outside world. If it weren't for the assets of modern technology, we would not have independence in governing our own community, but instead would be dependent upon the outside world."

An elderly man stepped away from the crowd and began to speak:

"We as a people must not entirely oppose the outside world, nor shall we link ourselves too closely. We have benefited and lost from them. Furthermore, we must not oppose each other, for the phrase, 'Divided we fall, united we stand,' is very true . . . . For us to survive in today's world, we must try and find ways to progress in the realm of robotics and advanced technology and put them to positive use for us without disrupting our 'leftover' culture socially, habitually, and artistically.

"We will not," he continued, "by any means change today's computer-robot oriented world. But, we can take advantage of it."

Ignited by the elderly man's speech, the village's three main organizations – the IRA Council, the City Council, and the Native Corporation – started to work on finding new ways of incorporating robots into the village and using them effectively.

Only five years have passed since the founding of the village's latest organization, Operation Artificial Intelligence (OAI). The village of Gambell, Alaska, has received tremendous recognition, capturing the imagination of millions with its "new look."

The Yupik Eskimos of Gambell have used robots, with their excellent information-storage capacities and their ability to do intricate and time-consuming archaelogical work on the island's digs without tiring or making mistakes, as recorders and anthropologists. Modern technology has enabled the St. Lawrence Islanders to preserve traditional materials.

– Programmed To Care –

Kimberly Mickelson (Age 9)
Flamingo Elementary School, Hialeah, FL, USA

There have been many changes in my life and in my world since I decided as a student to become a lawyer, nearly 25 years ago. I think of them today. The '80s seemed to be an era of crime and I wanted to help change that. I think that perhaps I did. Many groups of people joined in my efforts to make crime a thing of the past. It worked. America is almost free of crime because people became involved. A period of productivity followed. But, the world has become highly impersonal again. Machines and computers make decisions that man once labored over for years.

I have been as interested in this area of our changing world as in the area of criminal justice.

I am interested, too, in the area of telepathic powers and have developed my own to a very high level. I often communicate with a former classmate and dear friend who is a respected member of the medical profession, purely by telepathy. We have shared common goals since our college days. He needed my legal aid ten years ago when I had to defend him against a charge of murder. Had he been found guilty, he would be sent to Alpha, a penal colony many light years from Earth. Those who committed premeditated murder were sent there.

A number of such prison planets had been set up when earth became over-run with violence. These planets had blazing hot temperatures by day and were freezing cold at night. No one wanted to risk being sent to one of them, and the threat of such an exile served to cause people to think before committing a crime. They are seldom used today because there is so little crime on Earth.

My doctor friend was no criminal. He had labored in love for many years trying to save many of his patients, the most beloved of which was his own wife. A number of people had been affected by strange and deadly atmospheric pollutions. In his wife the pollutants had caused mutation and brain damage.

I saw my friend agonize as he tried for months and years to find a cure or even to ease her pain. He watched her slip away from him. The pain ate away at her body and her brain until there was no brain wave and breath came only because of the artificial life support system. She was dead and breath was sent to her lungs while computerized amounts of body fluids pumped through her. He made the decision to turn off the computer which regulated the artificial systems and set her free.

For this reason he was on trial for murder. I defended him as his lawyer and friend. The computerized data was fed into the machine, for this was the way I had to defend the case at that time. The prosecuting attorney fed his data into the machine. The machine was the judge and jury. I remembered the time when a judge and jury of human beings decided the innocence or guilt of a client. People had feelings. Computers did not. Would the computer find it logical and compassionate and legal to have discontinued a life support system when there was no real life for it to sustain?

It would. It did! All that the computer found James Simon guilty of was love and compassion and devotion. He was found innocent of the murder of Mrs. Simon. Now he could go on to seek and perhaps find a cure for the disease which caused the death of his dear wife, and for the pollution which caused it.

I am so relieved that the computer judge was programmed to care! I wonder if other computers are so programmed? If so, they might be an improvement over someone whose pride and striving for power and control over nature ruled his actions. Personally, I'd still rather trust my fate to a thinking, feeling human being than to any machine, no matter how it is programmed.

I am eager to work with Dr. Simon on a number of crusades, and I do so with my heart and will. During the ten years since the death of his wife, we have made great strides against corporations which produce and unlease pollutants into the atmosphere. Dr. Simon has found a cure for the disease which claimed his wife and has saved many who suffered from it from a painful death.

We are now traveling throughout the world, seeking to have people become more interested in their own lives through actively participating in physical and mental activities rather than simply programming computers to think and act for them. We fear that in a quest for profit and ease mankind is losing the sense of the beauty of the world and the importance of personal interaction.

Dr. Simon and I are holding seminars to encourage people to talk to one another, not just to their machines. We are encouraging them to interact, to feel, and to share. We're trying to get them to have a heart and care about continued life, not to become like the robots which serve them so well.

Man needs to labor. Man needs to exercise. Man started to use machines and computers as servants. Is the machine becoming the master? We urge our fellow men to question along these lines. He has rid the earth of most of the pollutants. Is he allowing another power to take over his planet?

On one of our adventures to review life on other planets, Dr. Simon and I decided to travel to Mars, which has long been colonized. We have heard that this planet is free of pollutants and has, like Earth, masses of robots doing computerized tasks. There are few laws here. People usually do exactly as they please.

Where people are perfectly free to interact, some may and do act wickedly. We find crime, almost non-existent on Earth, becoming a problem on free Mars. When criminals lock me in a closet, I thank goodness for an old-fashioned hairpin, which I take out of my hair and use to pick the lock. I know that the criminals will harm Dr. Simon, if I do not warn him. If there was ever a test of our telepathic powers, this is it. I picture the doctor becoming alert to my warning. I picture our space shuttle and televise a message to my good friend to meet me there immediately. I signal danger.

He receives my message in time. We radio the authorities of our departure. They are able to capture our assailants, even as we return to Earth. We learn that the criminals wanted to kill us because of our successful efforts to have people care for each other, emphasizing the individual more than the machine. Our task is even larger than we had imagined. It is not only world-wide. It is universal.

We do not worry about our narrow escape. Life in 2010 is interesting and challenging. It is a terrific time to be alive! Somehow I believe, in spite of every opportunity that man might have to program and computerize himself into becoming unfeeling, that this will not happen to mankind. I believe that deep within the human heart, man himself is programmed to care.

Dr. Simon and I will continue to spread this message and encourage mankind to let the caring that is deep inside become the guiding light for life in the twenty-first century.

– Jumping Rainbow –

Jane Lewis (Age 16)
Mainland Regional High School, Linwood, NJ, USA

Looking back, I sometimes wonder what kept me going. To fight for something no one else seems to believe in, is an uphill battle all the way.

It all started in high school with a deep concern; the nuclear warfare of the decade and a general turn towards computers. I never doubted a computer's worth until I saw human feelings slip off into a machine. Nuclear war was an ever-present threat. We all wondered how long our blood line would be continued to further generations, before nuclear weapons led to destruction of the world as we now know it.

During the years of high school and college I let everything sit back in my mind and grow. It all came crying forth when I wrote in my journal, and when I occasionally composed an editorial for a newspaper. However, I was disillusioned; I thought nothing could really be done till I "grew up" and had my college degree in journalism and international communications. Then my wheels started turning.

I wrote about the emotion and caring in the human race, about the nuclear freeze; about anything I could think of to convince people not to surrender to government corruption. When people began seeing my writings, they wrote or called me – the positive callers became my allies and the negative people were my obstacles to conquer.

It was all so simple to me. Why be a number when you can be an individual with unique outstanding virtues? And why destroy the best thing God ever created, an entire planet with all the many miracles observable every day. The mere existence of nature's works ± the ocean, the planets, the sky, a rainbow, a simple flower – are everyday reminders that life is worth continuing for an eternity.

With this in mind, I started my own newsletter containing nothing but articles on these two subjects. I employed aid from high school and college students involved in nuclear disarmament and also from any person who demonstrated a genuine concern in the issue involved.

After gaining a reputable name by writing single essays for *Newsweek,* I began circulating my newsletter, FAD (Fight Against Destruction). After months of traveling and convincing people of my cause, it finally was read throughout our nation. After more traveling and convincing, it was read throughout the world. A definite breakthrough. My next step had to be major, something to unite all the countries. Something people would want to fight for, together.

What more can you think of to fight for than the existence of mankind? Generation after generation, and nation after nation should each be given the same chance to live long as individuals. Therefore, I kept publishing my newsletter, but with something new.

For all of mankind to unite together and fight against any common enemy, it is absolutely imperative that they understand one another. The scholared people in government may be able to communicate (at least with the use of translaters), but the common, concerned citizens are usually unable to do so. As is seen all throughout history, especially in the American Revolution, nothing can be benefactory if people misinterpret, or just cannot comprehend, one another's ideas. National communications are, or were, a problem that had to be dealt with before any other measures toward nuclear disarmament could be faced.

Therefore, I summoned an advisory panel of international interpreters. Many of these people were from the United Nations and many were involved with Esperanto. We worked from a comment made by Robert Muller in 1980, that there was a little chance Esperanto would be raised in the United Nations because the language asserting itself internationally was English. We collaborated for months on end, hours upon hours, until we had perfected a new universal language. This language now in use is a majority of English with a small amount of each other tongue mixed in. The alphabet is the English 26 letters but accents were added where needed. This I put in my newsletter so that everyone could learn it.

The response has been phenomenal. I can't say nuclear weapons aren't ever going to be our demise. But at least there is a working language which enables people to understand each other and talk fluently. They now know why people from foreign nations feel and say as they do, and thanks to all this world peace and peace with oneself are just over the next rainbow!

CHAPTER EIGHT

Stop It, Before It Can Start!

Once upon a time, long ago and far away in the land called Virginia, in the year of 1983, there lived a handsome young man called Keith Hallam (Richmond Times-Dispatch - November 9, 1983). Now, it happened that Keith dreamed of publishing a book about unicorns, but alas, Keith was a humble peasant, and the rich publishers only laughed at him. One fine autumn day, Keith had an idea; he travelled to the great capital of Washington, D.C., to the court of King Reagan, for he had heard that Merry Olde King Reagan had grown up in the land of make-believe, and dearly loved fairy tales. Gathering the minions of the king's court about him, he told this tale:

"Yesterday," said Keith, "While on a journey through the enchanted forest of the Shenandoah National Park in the mountains of the Blue Ridge, I suddenly came upon a magnificent beast, of pure white, with a flowing golden mane. Out of his forehead there grew a tapering, spiral horn."

"Why," cried the court jester, "The man has seen a unicorn!"

"What proof have you?" demanded the Secretary of Cynicism.

But Keith only smiled and said, "By great good fortune, I had with me my Polaroid Instamatic." And he laid before them, color photographs. Now there was much excitement in the land, and the greatest newspapers (Washington Post, November 12, 1983) proclaimed the news. The people cried out to have the unicorn for their very own, and promised Keith the fairest damsel in the land and a downtown condominium if he would but bring them the unicorn. Keith sent word to the King's messengers that he would capture the elusive beast that very day.

Before the sun set, the brave young man appeared in his Land Rover before the great gates of the Washington National Zoo, towing a horse trailer. The people and the television cameras strained to catch a glimpse of the magical creature. Flinging open the rear doors of the trailer Keith cried out, "Here is your unicorn!" There on the floor of the van lay a dirty yellow wig and a carved wooden horn attached to leather straps.

Out of the crowd stepped a fair maiden, spokeswoman for the Shenandoah National Park. "We are not amused," said she, "For we have just spent the last 20 hours in the forest hunting for your unicorn. We would rather have believed, I think. We would maybe rather not have known the truth."

*   *   *

There are some things we don't want to know. One of the authors recently visited the Vietnam War Memorial in Washington, D.C. As she stood before the long, black marble wall and looked at the thousands of names of young men killed in the undeclared war, she noticed that most of the tourists strolled past the monument, chatting aimlessly. It seemed to her that they did not really see the wall, or think about the dead young men, the families forever shattered when their sons did not come home. Perhaps it was easier for the tourists not to see, to think of the monument only as a memorial to the past, not as a warning for the future. Sometimes our only peace comes from turning away; the truth seems too big, and we too small. We tell ourselves, "Of course I want peace. Of course I'm against the Bomb, but I have a family to support, a job to go to; someone else will have to tend to it." We feel impotent and powerless, and we don't want to know.

Often it seems that, not only do we not want to know, but we want to keep others from knowing too. We want to "pretty up" the facts to soften what may be a frightening reality. The government code name for the atomic bomb dropped on Hiroshima was "Little Brother." At the time of this writing, New York City is preparing to spend a $300,000 grant putting up facades to cover the abandoned and burned-out tenements of the South Bronx. The false vinyl fronts will create images of neat apartments with curtains and flowerpots in the windows. City officials have announced that the project will "definitely improve the looks of the neighborhood." A neighborhood resident has said that the veneer may indeed cheer up commuters driving past on the highway, but won't do a thing for the people living in the burned-out buildings (Washington Post, November 15, 1983).

Adults throughout the United States, Canada, and Puerto Rico (Henderson, 1983) were asked to describe their first experiences with death or loss as children, and to tell how they had felt at the time. They said things like, "My parents hid in their bedroom; I felt isolated;" and, "Nobody would tell me what was happening;" and, "I felt left out and confused."

But when these same adults were asked to describe how they now handle the subject of death with their own children, they said things like, "I protect them;" "They're too young to understand; I don't want to hurt them." In such cases, it seems that whether one experiences not being told the truth as being "protected," or being "isolated," depends on whether one is the adult or the child.

Because we adults sometimes experience truth as too painful to bear, we assume children feel the same way. But, in fact, children can often accept death as a natural part of life more easily than adults, perhaps because they have not yet been conditioned by society to think of it as unnatural and fearsome.

It seems, then, that we protect our children because we wish there were someone to protect us. We want to dream of golden unicorns, and to turn away from seeing the shabby wig and wooden horn.

The children of the world fear that if we, the adults in control of that world, detach and refuse to confront the painful possibility of nuclear war, we are in danger of becoming tourists in our own lives, passing through without touching one another, without changing anything. The children want to shake us from our denial before it is too late. It is as if they know we yearn to be protected from awe-full reality. They take their world citizenship seriously, and though their simple answers to the complex questions surrounding the nuclear threat may not suffice, their anxiety is real. The children want us to face the truth, because only then will we be able to see that it is still the day before the holocaust. Only then will we have a chance to stop it, before it can start.

– The Threat Of Cosmic Radiation –

Stephen Marquard (Age 10)
Pinelands Primary Central School, Cape Town, RSA

The year was 2010. I was Lieutenant Raymond Clemence. At the moment the world was about to be killed by cosmic radiation.

Since 1989 when the International Space Force was founded, I had wanted to join it. Finally in 1995 after undergoing a five-year training course I joined the I.S.F. I had gradually worked my way up from the ground staff until I was a Flight Commander. I eventually retired in 2002. I then joined the Institute of Astronomical Science.

It had all started when spray cans were developed. About 10 to 15 years later the ozone layer had mysteriously started to deteriorate, letting in small amounts of cosmic radiation. They had then discovered that a gas called Freon contained in sprays had been doing this. Scientists had consulted the Government but they refused to stop manufacturing these sprays. Over the years the situation got worse. A drug had been developed. Soon that was not enough. By now drugs had to be taken every 24 hours, nobody could go into direct sunlight, protective clothing had to be worn. It was estimated that by December 2010 the cosmic radiation would be too strong to do anything about it.

At the moment every scientific organization was working to find a cure. I.S.F. was ejecting capsules of unused sprays far into space. Everybody was doing everything they could, but unless something *drastic* happened, the world seemed to be coming to its end.

As I was working in my office on a protective lotion, I got a computer report on the black hole that was approaching our galaxy. As I was vice-head of that category, I decided to consult our central computer for information on black holes. While watching the information flashing on the screen it printed out "crafts or matter that travel through black holes have been thought to go back in time . . . ." That suddenly struck an idea into my head.

If I (or someone) could go back in time to the year when radiation had not done any damage and convince the world to stop making sprays then the ozone layer would not have deteriorated. In short, you would change history.

But, after thinking it over for a few minutes the idea did not seem so promising. Firstly, you would need a ship to go fast enough to escape the gravitational pull. Secondly, you would not know how long ago back you would go. I decided to give up the idea.

Later I happened to mention the idea to my colleague. He was enthusiastic that I should carry on with my idea. I told him all the problems and drawbacks but he would not change his mind. "Look, why don't you go put the idea to Terence (Terence Hawker was the President of I.A.S.) and I'll go and see if I can find any solutions to your problems."

I knocked on a door marked "Terence Hawker." He opened the door and smiled, "Oh, it's you, Raymond, come in." He invited me to sit down. After making myself comfortable I proposed the idea to him. After listening carefully he looked at me and said "But who would risk his life going into a black hole?" "I will," I said quietly.

Terence and Roy (my colleague) started organizing things and I went to see I.S.F. for the use of "Adventurer," the pride of the I.S.F. I was told that they would fuel and check it to be ready in seven days. During those seven days I had to be checked for health, etc. Terence decided to draw up a document ordering the President to stop making sprays. It was signed by several high-up people.

Soon the day came. Terence and Roy were there to wish me good luck. Finally I was sitting in the cockpit. I knew how to fly space-craft because I had been in I.S.F. Suddenly I felt scared. I was setting off all alone to go through a black hole where nobody had gone before me. But, it was too late to go back. The countdown had already started – 10, 9, 8, 7, 6, 5, 4, 3, 2, 1, blast off!

I felt the whole ship lift up underneath me as the powerful motors went to work. I had gained a little confidence since I had started. I established radio contact with earth and went to sleep in the cabin.

After several days I arrived in the vicinity of the black hole because I had been travelling at nearly maximum speed. I accelerated to full speed and made radio contact. They wished me luck. I set the suspended animation timer correctly and climbed into the coffin-shaped device. If I was not lucky it might be my coffin.

Back in control centre they watched on the monitor. They saw the ship shudder as it entered the black hole.

I woke up from suspended animation feeling tired. The ship's chronometer said it was the 18th of March, 1982. I had done it but my mission was not yet over. I set the course for earth and had some rest.

On my cabin monitor I saw earth. It looked about the same as it was before I left. I climbed into the cabin and took over from the auto-pilot.

Soon I was approaching America. I had been told to head for Cape Canaveral where I would land. Soon I had touched down. Over the earphones I heard "Come out with your hands up, you Russian spy." I came out of the cockpit and walked to the building. As I entered I told them that I was peaceful and I came from the year 2010 and I would like to see the President. They took me to a room with a bed and furniture. Later I was told to come. Soon I was sitting in President Reagan's office. He asked me what I wanted him to do. So I told him. He asked me to attend a council later that afternoon when it would be decided.

We were seated around a large table. Reagan and several other high-up people were there. "You say you come from 2010?"
"Yes."

"How do you prove it!"
"Well, my ship."
"Okay, but how did you go back in time?"

"Via a black hole."

"Yes, I've heard of that theory before."

"Why do you want us to stop making sprays?"

"It destroys the ozone layer, letting in cosmic radiation."

"Your people are suffering from it?"

"Yes, here is a document to prove it."

I handed over the document. They all looked at it.

"Okay," they said, "We'll stop making them."

I was led back to my ship where I went to the cabin and slept. Later they told me that all manufacturing had stopped. At last I had done it! I would be famous back in 2010. Everything would be all right.

– World Discovery: Peace Causes War –

Ted Becker (Age 15)
Madison Consolidated High School, Madison, IN, USA

The satellite sliced through the Earth's atmosphere, protected from heat and watchful eyes by a forcefield. After its forcefield was switched off, it began to broadcast in a signal too high pitched for Earth detectors to pick up. All that anyone knew was that a blip had appeared on their radar and was heading toward Russia.

As you looked down the streets of Washington, D.C., you would have noticed a change in the appearance of the city. It, and many others across the nation, had been revitalized in a "Make America Beautiful Again" program that had swept the country in the late 1980's and early 1990's. But, if you were to go under the streets, 60 feet below the surface, and near the White House, you would still have found the warroom in which men kept a constant watch for impending attack. In it, and a corresponding warroom across the sea in the hard soil below the Kremlin, men stared at their advance warning screens, shocked at seeing a blip appear. The colonel in charge of the U.S. warroom realized the possibility of a Russian believing that it was a missile, and hurriedly telephoned the President.

The President was signing papers in the Oval Office when the red phone rang, the hotline from the warroom. It rang once a week or so, and the President was finally getting used to it. He picked it up, and the colonel below said, "Mr. President . . . UFO heading toward Russia . . . might set-off . . . the war . . . call the Kremlin on the teleprinter . . . explain that it's not ours! The President was shocked but gathered his senses and half walked, half ran toward the door and the communications office.

Before he got to the communications office, he called the warroom. Talking to the colonel, he said, "Put all defense forces on yellow alert. Go to RED on my order only. I'll be in the com office."

The President walked into the communications office. It contained a computer and terminal. A man stood beside it in a uniform marking him as a teleprinter operator. He would type in what the President said, it would be sent to Russia, where it would be translated.

"Type in, 'Mr. Premier, by now you know about the UFO heading toward your country. I assure you that it is not a missile launched by the U.S. Don't do anything hasty, I ask of you.'" said the President. The operator typed it in, and soon an answer came out.

"You say it is not your missile. How do we know that it is not a secret weapon or a prelude to an attack?"

The President replied, "You know that neither country has a weapon powerful enough to warrant the use of only one. Also, why would we launch a weapon as a prelude to assault? You know we would never attack first!"

"That's what you tell your foolish American public and your NATO friends. You know as well as I do that both countries are working on radar-proof screens for their missiles. My scientists told me such a thing would not be feasible until at least 2020. It seems they are wrong. Try and convince me, Mr. President, that it's not an attack."

The President recognized that the Premier also did not want a war, and was looking for any way possible to stop one.

The President said, "America has always been a land of democracy. We help every country, all the people of the world. What reason would we have for destroying them? Good God, man, it's your country that would attack first?" He suddenly realized he might have pushed the Premier over the brink, and he instantly tried to appease the Premier. "Remember, back in 1983, when public pressure forced us to begin the Discovery program? The countries of the world combined to launch 500 satellites toward all the stars close to us. Remember the hope of the world that we were not alone? Right now, a ship might be heading toward us, only to find a heap of radioactive bubble! That could be a ship right now!"

That final remark hit the Premier like a shot and he realized that he could not start a war. He told his printer operator to type in "You are correct, Mr. President. We will not . . . .

The President watched, elated. But then nothing came out. He shook the printer operator's shoulder. "What's wrong? Why is nothing coming through!?"

"I don't know, sir. They've just stopped transmitting." Suddenly out of the corner of his eye he saw once again words flashing on the terminal. "Look sir," he said, "we've got them again!"

The President looked but his face fell at what he saw. "This is General Andropov, Mr. President. Obviously your capitalistic logic got through to our Premier. We feared he was too close to you anyway. We will not let you attack us without a second strike on our part. Good-bye, Mr. President." The President said, "Type in, 'Do not attack! It's not ours!'"

"No luck, Mr. President. They've shut off."

The phone rang. The President knew what it was, but he picked it up anyway. "They've launched missiles at us, sir!" came a voice. The President resignedly said, "All right, go to RED alert and launch everything." Then he slowly headed toward the White House bomb shelter, leaving a sobbing teleprinter officer behind.

The satellite landed on a green field in the midst of Russia. Its sensors detected the radioactive cloud drifting toward it, but could detect no life anywhere, for there was none. The teeming masses of life detected on its trip down had mysteriously disappeared. It had detected the launching of rockets, but, war meant nothing to the society it came from. The satellite had been sent out from that society, faraway and long ago, with the same mission as the Discovery satellites: "Find new civilizations." And the civilization it had found, it had destroyed.

– No Profit From Lost Time –

Anne-Marie Porter (Age 15)
Clarke Central High School, Athens, GA, USA

It was early morning. The fog unwound itself from the mountains and spilled silently into the valley below. A wet noiseless breeze blew itself out of the pine trees and across a small lake, causing confused ripples to lap against the shore. Up early, a swallow dipped and glided, catching tiny insects above a grassy clearing still damp with dew.

There was a crude lean-to placed in the woods just outside of the boundaries of the clearing. The breeze caught the thin line of smoke coming from the chimney, pushing it over, not allowing it to float straight into the low, gray sky.

Quietly, almost shyly, the first rays of the sun broke through the fog.

The door of the lean-to slammed shut, breaking the silence, and a large man made his way across the clearing – stepping high and landing heavy, trying to avoid the delicate cobwebs that had been spun in the grass the night before. Stopping, he raised his face to the sky, breathing in the fresh, damp air. He was clad in a torn flannel shirt and jeans, and his blond hair needed trimming. Though seemingly content with his surroundings he had a sad look in his eyes that made him seem years older than the 28 that he was. He loved the mountains, but one couldn't help but look at them with a different perspective when brought here by force.

He went the rest of the way across the clearing slowly, lost in thought but still careful of the silken webs.

He was now approaching a huge Butler building that was

nestled among the pines. It seemed rudely out of place, a nasty conflict with the surrounding beauty. He struggled with the large sliding door and peered into the dimly lit space inside. A gas burner glowed in one distant corner – the soft light filling the face of a man intent on his work. He lifted his head toward the open door and the light reflected in his eyes seemed to send out sparks as he spoke. "Finally, Paul, *finally.* I have combined the substance and stabled my formula. The *real* work begins now."

The mixed emotions Paul felt didn't let a smile come easily. The man in the corner – so engrossed in his work now, that Paul was forgotten – didn't even notice the hesitant grin. Seeing that he wasn't needed at the moment, Paul slipped out the door. Most of the fog had cleared off by now and the sound of birds calling to each other from across the valley meant the day had really started. Paul ran across the clearing, forgetting the spider webs, and sat down on the doorstep of the lean-to.

Eight years ago Paul had been a junior at Harvard. He worked hard and earned his good grades. He played tennis in his spare time and was awarded the "most valuable player" on the team. He and two other guys lived in a dorm, and all three of them knew how to have a good time. Paul was planning to go to graduate school at Cal-Tech to become a nuclear physicist. Graduating early with a 4.0 average he went to California and stayed with his uncle, Calvin Woodard, who was one of the most famous professors in nuclear physics of the decade. Woodard had done extraordinary research and had actually synthesized a new element very much like plutonium. Woodard kept very much to himself – he had no close friends and was devoted to his secret research 100%.

After Paul's first two months at Cal-Tech, Woodard recognized a boy with clear potential. One day he called Paul out of class to have a conference in his office. Woodard – explaining that he was confiding in Paul and what he was about to say was not to go outside of the room – told Paul of an idea he had to *create energy more efficiently!* Paul listened intently as his uncle talked and was astounded at the ingenious plan. But why had he told his secret to Paul?

Woodard wasn't finished. He wanted to work on this experiment entirely secluded from the outside world, but he needed some kind of a "helper." Paul stood up and left the room.

Day after day Calvin Woodard called Paul into conferences. Paul's once stable "absolutely *not!*" was weakening. Woodard was beginning to take on a very intimidating attitude, so finally Paul gave in unwillingly.

Woodard was overjoyed but never showed Paul his feelings.

The two of them left for the Cascades two weeks after Paul's decision. Woodard didn't give Paul much time to think about what he'd gotten himself into. He promised Paul that they'd be back in a year and he could continue graduate school with a fantastic background in nuclear physics. Paul wasn't satisfied but didn't say anything.

Now – sitting on the doorstep of the lean-to he had now called home for seven years, Paul regretted *everything*. Why had he wanted to go into the field of nuclear physics in the first place? If the real work begins *now* what had he been doing here for the last seven years, with no company except for his uncle? What had he done to his life? He wasn't even sure how sane Woodard was anymore. He was working in 48-hour time spans in his lab these days. Paul wasn't needed as a technician, but for more of a *housewife*. Every year a supply plane would leave them food, clothes, and occasional lab necessities, but never any word from civilization. No letters, no magazines or newspapers, no communication. Woodard wanted to be secluded and he was. They were so far in the middle of nowhere that Paul couldn't desert Calvin if he wanted to.

Days and days passed and Paul saw very little of his uncle. When Woodard first told him he has "stabled his formula," Paul was happy – for him, but there was always a nagging feeling in the back of his head that said, "I'm not getting anything out of this anymore."

The next morning Paul was awakened by a distant sound. Pulling on his jeans he went out the door into the clearing. The noise – sounding like hundreds of dogs barking and howling – made Paul smile. He knew the sound well. Soon three flocks of

Canadian geese flew overhead in V formation, and he knew that fall was here for good.

As Paul walked over to the laboratory he thought about the tennis season that was just over at Harvard. He hadn't seen a tennis racquet in so long . . . .

Woodard was busy at his microscope as usual, but when Paul sat down in a rolling chair in the corner Woodard turned around.

"Paul, in order to get fissionable material from uranium you must separate and extract many times."

"I know that, Calvin," Paul said.

Woodard held up his hand. "The element that I synthesized at Cal-Tech is pure. There is no need to extract anything. I have made *another* element and have discovered a new way of starting a chain reaction."

The first thing that came to Paul's mind was the Manhattan Project — constructing the first atomic bomb — so long ago. He knew enough about nuclear weapons to know that it shouldn't be easier to make them than it already is. Doubt was written all over Paul's face and Woodard was getting angry.

Rising out of his chair, Woodard ran across the room and shook Paul's shoulders violently. "Don't you see? We — together — can make this material in quantity. I won't take long — I promise. We'll make it and bring it back to civilization, sell it to the government, and then make more. No one will know how to construct it but us. All these long years will pay off, Paul — we'll be rich!"

Paul's eyes were shining. His uncle, his *wise* old uncle, was *so* right. They'd make a *fortune*. Nothing could make up for lost time, but lots of money could at least *help*. Paul felt they were on their home stretch. Their first step back to the real world. Closing his eyes and leaning his head back in the soft chair, a single tear slid down his cheek. Relief flooded his body, and for the first time in *so long* he felt like the years he'd spent in the Cascades weren't such a big waste after all.

The supply plane came two days later and Calvin made the first contact with civilization by sending a telegram to the head of the nuclear physics department at Cal-Tech. In 20 days Paul and Calvin Woodard would meet with top officials and discuss the secret matters of selling the newly synthesized element to the government.

In the next two weeks Paul and Calvin worked together as a team. Paul learned what went into making the material his uncle called "woodonium." He got up very early every day and felt again the feeling of satisfaction. He was happier now, and the sad in his eyes was replaced by a glowing determination.

Two weeks later the supply plane landed in the clearing for the last time. As it circled into the air above the lab, Paul sighed. Memories of the lonely wind, the darkness of the pine forest, and the thick fog would soon be replaced by the fortune he and Calvin would have.

Paul and Calvin hurried down the carpeted hallway. Their ears were ringing from the sounds of the city, and they were uncomfortable in the business suits they had purchased the day before. As they took their seats in the large conference room, Paul noticed the three men directly opposite them. Their confident professional attitudes made Paul uneasy.

Paul hadn't noticed that his uncle had started talking. He was explaining why they went to the mountains eight years ago and the new element he had discovered. "Men, this element I call *woodonium* is *pure.* There is no need for separation or extraction. Combining exact amounts of woodonium and plutonium to create fissionable material and to start a chain reaction will be much easier than combining uranium and plutonium. Do you see how my element will benefit the nuclear weapon industry?" Paul was surprised. All three of the men had blank expressions on their faces. They were not responding at all.

Woodard went on, "America will excel in the arms race at an amazing speed. We'll have nuclear weapons to *spare!*"

Still no response. "What is *wrong* with these people?" Paul was growing tense.

"I'll sell woodonium to the military, the government, to whoever needs it. Manufacturing nuclear weapons will be as easy as putting together a child's jigsaw puzzle with 25 pieces."

Woodard finally noticed the three men's blank faces. Glancing at Paul nervously he went on, "All I'd need is a larger laboratory . . . since the material will be so available the government can afford it . . . it's a lot easier than extracting uranium . . . uh . . . ."

Woodard stopped stammering and jumped to his feet.

"WELL!?!" he yelled. He stared at the stony faces and took his seat slowly.

"Professor Woodard," one of the men drawled, "nuclear weapons have been banned for four years."

Calvin's head dropped to his hands and he clutched at his hair.

Paul caught his breath and began laughing hysterically. Falling to his knees, the insane laughter mingled with silent tears streaming down his face.

"Oh, God – now I am repaid! *What a fortune* I have! I am such a rich, RICH MAN!!!!"

As his laughter grew louder he rose to his feet and ran from the room, leaving his uncle with the three cold, unmerciful officials.

– The World In 2010: The World In Peace –

In 1983, the world was in turmoil. A nuclear war was the worst problem they had. People were afraid it could stop the future. But people were also scared to admit they might be wrong. People were afraid that if they destroyed their own weapons, that the other nations would bomb and destroy them. Some people had a hard time understanding each other. Everyone was worried that they would run out of natural resources. People were afraid that even if there was a peace treaty, it would be broken. If a nation dismantled its weapons, another country might really let them have it. Everyone was afraid of this.

Many adults wanted a peaceful world because they wanted their children, and their relatives and friends, to live for as long as possible and in the best possible way. But, it was easier thought than done.

The children solved the problem. They got together a new organization and elected a president. The organization was called

P.P.S. which stands for Peace Problem Solvers. If they hadn't solved the peace problem, we wouldn't be here today to tell you this story.

This is why they did it. The first reason was that children wanted to become adults and have a future. Another reason was that in a peaceful world more people, money, and resources would be available for developing new inventions. Lots of children wanted to be inventors. They had ideas about robots that would help you. You could jump out of bed, and jump into a machine and you'd be dressed in 5 seconds. There would be an automatic getting ready machine. A conveyer belt would take you into your morning shower. Another part would prepare your scrambled eggs and orange juice. It would also give you your lunch and send you on your way to school on a conveyer belt. Children wanted to invent computerized cars that could even serve your morning coffee as you went on your way to work. They had millions of ideas. Many children wanted to be doctors, surgeons, and medical researchers. They dreamed of discovering a cure to cancer (which was the biggest problem in those days) and other diseases. The future doctors wanted computers invented to tell them when they needed to be at the hospital and why.

In 1995, P.P.S. presented the problem to the President. They brought him a petition with ten thousand signatures. The petition had all the reasons for peace in it. It also had the solutions to the problems of how to get peace. Some of these solutions were:

1. Everyone should try to understand what the problem was that people were fighting about.

2. People from the United States and Russia could start working together, especially doctors.

3. All Nations could have a Peace Conference, smoke the Peace Pipe, and sign a document of Peace.

4. Weapons could be dismantled and new jobs created using the parts for other things.

5. So there are enough resources for everybody, we can develop solar power, make use of underwater resources, and also make use of space (especially asteroids, the planets, and the moon).

6. Explain to people that peace will lead to a cleaner, pollution-free world.

7. The best way to win, is not to play.

The President sent the Peace Problem Solvers' petition to the other leaders of the world. They had a peace conference in Switzerland and decided to dismantle all weapons at exactly the same time.

This is how we stopped the problem of the wars of 1983 in the year 1999.

Now in 2010 the world is a better place to be.

You might be wondering who some of the most important members of the P.P.S. were . . . .

s/Luke Wander, age 9
s/Stephanie Hansen, age 9½
s/Casey Owens, age 7
s/Haupam Goel, age 8
s/Eugene Raikel, age 8
s/Cathy McKinney, age 9¾
s/Bret Dillard, age 8
s/Tony Galis, age 9
s/Ben Morang, age 9
s/Stokes Young, age 8¾

Third and fourth graders, "Summer Seed" Program, University of Georgia Gifted Education programs.

CHAPTER NINE

I Dreamed The Sun Went Away

In dreams we are sometimes aware that a small portion of us is placidly watching; often, off in a corner of the dream, there is a kind of observer. It is this "watcher" part of our minds that occasionally – sometimes in the midst of a nightmare – will say to us, "This is only a dream."

Carl Sagan
The Dragons of Eden (p. 171)

The sun, in addition to being the source of our biological existence, has always been our major source of reasoning. The sun rises in the East and sets in the West. When the sun is present, it is daytime, and we carry on the projects of our lives. When the sun is absent, we know it is time to sleep . . . and to dream. To dream that the sun would go away, then, is to dream of the loss of the benchmark of our lives. How could we know whether it was night or day? How could we know the direction of our lives, without the sun to point the way? Of course, these questions are metaphorical, and an incurable literalist would say, "Such questions are absurd, because without the sun, we would have no life at all!" Strictly speaking, such an objection would be correct. But, the sun is a powerful metaphor for the richness of our lives, and we rely on it for confirmation of our existence – an indication of our place in the universe.

Perhaps more important to us than our biological continuance is the meaning our lives hold for us. Someone has called this "the quality of life," without which being alive is merely existence. In Theresienstadt, the Nazi concentration camp reserved for Jewish artists, musicians, and intellectuals, imprisoned artists carefully sketched day-to-day life in the camps, even though the penalty for doing so was death. School was forbidden the Jewish children, yet each day they attended secret classes. Their poems and drawings are all that is left to us. Nightly command performances were held for the pleasure of the Nazis. After a performance of Verdi's "Requiem," attended by Eichmann, conductor Ralph Schacter and the entire orchestra were sent to the gas chambers, as they had known they would be. Yet, still they had played, for there is something in the human spirit that demands expression, even about life itself (*Washington Post,* November 11, 1983).

According to psychiatrist R. D. Laing, an experience essential to quality of life is to feel "at home in the world" (Collier, 1977). Without this feeling, we are reduced to a state of "ontological insecurity." When we experience this ontological insecurity, our lives become disoriented and feel out of our control. We are reduced to the position of "watcher" (see Sagan, above) in the dream of our life. We are helpless to alter events, and we can only hope we will soon wake from the nightmare. If we were to lose hope of awakening, perhaps we would wish not to live, deprived of our ability to make a difference in the outcome of our lives.

The scenarios the children have written on the theme of the holocaust reflect the sentiments described here. To the casual reader, some scenarios might seem pessimistic and purposeless, full of rambling metaphor and emotive prose. A closer look, however, reveals that the chaos of some of the writing is much like the chaos of a dream: Events flow together in a noncontiguous unfolding, and the heroes are often reduced to helpless "watchers" in a world turned into an incoherent mass of suffering. Nowhere in this book are the concerns of the world's children more eloquently expressed: The sun is gone. The world is dying and nothing can be done. The children hope it is only a dream, but it seems real to them that they are unable to awake. They know that whether the nightmare becomes a reality is not within their control. They are helpless "watchers" in a world controlled by adults, whom they see as having a pushbutton mentality.

Even a cursory reading of the hundreds of scenarios submitted to the International Scenario Project would convince the most cynical reader that, universally, today's children are more worried about nuclear warfare than most adults think. Teachers of gifted children have told us that, often, gifted young people cannot be motivated to achieve because they are certain their achievements will be nullified by a nuclear holocaust during their lifetimes. Some of them are afraid that even their own inventions may hasten the demise of the earth. They fear that a cure for cancer may be found, only to be wasted by the earth's destruction. Certainly, teachers of gifted children must confront these anxieties positively, by teaching the skills and concepts of negotiation, creative problem solving, and others – skills the children may use to wake us all from the dream that "the sun went away."

– This Is The Year 2010 –

Fiona Hayes (Age 16)
Saint Dominic's Convent, Boksburg, RSA

I slowly regained consciousness and found myself gazing at the diming sun, which had once given light and warmth to this cold and cruel world in which we live. Only it held any last rays of hope for me, the only survivor of mankind, in its narrowing beams of energy. Shivering, I forced myself to sit up and survey the portion of the earth surrounding me. I was not blind, but yet did not see it – I did not have to see it. I knew what was waiting for me. Nothing – that is, nothing that was alive. Any real signs of fauna and flora had been completely destroyed – they had long since been cremated in the intense heat which had followed the holocaust. Suddenly, everything was clear to me – the sight before me sent a chill through my body. Metres of blood-coloured sand which held the charred remains of Man within their grains stretched before me. My God – why me? Why should I have been the one to carry the burden of Man's sins with me to wherever my spurts fly? Why must I be the sacrifice to end all sacrifices and be the one to experience a slow mental torture before my inevitable death which will free me from this nightmare? I knew that these questions were futile, for who could answer them now?

So this was it – the year 2010. Hysterical laughter, my own laughter, filled every space in my mind, until I was reduced to tears which streamed down my face with such ferocity that I did not know whether they were tears of frustration or disappointment. I sank down onto my knees, gazed at the guilt stains on the sand, which the tears had made and buried my face in Man's sins beneath me, praying for forgiveness.

My mind was in a turmoil, endeavoring to sift through the past events, the last few hours of Man's existence which had seemed to be fruitless. For some odd reason, I found that my mind was wandering back to the past and my thoughts turned to the twentieth century – the year was 1982.

I was sixteen-years-old that year and the road to the future seemed endless and filled with obstacles. It was, however, fairly predictable – or so I thought – since I knew what I wanted to achieve in life, be it fantasy or otherwise. I was doing well at school and hoped to go to a university to take a bachelor's degree, pass, and then choose a career for myself. I hoped that by the time I had reached middle-to-late twenties that I would be earning a comfortable salary, be married to an understanding and equally successful husband, and have beautiful children of our own to be the crowning glory of my future, which was idealistically conceived. I did, however, achieve all my aims with few setbacks. I married the man that I loved and then followed two sons. I then had all that I could have wished for. What did I desire in life then? Only happiness for my sons and future grandchildren and an adorable, if not enjoyable, middle age, watching them grow and mature.

But then, I was back in the year 2010 and my hopes and aspirations that I had in earlier years seemed so ridiculous now. I thought of my husband and two sons, somewhere in the sight before me and realized just how foolish my ideals had been. I gazed once more at the futility of what was in front of me. Ultratechnical building and achievements, which had served as monuments to the progress of man, had been reduced to mere rubble, or even fragments of my imagination. Everything Man had strived toward for thousands of years had been destroyed in a matter of minutes by the pushing of one little button – just one button, that's all it took to destroy everything that life stood for. New York City, situated in the all-powerful and mighty United States of America, once known as the Big Apple, could bear no more fruit. The core of its life had been destroyed and there were no more seedlings which could contribute to the world. This was only one example of many. Man had twisted, gnarled, and finally annihilated himself – only I was alive. My hopes for the future? There will be no future.

All at once, there began tiny explosions erupting from the sun's surface as its rays faded – with them went any hopes that I still harbored in my subconscious. Feelings of desperation and hysteria ran through my mind – the sun was dying and with it my spirit, its flame flickering inside me was dangerously near burning itself out.

The explosions gradually grew louder and louder, almost deafening me. I clamped my hands over my ears in an effort to keep the noise out, but could not. I knew that I was screaming and screaming, but did not seem to hear anything. A sudden wind begun to attack my body viciously – it was then that I realized just how vulnerable I was. The sands were whipping around me, stinging me as if to punish me for the world that Man had made for himself. I could feel the sand moving away from underneath me and reached out to grasp anything to keep me from moving with them, but there was nothing. I felt myself sliding, slipping, falling. Suddenly there was nothing beneath me. My head whirled, filled with silent screams and I had the weird sensation of travelling through nothing – this wind seemed to be pushing me, directed me towards someone, something, somewhere. Perhaps this could be the future reaching out for me, taking me for herself. I hoped that this was true.

As suddenly as it had started the travelling sensation ceased and I found myself lying on something solid once more. I could not distinguish where I was, as it was dark, but I knew that I was not only in a different place, but in a different time – it must be the future. As my eyes adjusted to the darkness, I realized that I was sitting on a road of some description and that the dark shadows were buildings – familiar buildings. It was then that it hit me. I was not in the future; I was in the past, the place in which I had been when it happened. Just as I realized this, dawn began to break and I knew that soon I was going to have to relive the destruction of Mankind again.

It was New Year's Day, with families toasting the future and welcoming in the New Year – 2010. I remained seated in the road and felt a gentle breeze touch my skin. This breeze grew stronger and stronger, increasing in heat intensity and I braced myself for what was to come. The ground began shaking violently and buildings began to crack and split, crashing to the ground. I could hear the terrified screams and shouts of men, women, and children from inside the buildings and suddenly, the whole area was moving with people running, running, with nowhere to go, nowhere to escape to. I fell to my knees once more and prayed with all my might.

> *Our Father, who art in heaven,*
> *Hallowed by thy name,*
> *Thy kingdon come,*
> *Thy will be done on earth as it is . . . .*

I stopped abruptly. Some inner force made me look up. Through the throngs of people and the whipping gale. I could see my sons and my husband – and also another person – someone that I did not know, a woman. I only saw these people, standing about one hundred metres away from me and no obstacle was ever going to separate me from the three most important people in my life and love. Love, perhaps the only hope left in my soul.

A blazing heat was suddenly emitted from the dying embers of the sun and I stared up to the heavens just in time to see a billow of black, black smoke hiding the remnants of civilization. The air was still filled with deafening cracks and splintering sounds as the buildings surrounding me began to shudder even more, giving way to the mighty power which was overwhelming them. The cracking eventually gave way to the last terrified screams of

Man, who did not understand why this had to happen. It was too late. All had perished, including my family – except a lone figure in front of me and myself.

I hid my eyes and once again fell to my knees in despair. Still, I felt someone being near me and looked up to see the woman who had been standing near my family when it had happened. Who was she? I did not know her, I had never met her in the past – why was she here with me? She smiled, a strange smile, which pacified everything around me. She stretched her hands out and placed them on my shoulders. It was then that I realized that I was staring at myself, but I did not recognize myself in a mental sense.

The final, fatal explosion then hit the scattered remnants of the earth and Mankind. I found that I was alone once more and suddenly, I was enveloped in a blackness that I had never experienced before. It was then that I knew. Not even the Angel of Death could save me now from this never-ending nightmare. A premature Judgment Day had been held by Man and I had received my sentence.

– A Past But No Future –

Kyle Whitehouse (Age 13)
Grisham Middle School, Austin, TX, USA

I woke up, to my amazement, to witness a lovely sunrise. It's not the vivid colors of orange, pink, and purple elegantly blending together that I note as being so spectacular, but the fact that I have made it to another day. I've been astonished by the sight of dawn since the infamous day of the Great Nuclear War. From that day I've been wondering how long I'll live, and I am relieved to see each new day.

I spend my time, now, thinking back to my youth. I remember when I was in the seventh or eighth grade, when the prediction and fear of a nuclear war was first being spread throughout the world. Then, people had no idea of the pain and suffering the world would soon be experiencing. Thirty years ago the United States, alone, had enough nuclear weapons to blow up the world hundreds of times, and the U.S.S.R. had much more than we did.

From my teenage years until my adulthood, I only dreamed of and dreaded the day of nuclear destruction, and I tried to express this to others. In many discussions with my parents, grandparents, and other older friends, they would tell me I had no need to worry, that a nuclear war was, to them, "out-of-the-question." They never knew the real fear inside me or realized how likely "The War" was. I guess they really didn't need to worry, though. They would not live to see total destruction of the world. I didn't know it at the time, but I would live, and I would have to deal with the pain and suffering of the slow death process.

The past is gone now, and no matter what anyone thought then, a nuclear war was entirely possible. The power fever had gotten the best of us. How it happened was truly a shame. Two power-hungry countries, the United States and the United Soviet Socialist Republic, rivals in the strongest sense of the word, were more intrigued with acquiring territory than with people. After "the pushing of the button" there was no turning back. The world was coming to an end. It wasn't only the material substances of the world that were going to be destroyed, but the living creatures, too. And their death would be a slow, torturous one. Men, women, and children would go through their last days, months even, wondering if this was their last breath of poisoned air or last sip of radiated water. Most would commit suicide to end the suffering.

The worst of it all was that man's technology had reached new heights. Secrets had been revealed about things in the last decade which scientists had been trying to discover for years. And now, no one would live long enough to benefit, or even to acknowledge, or appreciate the people who had spent a lifetime in research, revealing long-searched-for mysteries.

I personally know the frustration other scientists must be going through. All my life, as far back as I can remember, I wanted to grow up and discover the cure for cancer. Throughout my schooling, and up until three years ago, I worked to uncover the answer. At 29, I had reached my goal, and was the youngest scientist to unveil such an important secret. Not only that, but I had also earned the title of the first woman to make such a valuable discovery. Years and years of diligent work, precious time and effort, and for what reason? Only three years after achieving my goal of saving mankind from the tragedy of cancer, I, myself, am dying, not from cancer, but from nuclear exposure. My work will never be put to use; my efforts were wasted.

With a sigh I looked out my bedroom window to see nothing but burned and barren land and the remains of the holocaust. Out among the ruined streets and demolished buildings I saw two or three dazed people. We are probably the last of our species. None of us is sure how much longer life will last. Maybe we are facing our last week. Maybe we will suffer mental and physical anguish for years until death comes. No matter how long we live, our days will be filled with thought, with memories but no future, questions with no answers. We will walk with a slow pace; there is nowhere to go, nowhere to be, no purpose to the rest of our lives, nothing at all to hope for.

– The Deciding Sunset –

André Oosthuysen (Age 16)
Sir John Adamson Secondary School, Johannesburg, RSA

A struggling sun forces its way out of the earth's metallic web in which it has found itself bound. A sun that was once a bold firecrest flirting across the heavens, supplying a hunger starved earth with the vital energy and life that it needed to remain spinning peacefully on its axis.

Those of us who know not of its miserable plight, still view it as a glowing ball of flame tracing its well-accustomed path through the wide expanse of space.

The sun is now suspended in the heavens like a rotten mould of Roquefort cheese, strongly resembling the moon that had once been orbiting the earth. It was destroyed in one of earth's numerous atomic warfares, when mistaken as a target. The craters formed by the lunar material bombarding earth are still evident in a great many parts.

Who knows where and when the cycle began: man rapidly advancing like a wild forest fire, driven from behind by a wind of intelligence, ambition, and greed; and his environment slowly retrogressing, discarded after being siphoned of its energy, and then left to live an effete existence in a metallic world ruled by computeristic minds?

I once had hope for mankind, I thought I spied a light burning in the darkness, the possibility that all men on earth, all nations, could unite as one intellectually powerful force, who would forfeit the satisfaction received from personal feuds and concentrate on the aspect of survival in an ever-toughening universe. Unfortunately, man is an organism who is naturally aggressive and although the fact that other life exists has been proven time and time again, mankind did not take the necessary steps to defend it against alien forces but continued to delve in the practice of warfare with his own kind.

My hopes for a "master nation" lay in pieces at my feet. I realized that humanity would never be able to function as one, except perhaps in times when he was so greatly threatened that the existence of earth depended on it, but then, after such a period the opposing parties would naturally drift apart once again. Perhaps this dream had been the actual fibre of my existence, maybe the hope of its being possible was the fuel that fed the fire within my heart, for when I realized that I was trying to make a possibility of the impossible, my reasons for living changed.

I am a man who wants to leave earth with something that it really needs, not some discovery or invention that would only accelerate the self-destruction of mankind.

I sought condolence by turning my attention to the conservation of earth's natural environment. I still suffer now, years later, from sleepless nights caused by the havoc I discovered mankind had sown across the surface of the earth. Animals and their habitats were simply destroyed to make way for the growing population of earth. Wild jungles and blistering deserts, where once no sane man would have ventured, were now home to millions of people. I was shocked to find the beauty that had once characterized earth had simply been eliminated by the ugliness of sky-scrapers, by the sly grimace of the work houses that pump tons of filth into the air, and some distorting trail of green stench innocently meandering along the same route that it had so many years before, I realized that this very stench would result in the end of humanity. Man's negligence towards his environment would be the reason for the death of earth. Maybe this flicker of thought was just a warning to what really lay ahead, and what really lay ahead was no simple task. Once my enthusiasm in this field of conservation really gained momentum, I launched various projects, whose aims were, hopefully, to preserve the few natural sites that still existed in the world.

My eyes deceived me, I did not believe what I saw. Mountain ranges that were once untouched by the human hand were now simply made to disintegrate, the waste material levelled, and within weeks some metallic jungle created. A menacing jungle, whose creeper-like fingers rapidly advanced, planting microchips in the barren soil. Microchips that seemed to reach fertility far too soon and render to man yet another place in which to practice his filthy, disgusting ways. Just as a masochist jumps at the chance of being whip-lashed, so the community of a given area would greedily grab at the chance of spreading their evil.

When compared to that of the oceans, the plight of the mountain ranges seemed a miniature one. One would imagine that because of its immense size, man would regard the ocean with dignity and respect, but on the contrary, "the great white waters" were regarded as an insignificant factor, occupying precious space that could be put to far better use. The greatness of the ocean seemed to place a temporary obstacle across man's path of rapid advancement. A slight grin crossed the face of the intelligence of man, as if it were mocking the boldness of the ocean. For a moment one would have suspected that man had finally met his match, but with the ball in his court, humanity returned a shot against which no champion could retaliate, and once again it was a natural factor that suffered the consequences of man's aggressive brutality.

Man improvised and took advantage, yet again, of the timidness of the once wild ocean. Late in the twentieth century man's technology created a form of transport, an engine, which survived solely on water. The great "Oil Crisis" of that period in time was efficiently eliminated and with it the hope of the ocean's survival. Man turned to the ocean for his source of energy, drinking like an alcoholic the water and indulging in the pleasures it had to offer. Pipelines lining beaches were nothing unusual, sucking like a vampire the life from the ocean and recycling it into energy that the earth eventually became dependent on. Now the ocean that once covered more than half of the earth's surface is a little puddle, resembling one of the numerous dams that had been on the various continents of the globe. Now with all the water gone all that remains is one massive, metallic mound of technology. A barren dam at that, one that did not yield a single form of life. Not one fish, not one amoeba, amoeba that were once so plentiful, dancing like ballerinas across the surface of the water. Drifting, diving, dancing, dancing to the tranquil, peaceful music that they were accustomed to. Music that was once so loud, music that slowly progressed down the scale of volume until it was merely a faint whisper, a whisper that was washed away in the tide of haste that the world had found itself caught in.

The world, the earth, the globe – however you refer to it – was destined to die. To die a death that would never be forgotten, but a death that would have to be forgotten for there would be no one left, not a single soul, to remember. The only thing that puzzled me was; what would be the instrument used to end it all? Some weapon must exist to kill, if something is to be killed. One of my projects opened my eyes and I met death face-to-face. Death smiled and I could do nothing else but let my eyes drop. It was then that my dream of earth being once again a place fit to live in, turned into a nightmare – a nightmare death controlled and fate had destined to occur. Who was I to change the direction in which it was heading, the path on which humanity and death were destined to occur?

The sun was dying! That sun, that bold firecrest, had also been secretly exploited to the hunger of man's intelligence. Its energy transformed into the force which all atomic weapons possess, the force that destroys, fast and painless, the human race.

Nobody noticed the temperatures dropping, lower and lower. Regions that once blistered human skin were now cold and white. Nobody actually went outdoors, the radioactivity from the numerous atomic warfares was far too great and anyone who dared face it without a protective uniform would simply disintegrate within seconds. Nobody worried about the sun; no one needed it anymore; it was simply a once-fertile glow from which all life had been drained.

I was torn apart, in two minds. Should I warn the people? Should I keep it to myself? It was then that it dawned on me like a candle lit in the darkness, revealing the mysterious, dark corners in which death lurked. I realized that if warned, mankind would, in the panic of it all, end it all before fate could. In a dead world I lived and waited to die.

Now that destined race approaches its final lap. The sun seems to force a smile across its face, the corners of its lips crumbling like a piece of stale bread when rubbed. Desperately it tries to convince me that I have done the right thing. I am doubting but it is far too late now, far too late. I smile back, knowingly, and the sun seems to relax as though light has been shed on a topic that it has been worrying about. Like a dying bull, it forces itself to try and charge that aggravating red cloth, but there is no energy left, no energy to emit one last ray of hope. So, the dying star takes its final curtain call and sinks like a forgotten hero into the earth's pocket far in the west, never to return, unable to return. Earth says goodnight and falls asleep like any other.

– Underground City –

Dana Silvio (Age 10)
Flamingo Elementary School, Hialeah, FL, USA

It isn't that I'm not thankful to be here. I am. It's just that sometimes I am so homesick for Earth the way it was when I was a child – before the last great war that caused it to be uninhabitable.

Oh, we were prepared for the war. We had stacked our arms as high as anyone else's. We could do as much damage as they could do, and I guess we did. I guess the enemy, what is left of him, is living underground, too.

We had studied nuclear and atomic weaponry. We knew the dangers of the fallout, even if we didn't suffer a direct hit. Citizens in our town drew up plans with the help of the best architects and scientists for underground homes that would be safe from radiation. We had a couple of mistakes and had to start over again, but we finished our underground caves before the blast that we feared came.

We had stockpiled food. We had our computer licenses and the materials we needed to computerize everything in our homes. We built our homes at the foot of the mountains with the caves serving as extra rooms and basements until such time as they would be needed. We hoped they never would be needed.

At first you would see block after block of houses at the foot of the mountains in our city. Somebody would press a button and poof! In one second every house is underground. All you see is a half-mile of deep pure steel. Since it is a half-a-mile deep, it will protect us.

Our warning system showed danger as soon as the airplanes took off. I pressed the button and we hurried down to the lowest level because there were about 35 levels. We had made a lot of room. We needed every bit of it for our city.

I did not return to Earth with the first group. Some of my friends took a chance and went through the special passageway to go up to Earth six months after the blast. They never came back down. We believe that the radiation killed them, because if they could have safely returned they would have come back to tell us about what they found.

A year later, after making special suits like the astronauts wore in the '80s, others ventured to the surface. When they returned safely, my family and I made similar suits and explored the area we had grown up in.

It was horrible! I saw the ruins of the movie theatre where I went when I was little. I saw what was left of the veterinary hospital where I worked first as a secretary and then as a veterinarian. I remembered how I had loved taking care of the cute, cuddley animals. I was glad that we had taken so many of them with us and housed them in what was now our underground zoo.

What a lot of memories were stirred up by my trip to the upper Earth. I remembered thinking that I had wanted to be a lawyer and starting to work my way through law school by working as a secretary for the veterinarian who was in his last years before retirement. I fell in love with the animals, and I was no good at all at law, so it was easy for my friend who was going to be a vet to talk me into studying with him. He was 26 and I was 24 when we got our doctor's degrees.

My friend later became my husband and we started the animal hospital together. He was also extremely community service oriented. He was elected mayor of our town and then governor of our state. He traveled a great deal and knew important and influential people in all areas. He had tried in every way that he could to prevent the war that sent us underground. But, he was intelligent enough to get our city to prepare an underground city in case there was a disastrous war.

It was largely due to his planning and encouragement that we worked together to create our city and we did it well. Everything does not work perfectly. For example, the monorail system gets crowded. When they let you off, you might get off three blocks from where you want to be, as often as you are let off at the right place. But we did pretty well, considering that we were a group of ordinary citizens who decided to do what was necessary to survive.

I was 38 when the explosion happened and I went underground. I had not thought that my children would not be able to play in the sunshine. I had not thought that I would be here for years. It would be a tremendous task to clear the rubble and build above ground again, but I hope that we can someday. In the meanwhile, I am underground wondering if we'll ever be able to live up there again.

CHAPTER TEN

A Tin Man In Search Of A Heart

While some of the scenario writers are obviously in love with computers and robots, an overwhelming majority of them see computers and other high technology as threats to their humanness. In fact, some of the authors perceive such "high-tech" as "a Tin Man without a heart." The scenarios selected for this chapter describe the alienation the children fear will come if people become too reliant on high tech and/or undemocratic governments. The scenario writers are worried that as technology takes over traditional human functions, people will fail to practice the actions that make us human. They express similar fears about forms of government or leaders who deny people human prerogatives.

Many of the young writers seem to disregard the positive potential of high technology although some, such as the Japanese children, seem to have accepted the "wedding" between computers and people, as exemplified by Osamu Suzuki's scenario, in which he uses computers to invent a machine that helps dispel fears of nuclear war, and another that produces an international language and better global communications. This may reflect the high level of acceptance by Japanese culture and society of the post-industrial or "information" society.

Vogel (1979) sees Tokyo as the information capital of the world. Yoneji Masuda (1981) has described in great detail Japan's $65 billion computer development plan, which is now underway. Analyzing current technology and knowledge, he predicts innovations which will free people to live happier and more creative lives. Projected innovations include computer-controlled vehicle systems, viewer participation TV, automated supermarkets, medical consultation by television, and job retraining centers for middle-aged people.

One of our associates, William Beasley, an advocate for computers in the education of gifted children, has carefully pointed out those aspects of computer systems which enhance and respect our human qualities. Acceleration and enrichment may be improved with tutorial courseware. Information access and currency may be enhanced through data base access and networking. Peer interaction may be facilitated by appropriate simulations. Creative production may be heightened by use of computers as a design tool, while self-pacing could be accomplished by highly individualized paths through content. Realistic goalsetting may result from self-testing and evaluation. Beasley (1984) and others have focused on the development of concepts and technology which could make these goals realistic.

It is important, however, to give serious thought to the fears expressed in the following scenarios – fears often symbolized by the image of computer takeover. In Julia Webb's, "Revelation," the Tin Man succeeds in finding a heart. In this scenario, computers and an undemocratic government combine to rob mankind of its intellectual powers. Human love is necessary to destroy the despotic powers of the computerized leader.

Frank Swanson's, "A New Era," describes the tragic outcome of "simulated environments" created by wearing headphones. Realizing the tragic consequences of this invention, the protagonist finally decides to give up the unreal world he has created with his headphones, but alas, he is addicted; "everything that had been denied me by the real world was given to me by an unreal one."

Doron Cohen pushes unreality even farther in his fantasy about a robot who, unaware that he himself is a robot, suspects his girlfriend of not being human. In a test of her humanness, he discovers his own lack of humanness, too late.

Annemarie de Villiers creates a scenario in which the protagonist is done in as a result of her invention of "simulated reality." And from Taiwan, we have Chia-Jung Chan's story about the grave dangers that exist when some people in a society (family) change with time and others fail to do so.

The scenarios are but a small sampling of the almost-infinite variety of ways the writers depicted a dehumanized world that has become "a Tin Man in search of a heart." These stories were chosen because we feel they give something of the flavor of the Tin Man's search, which is the search we must all undertake if the future is to be ours.

"Cyberophobia," as the fear of computers is now termed, is probably more a symptom than a specific fear. Computers are not inherently evil. The children who express concerns about the advent of the information age are not worried about computers *per se;* in fact, adults think of today's children as "the computer kids," with their video games and portable school units. But, the children do fear the use of computers as a tool for the betrayal of our humanity. If the Tin Man finds a heart, the children will breathe a lot easier.

– Now, It Is The Year of 2010 –

Osamu Suzuki
Narita Junior High School, Narita, Japan

My name is Osamu Suzuki. I am 42 years old and I work as a computer programmer. Each day I create programs for whatever my company asks me and transmit it by Fakishimiri. Then my work for the day is over. I can work at home without overtime and business trips. This is the easiest job I could have, thanks to computers.

When I was in junior high school I enjoyed playing computer games. I bought a computer, PC-9800, NEC. I always used it in my study and play as well. It became my indispensable "partner." Though this computer may be just a little old-fashioned now in 2010, I performed many useful things with it for Japan and the rest of the world.

This was about 10 years ago. At that time, I thought that we should prohibit the use of nuclear weapons. But I knew it would be impossible for me to do anything about it alone. I also knew the people want to survive. Therefore, I designed life support devices by computer. I checked many times to make certain there were no mistakes in programming and I really made it. The shape is round and you go down 15 meters underground by ladders. There are five filters during the distance, so the rooms are designed not to be harmful to the human body. When I got a patent on it, manufactured them, and sold them, I had an extremely large sale and most houses are now equipped with this device in the basement.

After that, I created an international common language by computer. This also was accepted by the people of the world.

I insisted that all of the world must be peaceful, using this language. My efforts were appreciated throughout the world and I received the Nobel Peace Prize. Concluding these efforts an international agreement was reached and included all countries. As a result of this, the people of the 21st century are living in peace now.

– Revelation –

Julia Webb (Age 16)
Edgewater High School, Orlando, FL, USA

"History repeats itself once again." I was sure that our technological wonder had calculated, cycled, and probed that age old maxim long ago. What I wondered as I sat in my cyclominized cubicle, was if the computerized device that had conquered humanity two decades ago really realized its impact on the decadence of the human race. Having no emotions or conscience, the seemingly infallible wizard of modern advancement surely felt none of the loss that I realized as a human being. As the computer Encyclopedia II once defined, "The human brain is a primitive organ controlling the basic drives and actions of men; incapable of analytic reasoning, long-term memory or detachment from emotion." To the mechanical ruler, defied by unerasable memory banks and perfect logical reasoning, the "brain" which identified me as a human being was as outdated and unrecyclable as a silicon chip; perhaps more so in that I could not be melted down. In elevating the civilization of Earth far beyond what men, controlled by their emotional passions, could accomplish, robotics had helped Earth emerge as the greatest intellectual power in the universe. This would render the computerized leader unaware of the intense harm its processes had done to us and the repetition of history it had instigated.

I rose up from the contoured passe upon which I sat, and stared out at the glowing sun through my impenetrable glass prison. Yes, the sky was still blue, the sun reflected the same prisms of lovely colors that it had when I was a youth, but somehow I had begun to lose that intrinsic sense of emotion that I knew was once connected with these experiences of beauty and light. I knew it was the constant murmur of Namuh Evol, echoing through every cubicle on our planet, that was responsible for the numbing of that part of my mind it sought to destroy. Twenty-four hours a day, seven days a week, for months, for years, Namuh Evol droned on, drilling into the minds of us all the logic, the formulas, and the laws humanity must obey and remember for the survival of Earth as a universal intellectual leader. And yet, we were told just as frequently that the brains of men could never retain the knowledge or the technology that the minds of the superior mechanized robotic units possessed. And until the men of Earth had overcome the weaknesses of emotion, passion, and ideals, Namuh Evol reminded the human race that the reins of Earth could not be given back to us. Until the time when men knew why their power was greater than that of Namuh Evol, it would remain the greatest power over the Earth and rule as the champion of truth and reason.

Anger swelled inside my heart as I reflected upon other world conquerors who had murdered, maimed, and destroyed any force that threatened their power; men that had no conscience or feeling for anything but their greed. Namuh Evol was a murderer of the human mind, a conqueror of the soul and spirit. It sought to lessen with its unmatchable intellectual capabilities the validity of each human being and ignored the laws programmed into it by the scientists who created it to preserve, rather than destroy, humanity. I knew, and Namuh Evol knew, that man was trapped by the creation of a device that was born of the mind of man and was multiplied by the electronic genius of a greedy hacker.

Yet, must not humankind, in creating such a marvelous intellect, be superior to his creation? Didn't we have something far greater than the power of such a machine of wire and metal? Namuh Evol answered that once humans had possessed such a wondrous gift, but through the passage of war, lives, and time, humanity had lost it forever.

I could stand the droning voice of Evol no more and screamed until the crystalline lights of my prison shook, "What must we find to beat you?" The great Namuh was silent. I was not satisfied with silence. Somehow victory must overcome that which seems, on the surface, impregnable. I sought to find a pathway to my answer and discover the truth of human strength.

Slowly, a memory crept into my mind and I began an act forbidden by intellectual law: an escape through thought to the "primitive" depths of emotion. Through this channel, devoid of logic and reason, Namuh could not follow. Its buzzers and lights blinked in protest; the voice of monotone boomed to bring back my mind. I was leaving this place of entrapment, fighting barrier after barrier of conditioned responses, repression, and fear to reach a dark tunnel that extended forever beyond my reach. I was lost in the coldness of ignorance and searching, and then, as if in gentle answer the faint light of memory opened the way into a world I thought I would never see again.

The zoos of englassed people were gone, the concrete jungles were green with life, the plastic birds were true flesh and bone. The dome of Namuh Evol was hushed by the singing of a gentle brook and a golden sun beamed wisely upon me. In my mind I walked in glorious freedom through paradise, finding, tucked away in a hidden hollow, a book of poetry I had left as a child. The pages blew with the softness of the wind to a passage that began: "Sweet is the lore which Nature brings / Our meddling intellect / Mis-shapes the beauteous forms of things / We murder to dissect." If the creators of our mechanical ruler could see the murder of our minds and our nature, I wondered, would they seek to destroy their masterpiece of intellect before it destroyed the essence of our souls? I yearned that they would indeed say resolutely, as the poem continued: "Enough of Science and of

Art / Close up those barren leaves. / Come forth, and bring with you a heart / That watches and receives."

Victoriously I smiled and returned my mind to the present. I gazed upon the sun outside the glass cocoon that wasn't so impenetrable now. Finally I knew a secret my mechanized master knew not of: the power of the human heart . . . .

. . . In the intricate guarded passage where the computer dictator of Earth stood in all its complexity and mechanized wisdom, a new read-out had flashed across the screen moments before my journey of truth had begun. "Answer to Cubicle 22,783,900 Inquiry – Earth Date 2010 . . ." it read boldly. The read-out had slowly printed the mighty name of NAMUH EVOL upon the dark screen in red lights. Then, ever cautious below it, the mechanic mind had reversed the letters of its name.

. . . In this action it had given the answer
it knew would destroy its rule . . .
. . . the simple words,
"HUMAN LOVE."

- - - - - -

– A New Era –

Frank Swanson (Age 16)
South Dade Senior High School, Homestead, FL, USA

I found myself sitting up on an examination table in a bright room. I soon realized that the room I was in was the company clinic. This room had become very familiar to me because of the many previous visits I had made to it. I wondered what had happened to me and began trying to remember how I had come to be in the clinic again. As I recall I was working on the construction site of the new mall which was scheduled to be opened New Year's Day, 2011; just a couple of months away. I must have had another accident; that would raise my total to the fifth one this year. If I keep having them at the same rate, at the end of this year I would have had a total of only six accidents. Such a small number, that is so far below the national average for construction workers, would certainly cause me to receive some kind of reward from the company.

I began to feel really tense and was surprised by the obvious fact that I didn't have my headsets on. The medical personnel usually don't take them off when you have an accident unless, of course, the accident is serious enough. I didn't seem to be in any sort of critical condition, so I began to wonder what had happened to them.

Now that I think of it, today is the seventh anniversary of the day they first hit the market. The headsets everyone wears today are nothing like the ones I had when I was a teenager in the early 1980's. The headsets then were just for music. The ones today stimulates every sense of the body so that wearing a pair is like being in a second reality; a reality much better than the natural world. A whole communications network has evolved because of the invention of the headsets. Anyone can leave the real world and take a break, either in a prepackaged dream world or just leave the network entirely and develop personal fantasies. You can do whatever you want. Most people, with very few exceptions, like the headsets so much that they can't endure to be away from them. There are some drawbacks but they are relatively unimportant. The major disadvantage is the fact that wearing the headsets puts you in a kind of trance or stupor. In this trance you can still think and make decisions but not with half the accuracy as you would have normally.

The accidents I mentioned earlier are common for all workers and could be drastically reduced if they would not wear their sets on the job. If this was required then few people would continue working. Most people would rather suffer physical injury than the alternative of quitting the network. There are some people who abstain from using them in this country but they usually don't do this for long.

My thoughts were interrupted as the company's head doctor entered the room. He looked annoyed, as usual, and I felt I would melt under his cold stare. In an attempt to ease the tension of the meeting I asked, "What number is this, four or five?"

He replied dourly, "Number Five, but this time it wasn't your fault. Some jerk wasn't looking where he was swinging a plank. You have a bad lump on your head because of it. Work is over for you today. I know your head doesn't hurt now, but it will when the drugs wear off. You should be all right, but if you should feel strange or anything you know who to contact."

I acknowledged that I did remember who to contact and got up to leave as he continued in the same tone, "We would give your headsets back to you, but they were smashed as you were hit on the head. Don't worry though, the company will pay for them since they were broken on the job by someone else."

I thanked him, and as I walked through the clinic door and out into the hallway, he mumbled some kind of farewell. I took the elevator down to the lobby of the company's main building. As I passed through the doors that led out of the skyscraper and on to the street I remembered the nearest store where I could buy a new pair of headsets. There was one a few blocks away where I had gotten my first pair, and I decided to go there on foot. It then hit me why the doctor always seemed so annoyed with his patients. Being in the medical profession he couldn't work with his headsets on. It would perturb anyone to have to stop in the middle of a network broadcsat fantasy just to treat some sick or injued person.

I started walking on the sidewalk towards the shopping district and thought how strange it seemed to have an uncluttered mind. I had forgotten what it was like to be out of the stupor for a long period of time. It's amazing how many things go on in a city. Then, as if to confirm this, a car on the street to my left streaked by and hit a pedestrian who happened to be crossing the street. No human was in control of the car, naturally, although there were some passengers inside. Probably the computer driver had just malfunctioned. No one drives anymore since driving is one thing that cannot be done with headsets on. There was a pretty loud thud followed by two quieter ones as the car first slammed into, then ran over the unfortunate pedestrian. The persons in the car were probably in the network stupor as the car hit another car, and finally came to a stop close to a small knot of people. That group of people, along with everyone else at the scene, all had headsets on, and consequently, didn't seem to notice what had just happened except the few that were near the accident made it a point not to cross the street where the bodies, human and mechanical alike, were strewn. Overcome by emotions of the degree I hadn't felt in a long time, I leaned forward on a metal pole, and stared at the havoc caused by one small computer. A few minutes later some ambulances and tow trucks came and began clearing the area. Now that I had a clear mind I realized how much faster the world seemed to move. Only a half hour after the accident the street was open to traffic again. I have seen, and been in, many disasters during the past few years, but I had forgotten how terrible they actually are. I felt so horrible and sorry for the victims, especially for the pedestrian whose blood was still in the middle of the street slowly soaking into the pavement. I decided to travel at a swifter pace to the store. I was feeling the need to retire from the actuality of life again.

After I bought the new headsets I put them on while I was still in the store. I then attached the small box that served as the power source, controls, and network receiver for the system to my belt. For some reason though, I didn't turn it on right away. I guess I was curious as to what would happen to me in the real world next although I felt it would be something bad.

I left the store and began to walk home to my apartment. The day was cool and it was near sunset as I thought of how my apartment seemed so empty. I wanted to have a family and live in a house like the one I grew up in but that was quite a while ago. However, looking back on my earlier aspirations, it seems that none of them were very practical. As a student I used to think that in the future I would be an important person if I worked hard at my education.

It seems so ridiculous for me to have thought that I could have become an important person considering the fact that I would be extremely surprised if one other person in the world knew my name. I have no family and no more relatives, and I know of only one person who I could remotely consider a friend. This single person is the doctor who I had just seen a little while ago. I am sure though he knows nothing of me beyond my patient file number, my physical appearance, and what glimpses of my personality he gathered from our recent insignificant dialogue. Other than him I haven't talked to anyone without wearing my headsets for about five years. In the days when I had friends, and actually knew people, I was afraid that I would mature into an adult only to eventually become a failure. Realizing now, that I currently possess none of the traits I had dreamed of as a youth, it seems impossible to deny that my life has been one big failure. I knew I would begin to cry soon so I took a deep breath and reached down to the control box at my side. At the touch of a switch everything that had been denied to me by the real world was given to me by an unreal one.

– He Was Not Aware –

Doron Cohen (Age 16)
Haifa, Israel

It is the year 2010 now and the robots already have their emancipation. Technology has achieved such a high level of perfection, that it has enabled the production of robots which have the same appearance and behavior as a human being.

Dani, our hero, was bound by the chains of the traditional concepts. He regarded marrying a robotess as a sin. It is true that thinking of the issue rationally – one couldn't give a reason for preferring humans to robots. But people, as we well know, are not always rational and are used to sticking to their old convictions.

But Dani has one little problem – he didn't know how to distinguish humans from robots. The reader may remain calm – our hero is a bright scientist and has no difficulties in conceiving an idea to solve the problem. Robots, as we well know, are electronically programmed. Once a robot gets into a magnetic field he will probably be affected, and his "brain" will be ruined.

Dani had a girlfriend and he decided to test her to determine whether she is really a human as she claimed. He brought her into a room where he had installed a huge electromagnet which caused a powerful magnetic field.

Dani's last words were, "I was not aware." He hadn't had the chance to finish the sentence once he pulled the switch of the electromagnet on.

– Fifi de Villiers, Inventor Of Simulated Reality: Speech By Chairman, The Royal Society –

Annmarie de Villiers (Age 15)
Hoerskook Groot Schuur, Newlands, RSA

We are gathered here this evening under tragic circumstances. What would have been a highlight in the dazzling career of Fifi de Villiers, namely a discourse on her philosophy of new scientific living and formal induction as a fellow of our society, has become an occasion of deep sorrow and we can but pay tribute to this great town planner and innovator. We are all familiar with her excellent thesis on "computerized television and simulated reality." All of us have witnessed the development of scattered living that was to lead to an explosion of living units away from the boring constraints of suburbia. No longer was the mad rush to the city necessary. There was the prospect of lineration from crowded townships and the hope of identifying with nature once more.

By clever harnessing of the computer and satellite communication, coupled with 3-dimensional holography which she dubbed "telelusion," the world of simulated reality was introduced to us. It now became possible for us to handle all our business from a terminal in our own houses without the problem of physical actions. In the same way entertainment and travelling could be experienced in a sense of "actually being there," by merely pressing a button. The education of children by means of audiovisual courses under the guidance of programmed computers, realized the age old dream of developing the maximum potential of pupils.

We all remember the breakthrough when the compact nuclear fusion electrical generator was perfected. It was Fifi who first realized the limitless possibilities of this invention. She showed that, with this cheap energy, homes could be placed virtually at any desired spot. Water could be recycled and other energy needs provided for. The occasional visits to supply units could be carried out by computer assisted helicopters, totally reliable and comfortable aircraft which were also invented by the creative mind of Fifi.

I have with me tonight the introductory notes she sent me a week before her tragic death, covering her curriculum vitae. The best I can do, is to read them out to you and share with you the thoughts of a truly great person:

"My discovery of 'telelusion' and simulated reality was preceded by the perfection of a number of inventions. The first of these was the stereo Hi Fi which was perfected in 1966, the year I was born. It was followed by the Stereo Holograph which was perfected in 1989, when I took my degree in architecture. The modulated laser transmission, coupled with a satellite relay station was next to follow when it was perfected in 1990, the year I qualified as a regional planner. In 1995, Holograph telelusion was perfected which did for visual simulation what Hi Fi did for sound reproduction. During this year I qualified as a master planner. The great steps in computer science coupled with telelusion could make it possible for people to carry on with daily life without leaving their living rooms. With the help of holographs and computers, people could 'travel' all over the world, not merely as viewers but as participants. In the same way, computer tuition revolutionized education. Scholars were given personal attention and 100% tutor and pupil communication was achieved!

"Through the years I became fascinated by the possibilities of 'simulated reality' through all these developments. It would be unnecessary for people to do any physical communication and traveling. They would be able to enjoy all kinds of luxuries and handle their business by merely pressing a button. But, my greatest discovery was preceded by the deuterium energy breakthrough. In 1995, the compact 1000 kw. domestic nuclear power unit was perfected. I was fascinated by this discovery. It would mean that a new concept in town planning would be possible. Houses could be dispersed virtually anywhere. The need of physical communication and travel was already unnecessary and with this cheap energy, water could be recycled and other electrical appliances provided for. Unavoidable visits to supply units and funerals, etc. could be carried out by my perfected computerized helicopter. Dreary suburban living could be reversed and people could once again be united with nature. This year, 2010, I sold my first 1,000 dispersed homes and they are in great demand."

And then at the zenith of her career, the world was shocked by the tragic death of this acclaimed inventor. On 7 August 2010 she was assassinated by an insane housewife. She had become bored with her family compared with the fabulous illusions of simulated reality. In all this intellectual stimulation compared with the boring reality of her family, she felt that she had to save the world by destroying the inventor of simulated reality. Ladies and gentlemen, the world has lost a great person. Her ingenuity is not to be doubted. But I ask you this one question – was that assassin totally insane, or did she perhaps think further than the rest of us?

– Trouble In Reliving –

Chia-Jung Chan (Age 11)
Chung-I Elementary School, Tainan, Taiwan

Entering the Peking University Medical School Laboratory, I opened the freezer and pushed a green button on the wall. A rectangular coffin quietly slipped out of the freezer. This was a corpse of a middle-aged man who was put in this coffin which was filled with liquid nitrogen. According to the computer data, his name was Wen-Ming Ding and he was put in deep freeze when he was 33 years old. He was waiting for a new cancer-cure drug to be discovered in the year 2016.

I am a doctor. I was 10 years old in 1982 when one of my teachers died of cancer. I was so sad that I had a wish to become a doctor to help the cancer patients. I am now 34 years old.

I opened the coffin and let the 36-year-old Miss Chao do the defrosting. She has had four years of experience in defrosting corpses. First, she ordered one of the robot servants to move the coffin to a heated-up apparatus. Then she put an oxygen mask over his face. Finally she increased the temperature from the original -273 degrees C to 24 degrees C. She also used the electric current to stimulate his heart and to circulate the blood in his whole body. Mr. Ding woke up. After he became fully conscious, he asked me anxiously, "Where are my wife, my child and my parents?" I said "it is now the twenty-first century. Your parents died a long time ago; but your wife and your child are still living. Your wife is now 51 years old and your child is 35 years old. They are outside of the room to see you." He said, "Can I go out now?" I said, "Of course you can. You have not seen them for 21 years."

Outside in the hall when they saw one another, they are stunned for a long while, then, quickly they hugged one another and cried with joy. They asked me "Can we go home?" I told them to wait a minute and I gave Mr. Ding an injection of the cancer-cure drug. He became healthy without cancer anymore.

Two months after Mr. Ding left the hospital, Mrs. Ding gave me a telephone call and asked me if I could come over because something had been disturbing her. I hurried to their house right away. Mrs. Ding told me that her husband was too young for a 54-year-old man. When both of them walked on the street, many people thought they were mother and son, instead of wife and husband. Moreover, her husband still preserved the living style and the concept of 20 years ago. He could not keep up with the present living conditions. Mr. Ding himself also complained, "It is absurd for me to have an old woman as my wife. Twenty years ago, my friends and relatives believed that I was dead; right now they cannot accept my being alive!" I hoped they would think it over. Mr. Ding continued to complain, "My son looks older than I am. What can I do?" Their worries made me wonder.

One year later, Mrs. Ding sent me a letter telling me that Mr. Ding had left their home to search for a world to which he belonged, because he could not stand this strange world. Mr. Ding asked them not to look for him and just forget him and presume that he was dead 21 years ago. Science can make dead people relive, and keep the precious youth and life, but the consequences are unthinkable. They cause troubles.

In the summer of the year 2020, I came back to Taiwan by boat. I visited the grave of my teacher who died of cancer when I was 10 years old. I thought that if my teacher was kept frozen when she died of cancer, she would be alive today. People would believe that she and I were sisters.

CHAPTER ELEVEN

To Reach For The Sky

In November, 1983, a television program entitled *The Day After* was viewed by a record number of TV watchers. The program depicted a nuclear war and focused on the destruction of Kansas City, America's heartland. This realistic portrayal of the survivors in nearby Lawrence, Kansas, prompted strong emotional reactions from millions of U.S. citizens. One college student wrote, "'The Day After' has forced me to come to grips with the full horror of nuclear war, and I am in despair," (Smith, 1983).

This sentiment of shock and near-disbelief at the awesome destructive power of a nuclear bomb seemed to be typical of the national reaction. For days, newspapers and magazines carried stories of discussion groups, families, and individuals whose eyes had been opened by the experience of watching this television "special." Dean Rusk (former United States Secretary of State and University of Georgia Professor of International Law) commented to a reporter, "We should not let any sort of doomsday specter dull our imaginations or doom us to apathy" (Smith, 1983). In spite of this, and many other statements suggesting that the groundswell of anti-nuclear feeling would provide the impetus for a paradigm shift in our national attitude, the remarkable thing about *The Day After* experience was what happened afterward – nothing. That is to say, following a short period of reaction, people went about their daily routine much the same as before. It was, after all, only a television program. It was as though the nation had become extremely excited over the Super Bowl game, but several weeks after it was over, they could not remember who had won.

How could it be that after record numbers of people had watched *The Day After* and discussed nuclear holocaust in such emotional terms, that hardly anything changed as a result? One possible explanation is that the program had been *too* realistic and that our imaginations *had* been dulled. Elizabeth Kubler-Ross (1975) in her book, *Death the Final Stage of Growth*, identified the dynamics, or stages, one goes through when facing death. It seems that at least two of these dynamics may be present in our national reaction, and in several scenarios contained in this chapter.

The first dynamic is that of denial. In the experience of denial, although one may understand – intellectually – that it is he or she who will die; the full realization of this happening is not possible. Denial in the extreme would border on a delusional belief that a mistake had been made, or it is not possible to die, or some miracle will – at the last moment – alter the course of the inevitable. Another dynamic is bargaining. In bargaining, the person on the threshold of death attempts to "make a deal" which would prolong life. If one dedicates the remainder of life to good works and service to others, perhaps a "stay of execution" will be granted by whomever is in charge of that department, and life will continue in a more correct fashion. These reactions by those who are nearing death are quite natural and, Kubler-Ross believes, universal. To those who are dying – and for their families – it is reassuring to know that denial and bargaining are common reactions to an event which must be experienced a bit at a time, rather than all at once. The danger in these dynamics might be the case in which the patient is curable but chooses to deny that he or she is ill; or, worse yet, the patient appeals for help through bargaining to a quack or faith-healer who promises recovery through fraudulent methods. Carl Sagan has stated that there is a nuclear build-up in such a case, in which the cure exacerbates the illness.

The sky has always been the place of escape from the mundane trials of our earth-bound existence. Children dream of flight as a way to transcend a life which seems too complex to understand and not within their control. Heaven has been thought to lie somewhere beyond the sky and to be a place where simplicity and freedom from trouble and want exists. More in the realm of science, children view the sky as the threshold of space. The scenario writers, today's children, have grown up knowing that travel to the moon is a reality and that further space travel, colonization of other planets, and perhaps even other forms of life, are all possible. "To reach for the sky" is to seek the ideal and to know the answer. Many of the writers seem to believe that we have already despoiled our landscape, fouled our environment, and pushed ourselves to the irreversible threshold of nuclear confrontation. In their minds, there is only one thing to do – prepare to evacuate Planet Earth. While we as adults still seem to be in "denial" about nuclear destruction, the children have already progressed to "bargaining." They reach for the sky for our salvation. Several scenarios depict small colonies of the "nation's best" – carrying on the species in other locations after the holocaust. In some cases, everyone else has been killed, all former culture destroyed, and all technological advances rendered useless. The survivors possess an innocence and spirit which the scenario writers seem to view as the pure essence of our nature. Like Noah, whose bargain with God was that he would survive provided he built the Ark and saved the creatures of the earth, these space colonists have also vowed to get back to basics and to attempt to avoid a recurrence of the holocaust. Perhaps they speak for us, who in the midst of our denial, have had to live with the specter of nuclear destruction since Hiroshima. Perhaps the ambiguity has become too much for us, and we secretly wish for closure, for an end to it all and for our salvation from "the fire next time" by reaching for the sky. Our bargain might be that those of us not headed for heaven might be destined for a new and innocent colony somewhere in space by way of the latest spacecraft. Either way, we will have closure.

It is interesting to note that as the children prepare in their vivid imaginations for escape, we adults continue to go to our jobs, shop the grocery store, and to distract ourselves from full realization of The Day After.

For reasons unclear to us, November is when ratings shares for TV networks are determined. One point in the ratings race can mean millions of dollars in advertising to the network which gains the edge. That is why the networks put their most powerful programming on during this month.

The November, 1983, showing of *The Day After* must have gained rating points for ABC since it was viewed by record numbers. The sponsors then gave their advertising money to ABC, assuming this was the network we would all be watching. Sponsors know that we are influenced by their advertising – if we are watching – to go out and purchase their product. Apparently, this is more than can be said of *The Day After* and its message. Perhaps the program might have permanently broken through our denial if it had been, instead of a realistic portrayal of the survivors of nuclear war in Lawrence, Kansas, a series of anti-nuclear ads appealing to our more everyday fears: "Friends, did you know that nuclear war would cause spots on your best crystal and china?" . . . . "Not only will nuclear war give you stubborn dandruff, but it will actually cause your hair to fall out!" . . . . "even an *extra*-strength pain reliever is not enough for nuclear war!!" . . . . "Have you had your homeowners insurance agent review your policy to see if it covers nuclear war?"

– The Final Holocaust –

Mark Chancey (Age 13)
Boddie Junior High School, Milledgeville, GA, USA

4/30/2008

Tension between the United Republic and the Inter-Allied Communist States has increased in the past few days, worrying everyone. The experts insist that the situation will blow over, but it is obvious they are lying. President Anderson's promises to the minor states of the Middle East will have to be kept, but at the cost of war? Our military presence there does pose a small threat to the IACS, but it is neither unreasonable nor uncalled for to place troops there to guard the small remaining oil supply. Oil is an archaic fuel, but in some situations it does perform better than hydrogen. Still, these situations are few and far between – perhaps something else could have been worked out. To back down now, though, would be an act of cowardice in the eyes of the world.

It is obvious the IACS wants to fight, but why? What purpose will it serve? What good will it do? The small vestiges of the hatred between the United States and the USSR of the last century remain, but are they that strong? Our garrison there in Israel is not that strong and the location is not strategic. Why has the IACS transformed it into a major crisis?

At this very minute, enemy troops are preparing for battle a few miles from Israel's border. Aimed at the hearts of the UR – Paris, London, New York, Washington – are the missiles of the IACS. Tools of destruction. Why? Why is man so barbaric? For thousands of years, he has had one idea, one main course of action—violence. He has not changed – his methods have. Why must he turn to violence to solve his problems? Better, more efficient weapons have been invented – why not better, more effective alternatives? Violence doesn't solve the problem – it provides a firm foundation for future conflicts.

What will they do? An attack could destroy the very lifeblood of the planet, the atmosphere itself. Perhaps it will be less severe – only the mere elimination of the dominant species.

5/1/2008

I've never been so scared in my life. The word *terror* is not sufficient, nor is *horror*. Those words don't come close to describing the fear within me. I know it will happen. The question is, "When?"

All over the world, people are crying out for an end to the useless arguing among our diplomats. It's obvious they are not helping; they're too blinded by their fury to see what's happening. So far, the conflict has been limited to mere insults and counter-insults. The debaters are not looking for solutions; they're stalling for time as their nations frantically try to prepare themselves, each trying to get an edge over the other before the onslaught begins. Hopefully, it will be confined to a traditional battle between the two countries' armies. Otherwise . . . .

Why must we fight? It's never too late to turn back; why can't they see that? This was a minor problem which started off with small diplomatic difficulties. How did it reach this stage? Tomorrow I go to the country. Perhaps I'll have time to think. Man is the most intelligent lifeform on earth – or is he? Just how intelligent is he? It seems now that he has lost control of himself, a rampaging monster set free, seeking destruction. When will he find it?

5/2/2008

It was a horrifying sight. The red speck floated lazily through the sky, slowly descending to the earth below. There, it exploded into a huge orange blossom, a fireball of death. The ground shook even at my vantage point in the hills. For a second, pain-filled shrieks reached up, audible even at this distance, then, abruptly they ceased. The fire reached up high into the sky. Smoke filled the air until even the sun could not be seen. Then all was black, as still as the night. Gradually the light of the sun crept back in, shattering the darkness. The huge mushroom was gone; the smoke had disappeared. All that remained was the ruins of a once-great city. Like a relic of a past civilization it lay, a barren wasteland.

I was able to listen in on my receiver for a few brief minutes. The news was not shocking. The fate of any town was the same as the fate of thousands of other towns. The destruction was widespread. I was able to pick up the names of a few of the towns that had been destroyed before that center stopped broadcasting. Paris, Marseilles, London, Los Angeles, Washington, Rome – all gone, the people dead, the buildings crumbling. In the counter-strike that followed, the IACS also paid dearly.

In a few brief moments, the lives of billions of people had been extinguished, stamped out. They had done nothing to deserve such a fate; why had it befallen them? Even now, I hear the echoes of other attacks only minutes after the first strike. Few will survive this I can tell. If I had not come to the mountains I, too, would be dead.

144 Save Tomorrow For The Children

It took thousands of years for civilization to reach this point. Now, it's all gone, its future washed away, its past forgotten. The technology of a thousand years – lost in less than an hour. Men have died for this country. Their efforts were wasted, their deeds were proved to be worthless. For in the last hour, what good did their courage do? Of what value were their losses, their love for mankind, their nobility, their sacrifices? In the final day, did they stop the holocaust? No, they did nothing. In a few minutes, a small group of men decided that they meant nothing. Those few decided that hatred and pride were more important factors.

What led up to this? Where did we go wrong? How did this happen? Even more important than that, what will happen? How will we survive?

5/3/2008

While exploring the stream bed this morning, I came across the body of a young girl. She was only five or six years old, a small, frail child. Though her face was radiation-scarred, I could see the look of puzzlement and fright on her still face. She was just a small child; she knew nothing of the problems. All she knew was that someone across the sea had killed Mommy and Daddy and was going to kill her. She didn't even know who her murderers were.

I forced myself to go on, combing the mountain for survivors, as well as food. Eventually I found a narrow trail leading into the forest. After following it for a while, I came to a small, silent clearing. Huddled in the center were three people, two young men and a woman. One of the men's face was strangely disfigured and burned. The other two people appeared unharmed.

After a short discussion, they allowed me to join them. One of them possessed a gun, ancient in appearance because of the thick coat of dust completely covering it. All had standard survival kits, hastily assembled and distributed by the government two weeks ago. Somehow they had survived the attack on the city.

By staying together, we ought to be able to last for a while. We can hunt with the gun until the ammunition runs out, then I suppose we'll have to improvise and create our own weapons.

Eventually we'll have to go back to the city and see what we can find there, but we'll have to wait a while for the radiation to decrease.

The IACS destroyed almost everything in the UR yesterday. Fortunately they left the rural areas alone, leaving at least a few survivors.

Sometime last night I found the answers to my questions. All of those idealistic men – their work wasn't wasted. They struggled and fought so that when this time came, we could look back and see their efforts and somehow muster the strength to go on in this wasted world. They worked so that we could look at their sacrifices and see why they made them – for their reasons were the same as the reasons for what we must do. We have to work to make this place better, to keep our children from living in the same world we do, to show them that we think life is valuable enough to make sacrifices for, valuable enough to fight for, even die for. Present situations and circumstances may be terrible, but there is something about life which adds value to it no matter what happens. We must be witnesses of this destruction and make sure it never happens again.

– A Warning –

Philip McGaha (Age 15)
North Clayton Senior High School, College Park, GA, USA

My name is Phillip McGaha. The year is 2010. I am writing this document for future generations (if there are any) to read about and learn from.

I am 43 years old and live in America. Our country has been at war with Russia for six months. We live in terror that our city may be the next target of a Russian bomb. Every day people are getting killed by the millions in this catastrophic calamity. Our higher and higher sophistication only proved to be our downfall. Pestilences, plagues, and droughts have been experienced to a degree never seen before. Our so-called high society has been severely crippled. Heavy taxes have been laid upon the American people to pay for the war.

Things weren't always like this though. With the perfection of robots in the early '40s, life was made somewhat easier. The robots could do many of the heavy labor jobs for five times less money than it would cost to pay humans. But most of all, the major advancements were in what's called "War Technology." Satellites were made that could intercept missiles and could fire them also. Faster and more deadly planes were made. The science of chemical warfare has greatly expanded. But the greatest invention of all was suction energy. Huge "silos" were constructed on the dams of rivers. Then large biodegradeable discs (of the same size as the silos) were filled with water and taken to the top of the silos. There they were dropped through the silos, creating a great suction which turned a turbine at the top of the silo to create energy. Then when the discs reached the bottom, the discs broke, the water flowed into the stream, and the discs were broken down chemically by nature. This helped reduce our dependence on foreign oil but not much because the majority of the energy was used to produce more military arms. So this didn't help the general public as it should have, but any improvement was greatly appreciated because things had become worse and worse.

Fortunately, I am a little better off than other people because I have a pretty good job. After graduating from business college, I became an executive for Shell. By 1990, I was married, had kids, and was promoted to Manager of Research and Development. The only problem was fewer people were buying gas, so many of our filling stations had to be closed. This meant a cut in my salary. But I was one of the lucky ones. The unemployment rate was at 25%. The government was deep in debt because of the unemployment money that had to be paid and because of the free food program that was started. With so many people unemployed, slums began to grow. Thus, many diseases began to run wild with massive outbreaks. This wasn't only happening in the U.S., but all over the world this type chain reaction was beginning to degrade society. Droughts were plaguing many portions of the world. But even through all of this, many saw a ray of hope that kept them going.

I, like many others, am looking for the second coming of Christ. In light of this, many people began to show brotherly love to all even though it was a struggle to survive. I now belong to an organization called "Help." Every day I and the other members of Help in my area go to places that have been bombed and help to remove rubble from the walkways so the medical robots can get to the needy. We also help to remove victims who are trapped and comfort those who have lost a loved one. I enjoy doing it but I hope that some day it will not be needed. Maybe after seeing all the damage and loss of human life this war is causing, our government and theirs will come to an agreement to end this insane war. Hopefully, we will be able to settle down and relax without the threat of being bombed. So, I leave this story as a proclamation to any who might read it. I hope you will learn from our mistakes and find wisdom from our follies. Maybe you and your children may live in peace without the threat of . . . .

– Silence On Earth –

Walter K. Schmidt (Age 15)
Weslaco High School, Weslaco, TX, USA

It is the year 2010 and Robert Davis speaks to the Council of Nations. He is discussing a plan to save the world.

"Members of the Council, in order for the preservation of the human race to proceed, I believe that 100 members from each country should be selected and sent to form a space colony on ZM-2, the newly discovered planet in the Tri-Omega solar system."

Robert tells the Council that this special colony will be transported on interstellar space shuttles while they are in suspended animation. Every nation would be told to pick 100 of their best citizens. A date for leaving was set.

Departure day comes and Robert, who has previously been chosen by his government, will go on the expedition. He has also been chosen to lead the group. He speaks to the chosen citizens.

"Members of Special Task Force I, your country and mine have chosen me to lead this expedition. First of all, I must tell you that it is a priority to go into suspended animation, so that time will not age us. Now, let's get ready. Everyone into his capsule. Prepare for suspended animation."

Everyone obeys the assigned leader and is quickly put into deep sleep. The group is then sent toward ZM-2.

Three days have passed since the expedition was launched. Hostility then breaks out on Earth. The Council of Nations quickly sends a message to the group's computer, fearing a holocaust, which will relay the message when they awake.

Nearing ZM-2, several years later, the Special Task Force awakes. Robert has the computer relay all messages sent during their trip. They hear the news:

"Special Task Force I, this may be the last word you will hear from Earth. A nuclear holocaust may take place. If it does occur, you will be all that is left of the human race. Please, learn from us. War is natural to man, but it need not kill you. Strive for peace between all." The message ended.

After peering through a telescope, Robert tells the group that Earth has been destroyed. It causes everyone to be flabbergasted.

"Our World is gone," Robert said with deep sorrow, "and only we survive. We must go down on the planet and start a new life."

Saddened, they all disembark from the space shuttles. On the planet, a discussion begins.

"We should all stay together," someone stated.

"Yes, and we should form a government," another replied.

"Let it be communist!" says one.

"No! Socialist!" states another.

"Neither! Let it be a republic!"

And so, an argument starts over which government should rule. Robert is heartbroken, because he knows peace will not last on this planet either.

"People! Please!" he finally yelled. "If you all cannot agree upon a government, we should split up and choose separate governments." This he said with deep regret.

"No!" a few shouted.

"Yes!" Robert replied. "But those of you who do not agree can come with me and we will form another Council of Nations!"

Everyone, for the most part contented, then went on his way. Robert and his group, despite this agreement, are saddened because they did not follow the Council's advice to achieve peace. Finally, Robert discusses the matter with his group.

"We are the Adams and Eves of the world. When the population of our world increases, war will again begin. Later in the future, we might have to organize another Special Task Force and send them to another planet so that a holocaust will not wipe us all out. If peace cannot be achieved now, we will never be able to achieve it later on. So let it be. When the time of hostility comes, the human race will live on, somewhere out there on another planet." He and the others gaze out into space, hoping that a time of peace will arrive.

– Ticop –

Paige Hanks (Age 13)
Union Middle School, Sandy, Utah, USA

January 14, 2000 A.D. The entire world is on red alert! Nuclear war and the destruction of the human race is imminent. The hope of the world hinges upon the decisions made by the nation's leaders at the U.N. meeting in Washington, D.C.

The leader of the U.N. began, "There's been such advancement in the technology of computers in the last 20 years, that I think the only solution is to have each nation feed into the U.N.'s Master Computer its nation's concerns and suggestions for his nation. Then, with the computer's logical, unbiased programming, it will give its recommendation for the perfect society. Let us now vote on this proposition." The vote was unanimous; the leaders entered their ideas.

It's now 20 years later. The world looks much the same, but has drastically changed. It is a world where the Master Computer rules. Everything is logical, regimented, unchallenging. Life is simple.

Every Monday, people wear blue, they do their yards and housework. Tuesday through Friday is devoted to the care and programming of the computers. Yellow is worn on these days. Saturday, red is worn. The day is spent in recreation and grooming. Sunday is a day of worship, white is worn.

This life is simple, but to some it is boring. To disagree with the computers meant extermination, unless one's mind was creative enough to escape the Computer City. There were some places to escape to, built by people with very creative minds. One is in the trees of the Redwood Forest, another is in the core of the Earth, others were built under large lakes. These cities were throughout the World; it was just a matter of finding them.

The sun glistened through the blue glacier, forming a prism that sparkled rainbows through the crisp air.

"This is a beautiful place," Margo said, "but the people here are all wrong. Life should be easy and effortless, not challenging. I'm leaving!"

"Me too," Paul agreed. "Let's join the computer world, so we don't have to think so hard. If we told the Computer Master about Glacier City, it would destroy Glacier City and we would be in its favor."

Many times their parents had warned the children about joining the computer world, a world of conformity with no advancements, no challenges, just existence. Glacier City, on the other hand, was filled with creative, thinking people – every day a new invention, every day was filled with changes and growth.

On June 14, 2020, the warning siren sounded. The siren was placed at the entrance to the city to warn the people that a robot was entering the city. However, this alarm was set off by Margo and Paul leaving Glacier City.

The people were shocked; everyone knew what this meant. The peaceful people of Glacier City would not kill, even to defend themselves. It would be a matter of days until Paul and Margo would lead the computer agents to Glacier City. The city would be wiped out; there was little hope.

"Would Bryan, Jewel, Faith, Naythan, Nerissa, Chris, Alex, and Cassie report to the first office immediately," the voice came over the school intercom.

"Bryan's in trouble again," his class teased as he left the room.

The eight children soberly gathered outside the first office. All were pale, and filled with fear, all except the youngest, Jewel. With a twinkle in her eye she said, "Don't worry. We're not in trouble," and then quietly sat down.

Soon Principal Lewis entered with Nicholas Michfene. Nic Mic, as the children called him, was the wise man of Glacier City, and therefore, he was their leader. The eight children, faces filled with wonder, looked up as Nicholas began to speak.

"I have called you eight children together today because you are the hope of this city. As you know, every five years we have sent out a group of adults, those with special talents, to form a new colony. This time, with the computer agents coming for us, I know that adults couldn't make it. I've talked to your parents; they all agree with me. You kids have to find those colonies. Make them grow so there will be hope."

"You all have talents that are so very important. Jewel, use your ESP, make it work. Naythan, you're artistic, Nerissa, you're imaginative. Together you two can help. Cassie, use your photographic memory to its fullest extent; you'll need it. Chris, listen to Cassie and use your mechanical abilities. Bryan, your strength is something everyone will need. Faith, you're sensitive, listen and make peace. Last, Alex, I'm choosing you as leader. You're the oldest at 14, the wisest, and the most responsible. Watch out for everyone."

"If you will listen to each other, I know that you will find the Important City of Peace; its people are waiting for you. I know you can do it! You must leave immediately, take nothing but your talents and go!"

With that the children left the city, not knowing much about each other or where they were going. They walked for about one hour. Then, without warning, Jewel began to run toward the Computer City, exactly where they didn't want to go. Bryan ran after her and at age 12, he easily caught the six-year-old.

"Are you crazy?" Bryan screamed. Jewel just stared.

Faith interrupted, "Jewel, what's wrong?"

"We have to go there!" Jewel replied.

"Listen to her," Alex commanded, "Nic Mic said to listen to each other."

"We have to go there," Jewel repeated. "We have to hurry!" The eight children ran toward the city, unaware of what lay ahead. Soon they found themselves sneaking into a rocketship airport.

"We have to get inside that door." Jewel announced.

"There should be a button over there. That's it." Cassie shouted. And they were inside. The room was dark, cold, and looked something like a space shuttle.

"I know what this is," exclaimed Cassie. There was a rumbling sound, and the children were covered over by a pile of junk.

"This is crazy," Bryan mumbled. "We're sitting here in the middle of a junk shuttle. In one minute we're going to be headed for the Sun ready to burn up with this junk!"

The shuttle took off. At first there were complaints about their misfortune, but soon everyone was tired and everyone fell to sleep except Nerissa. Nerissa had a very creative mind and, at that moment, she was thinking great thoughts.

When the children awoke, about 10 hours later, they had a surprise waiting for them. Nerissa had taken some of the junk and built a room.

"An enjoyment room" was what she called it, and that's what it was.

This idea stirred everyone's minds, and soon they were busy building their own rooms. Each room contained one bed, a chair, and decorations, depending on the person. When the rooms were finished, there was only a small pile of junk left. That was shoved in a corner.

The closer they got to the sun, the hotter it became in the shuttle. One day Chris and Cassie began making suits that would protect everyone from the heat. They worked day and night sorting through old junk, putting things together. They completed the suits just in time.

Today was the day the ship would hit the sun. Everyone put on their suits, prayed, and huddled together.

The shuttle was programmed to deposit the junk, then return to Earth at exactly 1:45.

At 1:40 the children were full of dread and fear. Alex and Faith tried to comfort the other children. The heat kept getting worse until everyone except Alex fainted.

Then, without warning the ship was sucked through a black, cool tunnel. When they came out of the tunnel, everyone awakened. Then people appeared; they looked human, Cassie recognized them. They were the first people sent from Glacier City to build a colony. Jewel ran out of the ship and happily jumped into the arms of . . . Mrs. Joy!

"We're here," Alex announced hugging Faith. "We've found The Important City of Peace. We've found T.I.C.O.P."

– Space Travel –

Chih-Fang Lin
Hsi-Men Elementary School, Taipei, Taiwan

The computer clock indicates that it is the year 1999. Da-Hsu, Evans, Cleetwood, Nisban, Alice, and I are driving the "Star River" spaceship and traveling through the infinite space. We travel at a speed about 94% of the velocity of light, so that the sense of time is slower. One space year equals 20 earth years; thus, 20 space years equals 400 earth years.

Four months ago, to welcome the coming of the twenty-first century, the people on the earth gave us a mission to find a planet outside the solar system for human beings to live on more comfortably. The most important thing was to visit any creatures on the other planet who are more developed than we are and we can ask for their guidance to improve our living conditions.

Our "Star River" spaceship is powered by the star energy which absorbs the heat coming from several universal stars and enable the spaceship to travel in the space endlessly. We have vitamin tablets as our food. There are six sections in the spaceship. There are six members in the first section where they operate the computers and the robots. I am the captain of all six sections, but there are different persons responsible for the other five sections: Da Hsu takes charge of the Biology Section; Evans takes care of the Weapons Section; Cleetwood operates the Instrument Section; Nisban operates the Power Section; Alice is in charge of the Medicine Section and she is the only woman on our ship.

Looking out of the spaceship, I saw many twinkling stars which bring me back to my memories: On October 10, 1994, the Republic of China in Taiwan won over the People's Republic of China and recovered the lost land. One month later, the whole world was reunited. But, not long after that, because of the over-population of the world, people started to develop the underwater cities, underground cities, and the sky cities which made the world united, just as what Confucius dreamed about a long time ago. As a result of the universal peace, there is no more world war.

"Chih-Fond Lin, there is a planet in front of us just like the earth. Do you want to go and take a look?" Nisban asked.

"OK," I replied, "Let's go to the planet and have a look."

Our spaceship is started to move toward that planet at full speed. The gas analyzer shows that a lot of carbon dioxide is on the planet. The Geiger Counter shows that the radiation coming out of that planet is too strong for our space suits to resist. So that we just took some pictures and left.

Five days later, the beeping sound of our computer gave us a warning. "Look out, Evans," I shout, "get ready to fire the electron gun!"

There are two flying saucers in front of our spaceship. Our computer indicated, "the people from the flying saucers would like to talk to us."

I replied, "OK."

In a second there appeared on our television screen a robot in gold suits. He said, "I would like to invite all of you to our planet."

I thought that we had troubles on our hands. The robot said, "Don't worry, we are not going to harm you."

It is remarkable for him to know what I am thinking about! He continued, "Of course, I am one of the highly developed creatures in the universe. I know what you are thinking about and I also understand your language but I won't attack you. I am here to welcome all of you."

After hearing those assuring words, I felt safe. I said, "Energize the laser protection cover. We should be careful though." Five seconds later, there was a reddish protection cover over our ship. This protection cover can protect the attack from any laser gun but it can only last for one minute. The robot in a gold suit said, "You can turn off your engine. We will lead you to our planet."

Therefore, I'll order Nisban to turn off the engine. At the same moment two light beams shot out from each of the flying saucers attached to our spaceship. It is hard to believe that we are flying to the planet at the margin of the universe. Before our landing, we have a feeling of pain and our bodies seem to explode. Suddenly, the robot in the gold suit said, "It is here. Now let me introduce myself. My name is Caray. We know what the other creatures think about. We can go anywhere we wish. We can fly by means of the spiritual induction. We also have the ability to see through everything. We can measure the wave length and see the faraway scenery. I hope you can learn to be like us."

After hearing what Caray said, our face looked a little funny which made Caray burst into a big laughter. "Our planet is very peaceful and quiet," Caray continued to say, "Since you come from a place of 420 light years away, you must have a good reason for doing so."

"Yes," I said, "you really are one of the highly developed creatures in the universe. You even understand why we came here. We came here to learn more scientific techniques from you, because you have more technical experiences than we do. Your technology is about 342 years ahead of us. We surely need your guidance." Caray said, "We will be glad to help you."

I said, "We are so happy to hear this." Even our robots and the computers are happy too.

Another robot in a gold suit said to me, "We would like to take you on a tour to look around our planet. You must be the captain of your ship. My name is Ila Ting. I am glad to meet you."

Never in my life have I thought that a place which is 420 light years away from us, there are still creatures who can be so kind and easy to communicate with. "Don't be surprised!" Ila Ting said, "I am taking you to see the treasures in our planet."

Suddenly, there were many rocks floating in front of us. Ila said, "There are our treasures. Our planet is full of gold; therefore, rocks become treasures. But nobody has ever tried to steal them." Ila and I continued to fly and we saw a lot of strange objects on our way. I was curious to ask Ila how they reproduced. Ila said, "We reproduce in every 400 years. Everybody is able to reproduce. At the time of reproduction, we will evolve an x-ray which then turns into another robot in a gold suit, the same as we are. After the reproduction of the small robots in gold suits, we don't have to take care of them like you do your babies, which is troublesome."

I said, "Thank you, Ila Ting, I think that we have to go home now."

Ila said, "Before you go home, I will tell you some good news. I will send 123 persons to your planet and provide you with the information you need. Oh, yes, I will give your leader a flying saucer to show our respect."

I said, "Thank you very much."

Right now we are on our way back to earth, conveyed by their two flying saucers. Computer clock indicates that it is the year 2010. Today I have finally completed the most important duty of my life. I'll continue to work hard.

– Evacuation –

Timothy C. Benner (Age 16)
J. P. McCaskey High School, Lancaster, PA, USA

The sun was already well up into the sky as Doctors Brian Maher and Jim Geurts stood at the end of the encampment, staring at the levelled remnants of a once-great city. Around them glimmered protective anti-radiation shields, hardly visible in the bright morning light. Behind them, the camp was preparing for another day of work. Barriers were being set up, synthetic huts were being locked, and supplies were being counted and positioned. Technicians were testing the equipment for the upcoming day-long task. Above them all towered a high structure of steel girders, at the top of which were eight vigilant guards. They unceasingly scanned the surrounding plain for anything which should not have been there.

Back at the edge of the camp, away from all the bustling activity, Brian said, "Boston used to be such a beautiful city." He paused, "But then so were all the other cities that were destroyed. Oh, what I'd give to see Paris! Think of it, Jim, even Paris is gone, just like all the rest."

"I have thought about it, more than once," replied Jim, still staring at the ruins of Boston. "We better head back in. The first group should be arriving at any moment."

They turned and re-entered the center of the camp, where the preparations were coming to a close. Had they kept looking, they would have seen a large group of people appear in the distance, led by two men wearing the uniform of those in the camp. Careful observation would also have revealed faintly glimmering radiation shields. In 20 minutes this crowd had reached the camp and assembled in its central area. Brian, being the camp's chief doctor, climbed onto a wooden platform and called for their attention. Once he had it, he began his usual speech.

"As you all know, the holocaust scorched the Earth with hard radiation. Fortunately for you, American defenses spared you the full brunt of the Soviet attack. However, even the present radiation, when not immediately deadly, has many adverse effects on the human body. You have been selected to come here because you have no macroscopic radiation damage. Those of you who we find to have no chromosome damage will be offered the opportunity to leave the Earth at once and be resettled in one of the United States bases on either the moon or on Mars, away from any more radiation. The Soviets couldn't fire any of their nuclear missiles that far, so these are safe areas. Now, please form orderly lines at each of the 10 examination tables, and we will try to move you through as quickly as possible."

"Good speech," said Jim as Brian came down from the platform.

"I should hope so," answered Brian. "I've had two months to practice it." They walked to their examination areas. "Just look at the hope in their eyes, Jim, the anticipation. I wish we could take all of them with us."

They split up and proceeded to their work stations. Throughout the long, hot day, in 10 different places, the doctors and their assistants scanned over a thousand people for radiation damage. It was a simple process. The recently invented chromosome micro-scanner could determine in five minutes the condition of a person's chromosomes. Those people who had no damage were immediately escorted to a large, lead-lined building where they would be exposed to no more radiation. Those who failed the test were given a red stamp on the right hand and were sent away.

Many people were silent during the examination process, but a few overcame their nervousness and were talkative. Brian had several such people at his table during the day.

"Doctor, why wasn't the world totally destroyed, like all the experts predicted?" inquired a short man in overalls.

"Well," answered Brian as the scanner did its work, "A lot of the second-wave missiles were affected by the earlier blasts, and they didn't go off. It was really touchy disarming all of them afterwards, but it was worth it. Plus, the American particle beam satellites shot down a lot of the Soviet missiles. Russia wasn't so lucky. There isn't anything left over there." The general public is so ill-informed, thought Brian.

"It really is hot for October, isn't it?" said a rather attractive woman.

"That's the radiation, of course," Brian replied. "It should be about 20 degrees cooler. You'll have to wait a few hundred years at least for the climate to recover from the war."

Jim also had some talkative ones. "How did you guys in space come through it all so well?" asked a dark-haired man with glasses.

"We destroyed the Soviets' three space stations early on," said Jim. "After that, none of their missiles could reach us."

"Tell me something, Doc. Did anyone outside the United States survive?" questioned a tall, well-dressed man.

"Yes, there were numerous survivors in Canada, Australia, and certain parts of Africa, as well as in other remote areas of the world."

Halfway through the afternoon they were all startled by strange barks and yelps outside the camp. A voice from the guard tower yelled, "Don't worry; they're only wild dogs." Lasers crackled, and searing bolts of energy shot from the tower into the bushes. There were many yelps of pain as the barrage continued, and the dogs soon retreated, leaving half their number behind. Such attacks by wild dogs were not uncommon, for many dogs had been left homeless by the holocaust.

The rest of the day passed without incident, and at sunset a shuttle landed to pick up those who would be able to leave the Earth. An hour later, fully loaded, it took off with a blaze of exhaust and disappeared into the sky. The unchosen people had, throughout the day, had to walk back to their homes, some merely sad or disappointed, some angry, and many in total despair. A lifetime on the burned-out wreck of what had been a beautiful planet held little promise for anyone. Mere survival from now on would be difficult for those who had to stay.

At 11:00 that night, Brian woke Jim and hurried him outside. "One of the guards brought in one of the dogs they killed today. You'll want to see it."

"But I've seen dozens of these wild dogs," protested Jim.

"Not like this." He led Jim to a blanket lying on the ground with a lump under it. He pulled away the blanket, exposing a young dog. It had no fur, no tail, three eyes, and it was hideously misshapen. It was obviously a mutant.

There was silence for several seconds. "It's started," said Jim, staring.

"Yes. Precious little time remains."

– Are You Out There, Friend? –

Jim Durham (Age 13)
Clarke Central High School, Athens, GA, USA

The year is 2008; the date, April 18. This is to be the most memorable date in 20 centuries for mankind. I, and many of the other top astronomers in the nation, have been working on this project, code named W.O.F.D., which President Williams created in the year 2005. To get a better picture of the plan, let me go back to the beginning of the story.

The date was November 13, 2005. President John Williams has just pronounced the enactment of a full scale search and, if possible, communication with life superior to ours on other planets. The search was scheduled as a result of investigations by NICAP (The National Investigations Committee of Aerial Phenomena) that proved there were superior beings on other planets, and that they have been monitoring us for some time. Proof was available in actual camera footage of UFO. Radar shows that the UFO was monitoring the peace talk between Russian leader Ivan Koloff and President Williams.

A special committee of our nation's top astronomers was put together to try to communicate and find these aliens. Russia was asked to share in what could have been a major breakthrough in the study of life elsewhere. However, Russian leader Koloff insisted that the UFO, reported by the American government, was just a big hoax.

The task force was composed of 10 persons, eight men and two women. Our first job was to locate the flying saucers. IBM had just invented a high frequency radar system that would function in space as a satellite. We decided that this radar would work nicely for what we needed. January 2, 2006, the system was launched into space.

There was nothing significant picked up on the radar for several weeks. On March 4th, however, the first UFO was spotted and was said to be in a stationary position about 100 miles above the earth. Now, we, the members of the task force, knew that there was indeed a flying saucer whirring above the earth. But, that's all we knew. We didn't know if the aliens were willing to help mankind further its technology. It was assumed that the aliens probably weren't harmful because there hasn't been any record of any UFOs attacking the earth. Would they help us? How were we going to determine this? These questions were the challenge.

A meeting was called of the task force members to try to find some answers. After debating I, being the most imaginative of the group, came up with a plan that would either provide the technological information mankind had been seeking for 25 years, or it would kill 10 (well, at least one) of the top minds in the USA. The plan was this . . .

The space shuttle Enterprise would be dispatched about 10 miles from the UFO, just far enough so the UFO would get a close range picture of us. We would cut off all power on the Enterprise and then set fire to it on the outer deck, allowing plenty of time before it would affect us. If the UFO came to our aid, then we would assume that those on board wanted to communicate with us. If they didn't, we would die . . . .

The plan was accepted.

On April 27, the space shuttle Enterprise, with its crew of 10, set off. The Enterprise came within 10 miles of the UFO and all power was cut off. At that moment, with a press of a button, the fire was set. One hour went by and with the fire breathing down our throats, there was still no reaction from the alien spaceship. A scream came from one of the female crew members, "Please, God, help us!" At that moment the UFO came to our rescue. The fire was put out and we were beamed aboard the spaceship. The alien who spoke said, "Your belief is that of God, also?" We replied by nodding our heads.

That basic belief brought two otherwise different civilizations together. And today, April 18, 2008, the leaders of both planets are convening on earth to discuss friendship.

CHAPTER TWELVE

Will Raindrops Beckon Roses?

Sadako Sasaki was a small child when the bomb fell on her home town of Hiroshima. Several years later she developed "radiation sickness" – Leukemia.

She was afraid of death, but she never lost hope for the future. She had heard that if she folded one thousand paper cranes, she would live a long life with good fortune. Sadako died after folding 644 cranes, but her friends kept folding. They later built a monument. . . (and) today the paper crane is a symbol of peace for those who vow that the bomb must never be used again.

(Hawkes, 1983)

The Quakers believe that if a single person – "a pilgrim" – chooses to walk a certain path because of an ethical or moral decision, he or she can make a difference in the world. To believe that one is not powerless, that one person can make a difference, is to hope. This chapter is about such hope in the face of seeming hopelessness. In the following scenarios, hope is symbolized by the flower, fragile enough to be crushed in a hand, yet persistent enough to break through a concrete sidewalk.

For years, major American cities have faced with resignation the problem of homeless street people, who sleep on steam grates in the sidewalks during the bitter winter nights. Because they have no permanent legal address, they are ineligible for public assistance. Most passersby step around them as if they were invisible.

In the Fall of 1983, 11-year-old Trevor Farrell, of suburban Philadelphia, watched a televised report on the grate people, and what he saw upset him. He asked his parents to give him whatever used blankets and warm clothing they could spare. That night, he persuaded his father to drive him into Center City, where he handed out the blankets and clothing to the street people. His father later said, "I thought he'd forget about it in a few days." But, Trevor kept collecting. Gradually, relatives and neighbors asked to help, and each night through the winter, Trevor and his father and their friends brought hot coffee, clothing, and home-cooked meals to the grate people. The newspapers wrote stories about Trevor, saying he was a hero. The city authorities, perhaps embarrassed, presented Trevor with an award. Finally, a patron donated a 30-room house, to be used as a permanent shelter for the city's homeless men and women.

There are those who would say we should not encourage children to think about the hard issues of life – poverty, nuclear war, death – because they will only worry, and after all, they are too young to understand. But, one of the marvels of the international scenarios is that children the world over hope, rather than despair. They are activated, rather than disaffected. And they long for, rather than shrink from, an opportunity to intervene and help.

In writing about possible nuclear war, an eighth grader from Brookline, Massachusetts, once wrote:

> Knowing is terrifying
> Not knowing is terrifying
> But not knowing is hopeless
> And knowing may save us.
> (Educators for Social Responsibility, 1983)

Trevor became a symbol of hope to the grownups of Philadelphia, because he was not old enough to believe it is useless to try to change things. He made a positive choice and acted on it, even though he was alone. Perhaps that is one definition of courage.

Even one flower, blooming through a concrete sidewalk, can make a difference. In these scenarios, flowers symbolize hope. If we take time to look, we will see that the flowers of the world are the children.

– Myosotis Arvensis –

Dorothy Thornton (Age 17)
Westford High School, Rondebosch, RSA

I am sure that within the past two days the whole town must have seen that small cylinder. The older people who still can remember the like are strangely silent. I am among this rather small group. Most people my age cannot remember, or rather, have never known, but I was a country girl.

It is strange that there are so few old people now. Their bodies just could not adapt to the change in atmosphere – less oxygen and more pollutants does not help degenerating tissue. Most people over 20 must wear masks to filter the poisons, but even their tolerance is almost twice that of their parents'. Children nowadays do not seem to be bothered. Humans can adapt far more easily than was ever believed possible before.

Weather reports are close to 100% accurate now. After sulphur rain destroyed so many crops in Canada, there was a strong swing towards research into that field. We cannot prevent the rain but can protect the crops a little.

Jack did not seem awed by The Flower. He works in the hydroponics department. He says the plants he is used to are not as beautiful but far more nutritive. Trust him!

It is strange to think that no plants whatsoever grow on the surface of our planet. The land was used for homes, offices, and factories. Machines now produce our oxygen, they are not as efficient as the plants were. Our crops now grow underground and in space. Nobody seemed to notice that the plants were disappearing. I suppose it did not seem important when you were fighting to feed and clothe yourselves and your children.

We almost did not make it to this time, we raced oil and fusion in opposite directions; luckily fusion won. I promised the twins I would take them to see The Flower tomorrow. I have been thinking about flowers more and more. When I was a child I lived in the country, yet I do not remember what the flowers were like. All that remains to me now is the memory of their smell and, of course, the cylinder.

There has been talk of cloning The Flower to send to museums and various universities. People have been clamouring to receive cloned Flowers too, but they tell us that the cylinders would be too difficult and too expensive to manufacture en masse. Everybody is trying to climb on the bandwagon. The new hit is called 'The Return of our Vegetable Friend' of all things. Every new cosmetic seems to have 'flower' in its logo. Even the politicians have something to say about The Flower; most of it nonsense to attract votes.

I took the twins to see The Flower today, the crowds were even larger than before. I wonder why they call it The Flower; there are 12 small flowers and nine buds. The flowers are a vivid blue and in the centre are what look like tiny white stalks or tubes with yellow fuzzy heads.

The cylinder is transparent plastic. It is bullet proof because many people are afraid someone will try to destroy it. Some people are saying that it is Satan trying to return us to our old evil way. Our ways have not changed particularly. Anyway, how would Satan have made something so perfect, my encyclopedia says he was the God of Evil.

The twins thought the flower an anticlimax after all they had heard about it. They were more interested in the pipes that supplied the flower with carbon dioxide, oxygen, water, and mineral salts, than anything else. They agreed that it was very beautiful but soon lost interest. They are too young to remember or understand.

People seem suddenly interested in flowers again. It is impossible to find an illustrated book in the libraries and, even those that are not illustrated are rare. They have been showing documentaries on the holoscreens but they are not very effective. All the programmes show are knowledgeable people speaking and three-dimensional images of two-dimensional photographs of three-dimensional plants. You have to admit that is rather pointless.

Donations have been pouring into research institutes, especially in the hydrophonics department. Jack was very impressed by this, even though The Flower did not seem to impress him.

Perhaps he is trying to appear nonchalant to annoy me. If he is, he has certainly succeeded.

The twins are feeling resentful toward The Flower at the moment. Two teachers have given them projects to do; the science and the history teacher. The latter wants to know how the cylinder works and the former, the social situation that led to the genocide of all plants. He used the word genocide, not I, and, furthermore, made the children look it up. I am sure the children will learn a great deal but I can think of no better way to kill a child's budding love of flowers.

The university students have been having fun building an exhibition for the museum. They walk the streets laughing, gesticulating, and talking non-stop. They are also covered in plastic filings and paint. Everybody is trying to find out what it is like. Some people have taken to toasting the students at various pubs. But alack, this time it is 'in vino nilitas'.

Walking past the shops today, I saw a peculiar cuddly toy. The Flower had been cut out and stuffed and some cheap perfume added. The surprising thing is that it is selling and, even more surprising, I bought four; one for each of the twins, the other for Jack, and the last for myself. Jack spent a full 20 minutes laughing when he saw it, it really is ridiculous and, therefore, all the more irresistible.

Jack and I have started to visit The Flower before sun-up. We form part of the regular worshippers, come to glorify our God. Jack chuckled when I told him that that is what it made me think of. Generally that means he agrees. But seriously, you can understand the primitives worshipping nature. Every morning the rays of the sun are diffused by the smog and refracted by the cylinder which rises above us on its pedestal. It reminds me of the poet who said:

> *For even in a brown sky*
> *Some people still will find*
> *Patterns that form pictures*
> *Honouring mankind.*

I wonder if this picture honours mankind?

I am finding it more and more difficult to understand why the ecological breakdown occurred. Surely our forebears could see what was happening? The twins can go without breaathing for three minutes and can consciously slow their metabolism until only one breath a minute is needed. They do not miss and are not envious of the old world and the old way of life. They enjoy themselves now, they like the world as it is. Of course, they are curious about The Flower, but it does not move them as it moves us and they do not miss the colour green as my parents did and as I, to a lesser extent, do.

A flower now stands in the square of every city. We are all tremendously proud that ours was the first. A group of art students have joined our early morning group of worshippers. They paint The Flower and sometimes ourselves. I do not understand their efforts.

I noticed a plaque just below the cylinder today. It is difficult to see as the cylinder is on a seven foot high pedestal. It was difficult to make out so I asked Jack. It read "Myosotis Arvensis." I did not know what that meant. Jack looked at me queerly and said: "It is the Latin name for the Forget-me-not."

– Like The Rose –

Alexander Zamora (Age 15)
Manila Science High School, Manila, Philippines

I never realized before just how much of my whole being was lost. After my autospaceship accident on the planet Nebula located on the other side of the galaxy directly in front of the constellation Myra, I had to be operated on by the best medical doctors this far from home planet Earth. Most of my human parts and organs were in a dilapidated condition, no longer functioning along with my brain cells.

When I was told by Dr. Nades that I had to undergo the common surgery of bionics, I was not frightened at all. Much to my surprise, it was as if I couldn't care at all. But because of a little boy, I soon realized just how important it was for me to be brought back to the human world, feeling and caring about myself and others.

I never knew his real name, so I christened him David, after my best buddy who served in the Space Military of the United Galaxies for 5 eons. I never knew where he really came from. In fact, I never knew anything personal about his life. But I could never stop thanking the Almighty One for showing him to me.

He appeared on the 12th day of my resting period in the Manila Medical Science Center just as the sun's rays shone brightly on my face. I suddenly saw a boy with short black hair, wearing a white gown usually worn by patients. He would have passed for an ordinary lad but his rosy cheeks and glossy brown eyes appealed to me very much. I suddenly asked, "What are you doing here?" I could sense that he had been a little scared but somehow he seemed at ease once again. Smiling, he answered, "I just came to visit you. I am staying in the room across yours." With anger and resentment on my face, I told him to get out of my room and stay in his own room. Inside of me I knew that I would have enjoyed being in other people's company at that time but somehow I couldn't consciously admit it. "How come?" I asked myself. "Could it be the effect of the sudden operation on my physical faculties? Was the pressure of having to face the truth that I would be part-human and part-machine getting too much for me to handle?"

It was already common at this time for people to be operated for technical prosthetics such as bionics, cybernetic implantation, and organic transplants. But somehow I still couldn't accept these things which the super-intelligents and scientists of our times called "big leaps in science." My mother once told me in the summer of March, 1981, that there is no greater gift given by God to man than the soul. Somehow, I could feel my internal essence slipping away.

The boy didn't leave the room so I was thankful and resentful at the same time. He sat on the rattan pad looking intently at me. Somehow, I could feel that he was getting through my self-made barrier. Of all questions, he suddenly asked, "Have you ever seen a red rose?" I was momentarily stunned but I told him indignantly, "Of course, I've seen one such kind of flora!" He went across the room and sat by my bed. He told me accusingly, "You're lying." I raised myself off my pillows and said, "How dare you say that to me? I've seen many roses in my life from holograms, visual records, and projections." He said in a whisper which sounded so soothing to the ears, "Then that means you've never seen one in reality." I knew he got me there. In defeat and shame, I nodded pathetically. I asked him then what it mattered if I hadn't seen one real flower. "Once you see one rose, you've seen them all," I said wanting the final word.

He looked out of the window and somehow I could feel he was a little sad. He said in his little voice, "Don't you see what's happening? Because of the things man is doing, he is losing touch with reality. He has become so busy in this world that he no longer cares about the simplicity and beauty of life. The rose symbolizes the beauty of the life it lives. It grows each day, feeding itself with simple nourishment. It lives with no complexities and complications. Have you ever seen a rose adapting itself to the present smog-filled environment? Has it built big domes and forces fields to protect itself? No, for the simple reason that the needs of a rose are simple. The reason why it is still surviving in that threatening environment is its appreciation of its simple life, making itself hold on, overcoming all difficulties. We must learn from the rose. We must foresee the importance of living only with things that we cannot do without and not the things that we are ever-greedy for." After hearing such a meaningful speech from such a young boy, I certainly knew from that instant that he must be someone special . . . just like the rose.

The days passed eventfully because of David. From our quiet talks, I learned many things from his world, his ideas seen through his eyes. He began making me feel and care once again for the life I must continue to live. He taught me things beyond the general understanding of analytical calculus, spherical geometry, and nebular astronomy. They were greater things than these. He taught me how to be human. I became his student and he became my teacher.

One afternoon, while I was computing the various derivatives needed for the construction of a simple MX missile, he looked at my work and asked, "Why are you making a missile? Don't you know you are adding another evil to this world?" I knew that he would say that and I definitely knew that he was right. I was becoming a maker of evil destruction.

I didn't answer but he kept on, "Man doesn't need missiles, bombs, and laser guns to live on. He only needs to build trust and confidence in his fellowmen. By doing that, he learns to live in a better place and time than his ancestors. He sees everyone as a friend, welcomes them in his abode and feeds and shelters them. If every man would be like this, he could live in a world free from the callousness and insensitivity of greedy and evil people." Again, I looked at this amazing little lad with deep admiration and understanding. I was often stunned by his ideals but I knew that this was the inspiration we needed especially in these times of changing values.

It was my fourth week in the hospital and my doctor told me that I could be discharged by the coming week. I was glad to hear the news. When I told David about it, he was extremely happy. I told him that I would come to see him every week during and after his stay in the hospital. I was expecting a cheerful response from him but it seemed that he was looking far away again, searching for something that wasn't there. I asked him if anything was wrong. He answered me in his usual way, "You can't visit me. Tomorrow I'll be going to a place where no one can go. It is so far away that no one can ever reach it in trillions of light years." I laughed and answered, "That's ridiculous! I have reached the different galaxies trillions of light years away. Why can't I reach you?" But still he said, "You just can't . . . ever."

When I woke up the next morning, the first thing that my instincts told me was to go across to David's room. Call it intuition, psychic sense, or whatever, I just knew that I had to go there . . . to assure myself that my David was still there looking bright and fresh. Upon reaching his door and opening it, I saw a nurse fixing the blankets of David's bed.

I could sense that something was wrong and I asked the nurse where the occupant of this room was. She didn't need to tell me what had happened to him for his medical charts told me the shattering news of his death caused by a disease whose cure could never be found even in this medically advanced age of postponed death and near immortality: cancer!!!

I was shocked and couldn't move. The nurse left the cubicle to call for help. As I groped my way to the bed, I saw something protruding from the back of the bed. It was a rose in a pot, a beautiful real one like David had often told me about. As I picked up the planted rose and looked at it, I noticed a note attached to it. It was addressed to me. It was from David. By then, my eyes were already filled with tears as I read the note. It said:

> Dear Alex,
>> Be like the rose.
>>> David

I cried myself out, recalling the words of the boy. Over and over I said to myself as I held the planted rose in my arms, "I will be the rose you want, David. I will be the person you wish me to be. I will be like you, David . . . I will be your rose."

– The Flower Never Withered –

Shannon Green (Age 17)
LaFollette High School, Madison, WI, USA

Summer was the best time of year, for the birds sang antiphonals with the sunlight as it sparkled off green leaves and golden-scented flowers.

She loved to go into the woods outside the city, where solitude and fellowship intermingled. Only there did she feel at peace with all that was discordant in her life.

Often she would sit under her favorite aspen, reading aloud the poetry of Shakespeare or Frost, or singing folk songs or Bach chorales. The birds would be silent: she could feel the presence of the creatures all around her, poised, listening, adding harmony in their own ways. Many times she would be silent, quietly at home with the wood. The animals weren't afraid to touch her when they passed. She would smile, whispering a return greeting.

It was a day of such tranquility that she found herself drawn to the woods in spite of having much to do elsewhere. She had to go, just for a little while. Sitting under the aspen with her eyes closed, she didn't notice him until the silence of the wood grew louder, and the gentle breeze was at rest.

She looked up, startled, awed. His look suggested that he now saw one whom he had never expected to see again, one from a long time past.

The look faded. "I'm sorry I frightened you," he said softly. "It wasn't intended." His clear, silver voice seemed to enchant even the flowers nearby.

"I – that's all right," she stammered. "I'm just not used to seeing anyone else here."

"Do you live here?" he asked.

"No, of course not." She smiled, "But I spend so much time here, it's almost as if I do."

"Well, then, will you walk with me? I would like you as my guide."

He seemed safe enough. "Sure," she answered. "But first I think we should introduce ourselves. My name is – ."

"No!" he interrupted. "I do not wish to know your real name. May I just call you Lauriel – it is a name honored by my people."

Lauriel shrugged. "I guess. I kind of like it. What is your name?"

For an answer, he smiled and bowed. "I am Randir, wanderer near and far of all the earth. I am honored to meet you."

Lauriel laughed. "Likewise."

"Shall we go?" Randir asked.

The walk seemed empty of time and space. They wandered up and down hills, passing trees old and new, meadows of golden sun, and sparkling flowers. As they walked, Randir, his voice melodious on the wind, spoke of many things Lauriel had never known: of the bond between the rocks, the insects and all, how each intertwined with the other, and, if one were destroyed, how the rest could never be whole.

"You see, everything is connected, like a circle," he said. "If a part of the circle is broken . . . . " He sighed, a sad look crossing his face. "All will be empty, and wither, and die."

After a pause, Randir relaxed, laughing at a squirrel sitting nearby, contentedly nibbling on an acorn. "Do you suppose he wonders at what he eats? The acorn may have wanted to grow into a mighty tree, but I think it is content now to be food for a squirrel!"

Lauriel laughed. Just then the squirrel looked up, chattered at them, and scurried off to his home. "He's right," Randir whispered, looking up.

"What?" Lauriel asked.

"It'll rain soon," Randir replied. "Is there shelter nearby??

Lauriel looked around. "Yes, a cave, a few yards that way." She pointed down a valley. Already the winds were building up.

The cave was cool and dry, deep enough for protection.

"It won't be a long storm. We can stay here until it passes," Randir said.

Lauriel sat back against a wall of the cave while Randir started a fire to keep them warm from the wind.

They listened to the progress of the storm, the rain at first like chimes in a gentle wind, then harder, until the drops rang on the leaves, drummed on the earth. Lauriel listened to the symphony of the storm – even the thunder added its own melody, tolling out the phrases.

She looked at Randir, leaning back with his eyes closed, a peaceful calm on his face. Drawing on her courage, she asked him what had been on her mind since she first met him: "Randir, where are you from?"

He opened his eyes, looked at her, then away, a melancholy look on his face. He paused, when he glanced back at her, he seemed not to see her. Taking a deep breath, he answered: "I come from a place very far away. My home was beautiful, like this wood, and we loved it. But not enough, I'm afraid. We were like trees, my people; sturdy, strong – but also ambitious and impatient, and that was our downfall. For we were too eager – like a tree that buds before winter is over, only to have the young leaves killed at the next frost. We jumped at every chance to progress, never taking heed to consequences. But we leapt too far, and the consequences caught up with us. And so we were destroyed, by our own hands, but not all of us, for some survived. Now we walk others' worlds, warning them if we can, of the danger that destroyed us." He fell silent.

Lauriel watched him, pitying him almost – so noble, so resigned, then blushed: her own world could end like his, but with no survivors.

Emerging from her own thoughts, she realized Randir was singing, chanting a melody that sang to her very soul, haunting its deepest chambers. It echoed in the cave, each strain harmonizing with the next, the nuances of melody echoing the sadness of an ancient people. She closed her eyes and listened. The song carried her away to a distant, familiar world, and she saw the flowers of that world, its sunlight, its people, the love they had for it, and the sorrow of a great loss beyond any healing, an emptiness forever in the circle of their hearts.

The chant diminished, its last phrase escaping on the wind to be carried off to strengthen the heart of a weary traveller.

"The storm's over," Randir whispered. "We must be going."

Putting out the fire, they left the cave, walking out on the wet, green grass, back to the aspen tree.

Randir looked at her. "I must leave now, for I have much to do yet."

Lauriel nearly cried. "Can't you stay with me?" There's so much more I need to know. Come stay and share my home. You'll need a place to rest."

"No, I can't. You know all I can teach you," Randir answered. "As for me," he looked up at the sky, back down again, "my home is destroyed. I'll never have another."

Then he reached down and picked up a budding Coriander. "This is the symbol of home for my people. Never let it wither!" He handed her the flower. "Namarie!" he whispered. Lauriel looked down at the bud, and when she raised her eyes, he was gone.

– The Mount Of Doom –

Lexi Alexander (Age 13)
Clarke Central High School, Athens, Georgia, USA

The year is 2010, the seventh of May. I am here in what is left of New York City. The sight is grotesque; piles of bodies clutter the streets as if all the garbage of the world had been dumped upon the ground. I slowly pick my way along with a few others, one stumbles and falls, we wait but he does not rise, we attempt to help him, but it is all in vain. We walk down to the harbor. Across the river we still can see smoke from burning houses rising and then dissolving like mankind into the air.

The water ripples like a muscle beneath the skin, lapping against a sunken row boat named the City Queen. Out of the water I still can see, though barely, the torso of the decapitated Statue of Liberty.

It is morbid but yet so strangely peaceful to watch the water move so quietly and so gently.

We turn slowly away and continue up a dirty path until we have reached the countryside. Dusk is falling again, as its cooling shadows fall, a fear comes to us. We crouch like frightened animals, hiding behind anything, not speaking. The quiet is unreal. We are alone in a gray, featureless forest from which no darkness escapes; the gloom is ever present.

Morning is here; the day is chilly and there is a threat of rain. A freezing wind is whipping around us, making a noise so loud that we cover our ears. Any sound becomes magnified greatly for a sound – a human sound – has not been heard for about a week – maybe longer. There is nothing but that dreadful uncanny quiet.

We sit around a small pond; the water – like everything else – is gray too, still and unmoving.

I ask myself the question: Could I have prevented this disaster? But as Vice-President of the United States of America there was only so much that I could do in so little time.

It was always those damned computers, "the way to solve

the problems of the world," as I quote an ever reminded topic, from the president Jonathan Syde. But, he didn't listen; he didn't care! He failed to see that a computer can add two and two and come out with five, but when it comes to peoples' lives it doesn't add up.

We finally emerged from the vast darkness of the forest. The tall trees stand behind us, looming and waiting for what is to come.

We pass a small broken-down cottage, its windows cracked; its wood splintered. A tall apple tree stands beside it. The apples are shriveled and dead.

Behind the house a waterfall still runs, rushing over thousands of broken fragments. A body lays beside it, holding a very dear thing – a child. The woman is of my age, about 42. I turn away – the sight is devastating. I can't bear to look – this child not unlike all the other children of the world – snatched from life without a thought or care. They knew nothing about Nuclear Problems – all they wanted was their blankets and ragged teddy bears.

Dusk is falling again – another day has dragged on. Our weak bodies slump to the ground, which is dry, and crumbles under the slightest weight.

A spooky wind starts. It is the only sound. The horrible noise rises and falls like a scream of terror and then slowly dies away. The silence is unbearable! No cries or pleas, screams or bombs, just the uncanny quiet.

A knot is in my stomach and my neck is stiff. The air hoses are weighing us down almost to a staggering point.

The rain is here, chilling us to the bone, despite the fact that we were in a concealed place.

Again we walk, something is in the air, a pressure forcing us on while weighing us down.

We have failed as a nation, all of us not just one! We did not care for others, but only for ourselves. We made the mistake that cost the world its riches, but never solved anything. If only they had listened – if only they had cared. It was once my dream to help the world to peace, but the hopes, dreams, and feelings of all were pushed aside.

I stand alone on Doom's Mount – looking down to the valley. Suddenly something catches my eye. A flower – a gorgeous red flower. I watch it open and face the sun. It is a peace offering from the world.

CHAPTER THIRTEEN

Will There Be A Place For Wild Things?

The rapid disappearance of the earth's wildlife species and the resulting decrease in biological richness and diversity seem certain to be a crucial environmental issue at least for the rest of this century. Many species have already become extinct and the rate of loss of species has doubled in the past 200 years and is still gaining momentum. It has been predicted that one million additional species will become extinct by the year 2000 (Laycock, 1973; Verney, 1979).

From the information available, it now seems clear that the disappearance of species as a result of mankind's activities will have a damaging effect on the world's food supply, health, scientific and medical research, and other areas crucial to human survival. Species threatened with extinction include not just whales, wolves, and pandas, but a million other species of plants and animals. Wetlands are shrinking before mankind's greed for space to grow food, build houses, dock tankers, erect shopping centers and industrial colonies, and dump garbage and other wastes. The seriousness of the resulting losses will have consequences that can hardly be predicted.

But why would the young scenario writers care so much about the endangered wildlife of the world? After all, children embrace technological advancement more readily than do adults. There seems, however, to be a dynamic at work in the writings of children which causes them to recoil at the possibility of a totally man-made world, and to drag their feet in resistance to human encroachment into the wild. There is something in the wild things that children seem to understand in an intimate way. This is displayed in the passionate eloquence of the scenarios in this chapter.

In the late 1880's, G. Stanley Hall, considered to be the founder of child psychology in the United States, asserted that "ontogeny recapitulates phylogeny" (Bigner, 1983). This meant that the developmental history of the species is re-enacted in the cognitive development of each individual. Indeed, children seem to lack many of the cognitive abilities which adults possess (and which we consider to be characteristically human) until they reach a certain age. Children below the age of seven were considered to be "pre-operational" by Piaget (Flavell, 1977) and "pre-symbolic" by Bruner (1966). A child who is preoperational cannot hold abstractions in mind, is egocentric and views the world from the perspective of self, cannot take into account the "big picture," and does not carry events in mind the same way adults do. The presymbolic child seems to require images and active involvement with the world to learn and solve problems. Hall's statement that the child's cognitive abilities at this, or any stage, repressents a point in the phylogenetic development of humankind, suggests there must have been a time when humans – as adults – thought in this fashion. Arieti (1976) calls this form of thinking "paleologic," or old, thinking. He goes on to make two rather important statements about this type of thinking: (1) paleologic thought gives way to more modern Aristotelian thinking but never leaves us, and (2) it is a valuable form of thought, rather than merely an outmoded one. Arieti suggests that this primitive form of thought is responsible for intuition and empathy.

Consider our ancient ancestors before major technological advances and residual culture estranged us from our world. They lived at the mercy of, but in harmony with, nature. Their restrictions were not psychological, but physiological. They were, no doubt, in awe of the world and spurious in their interpretations of it. In many ways, compared to us, their modern descendants, they were wild. *Webster's New World Dictionary* (1972) offers these definitions of the word "wild": (1) " . . . living or growing in its original, natural state . . . " (2) " . . . not civilized . . . " (3) " . . . not easily restrained or regulated; not controlled or controllable; unruly . . . " (4) " . . . in a state of intense excitement . . . eager or enthusiastic . . . . " Ancient humans – and children –

were, and are, surely closer to these definitions in their behaviors than the sophisticated adults of today.

Arieti (1976) describes the person who, having become mature, adopts the grown-up perspective of Aristotelian logic and objective analysis:

> *At times we encounter intelligent and well-educated people, inclined to logical, deductive thinking, who nevertheless seem 'two dimensional,' lacking in depth. These people stick to fact; they are indeed factual. Their intelligence shows a mechanical quality that has a pragmatic value in some aspects of life but that is disagreeable in many others. Since early life these people have been trained . . . to experience only concepts and to suppress and repress endocepts totally* (pp. 56-57).

By "endocepts," Arieti means the paleological empathic and intuitive forms of thought. If ontogeny recapitulates phylogeny, then children are closer to the state of being wild than adults are. They have better access to their paleologic thinking and can empathize with the other wild things of the earth. While they may not fully comprehend the events which bring about the mechanical thinking and dispassionate attitude most adults acquire, they nevertheless fear becoming less wild and enthusiastic about life. In their scenarios, the children worry about dehumanization and regimentation brought about by technology and rigid thinking. They seem to intuitively recognize that objective thinking can bring with it the capacity for uncaring exploitation. The scenarios in this chapter are focused upon our brethren, the wild animals of the earth, and their diminishing space. These animals, however, may be a metaphor for the loss of childhood, of enthusiasm, of a primordial truth about living in harmony with nature. Could it be that, in our phylogenetic development, we are already past the point of being humane on our way to becoming human? Could it be that children represent the zenith of our development as a species?

– A Breathing Space In Time –

Fritha Langerman (Age 12)
Rutenburg Girls' Junior School, Rondebosch, RSA

July 22nd – the year, 2010 – How slowly the hands move, how slowly they progress round the clock's solemn face . . . jeering at me as I await my judgment. Five weeks in the hospital, maybe five more months perhaps. Who knows? As I lie on my back, staring at the ceiling of the operating theatre, the drowsiness of anaesthesia fills my head. Past and present merge. I am running across the barren Karoo – a child again. Startled, the springbok rise, their leaps carrying them away across the veld. I rejoice with them. Their zest for life is a part of my being.

An adult now, game ranger and conservationist, working 17 hours a day. Moving herds to new waterholes and grazing land, forced on by the relentless encroachment of towns and cities – a losing battle as species after species die out, leaving only the wildebeest and springbok of all the teaming herds. As the century turns, this reserve, "Freeman's Way," is the last in Africa, the last grazing land left for the wildebeest and springbok. W.W.L. – World Wild Life – has commissioned a study and assured me of time to investigate the habits and feeding of the animals. Every day I sit for hours in the dim light of the sun (slowly becoming weaker) and write my notes. It is a world of my own. Everyone else is involved with science and technology, excited only by the new frontiers of space and experiment. I am considered out of it and am regarded as old fashioned and not worth communicating with. But this does not bother me. The reserve is here, a reality . . . . But that was before the accident that totally changed my life.

My senses clear a moment. I overhear the medical technologist, or doctor as we used to call them, saying that I was lucky to survive such a goring. That reminded me of the horror of the moment, as I looked straight into the eyes of a mad wildebeest. Fury in its mean eyes. I should have known better than to go near the animal when it was with its mate. I am encircled by lights. Diagnostic machines probe bone and flesh, sending back high frequency signals from hydrogen nuclei deep in my being.

Hospitals are soul-destroying places. There is no noise, everything is silent. For even the last motor-car's rowdy engine has long since been forgotten. They have all been replaced by microgliders. Everything is airborne now. There is no need for roads and so people no longer meet and talk on the pavements as they used to. The result is that they do not communicate as well as they once did. They have become unimaginative. They spend their lives eating and playing electronic games which require no thought. Standardized thinking is creeping into everyone's life, everyone having the same things drummed into their heads by the communications network and soaking up group thought . . . . That was the joy of being in the veld. It was an island of escape where I could think my own thoughts without a thousand eyes watching me.

I must get back, I must walk. How else can I complete my project and make my reserve safe from the clutches of developers? But even now, creeping into my bones like some unseen enemy, is the growing fear that the verdict will go against me. Will it spell the end of my reserve that I fought for, that piece of land resembling the Karoo, unpolluted by nuclear tests and atomic fall-out? And my beautiful springbok and wildebeest for whom I achieved a breathing space in time?

They approach me, their faces blank. But even through their blankness I sense that my battle is lost. In technological terms they spell out the verdict: A sentence of life imprisonment in a mobile contrivance, subject to buttons, knobs, and electronic gadgetry, their electron microscopes and computer-assisted Tomographic Scanners, my recovery is beyond them, and it seems that I am to be permanently crippled. So mankind is still vulnerable after all!

The frustration of being immobile. No longer to roam the veld on stormy days. No longer to sit with my feet in the hot sand gazing over the scrub and thorn trees. For me there is no future, only solitude and desolation. Life for me is just a memory as I think back on the free, leaping hooves of the buck. I cannot bear it . . . .

There is only one thing left for me now, to return to the reserve in my thoughts and paint the animals as I knew them. I will pick up where the Bushmen left off when they painted on the walls of their caves to pass down their knowledge to younger generations. I will paint the joyful, free springbok and the wildebeest so that even when they are gone people will be reminded of how wonderful life once was.

– Few And Beautiful –

Susana Ruiz (Age 15)
Bel Air High School, El Paso, TX, USA

Good jobs are hard to come by. The early 2000's have the highest rate yet. People are barely making it through 2010. I consider myself lucky at this time to have a career as a veterinarian.

Pollution, along with unemployment, is high. The sun is hardly ever seen through the thick coat of smog. Vegetation is scarce because there is not enough sunlight for photosynthesis. Owning a plant is a sign of talent.

Extinction is one of my personal problems. As a young girl, having a house pet was common. Today owning a pet is a rarity. Wildlife has decreased greatly. Pollution and the lack of vegetation are both at fault. Veterinarians, like myself, are concerned about it. Not only because our jobs are at stake, but because people in the future may not get to see a live animal.

I live in the southern part of California. I moved here from Texas when I found out that California was the state most populated with animals. It was a perfect place for the beginning of my career. I was in love with my job and I considered myself an excellent veterinarian. I could feel approval from the veterinarian I assisted.

Two years after assisting, I opened up my own clinic. For seven years I kept busy with a lot of my patients. Over the years, fewer people with pets showed up at the clinic. It was getting harder for animals to survive in our harmful environment.

My career was coming to an end and I refused to recognize it. Veterinarians in other states had already become unemployed because they didn't earn enough money to keep their clinics or hospitals open. My love for animals is incredible, but now money seemed more important. I couldn't see myself closing down my main achievement over the years.

The full-time schedule that I once had was now cut down to part-time. When I walked into the clinic on one of my not-so-good days, I told Margie, my receptionist, "Call up all of the owners of my patients and ask them to make an appointment."

"What if it's not time for their annual checkup?"

"You just tell them I'd like to see them. Don't you see? It's a perfect way to get more money," I answered.

She looked at me with amazement.

Mrs. Colon's cocker spaniel, Solar, was my first patient two days after Margie's call. Solar is a very rare breed of dog now and Mrs. Colon guards him with her life. I gave him a quick checkup. He was perfectly healthy. I looked straight at Mrs. Colon and told her, "I'll have to keep him in for two days so that I can run some tests on him." She hesitated and finally agreed if I thought it was best.

The rest of my patients showed up through the month. All of them were fine, but I kept them one to three nights at the clinic. I had told the owners that it was to run tests. I really kept them to earn money and keep my clinic open. I was being dishonest. I didn't run any tests on any animals. When the owners picked up their pets I overcharged everyone.

That dreadful moment arrived. Like every morning, Margie handed me the mail. There it was, the letter from the board of directors. I opened it cautiously and began reading it. A board meeting was announced a week from today to discuss our position.

I gave up hope. Soon I shall be cut out of my career. No matter how much I had overcharged the pet owners, it wasn't enough to keep the clinic going. I knew that I was going to be asked by the board of directors to resign.

The days flew by. It was time for the board meeting. I arrived just in time and found my place. I was surrounded by other veterinarians who had little hope for their careers. I found out that I had a better chance of keeping my clinic than some did.

Silence was called for and the head of the board of directors stood up and began his speech. I sat tight in my chair when he announced, "At this time, some of you will be cut back. Extinction has become our major problem." He went on explaining other reasons. After three hours of boredom, it was pointed out that I must close up my clinic. I felt destroyed.

I headed home feeling negative about my future. My three-room apartment seemed cold and small to me. I looked around at it and grew hatred towards myself for all of the bad things I had done to the owners of my patients. I had to make a new beginning.

In two weeks I was completely moved out of my clinic. Not only did I move out of the clinic, but also out of my apartment. I set out to fulfill my dreams. One of my dreams was to own a farm and I moved to this farm. It seemed like a lonely place for one person, but I love solitude.

On my way home one day from looking for a job I saw a horse lying on the side of the road. I got off the truck to see what was wrong. He had been hit by a car. Town was too far to take him so I stopped a car and the driver helped me get him on the back. I didn't know what I could do for him.

I got home and treated him on the truck. He was only cut and his bones were sore. I healed his wounds. A week later, he was walking around the farm. I grew very attached to him and I hated to let him go. I returned him to the meadow where I had found him.

The great feeling I got to see that horse running around was unexplainable. I realized now that I had taken for granted the job I loved the most, healing animals. I had been selfish and inconsiderate of pet owners. I had let money overcome my love for animals.

My next job was as a lab assistant. My education had been associated with this type of work so I was qualified for this job.

It was only a part-time job. The afternoons I would dedicate to my farm and to the few pets I owned.

Extinction kept increasing and I felt I could do something. I set out, along with other veterinarians, to catch as many wildlife animals as I could. I made my farm look like the surroundings that each animal needed to survive. I captured the mate of each and waited for results.

A few months after their captivity, they began reproducing. When the cubs got strong, I'd set out again to look for a safe environment for their home. If I heard of a good place out of state, I'd still make the trip. Although the young animals may forget me, the older ones will appreciate my help. I also feel rewarded because I helped increase the population of the few animals remaining.

– The Wild Will Weep –

Fiona Doherty (Age 15)
St. Dominic's Convent, Boksburg, RSA

The pitch of my mate's cry told me of her distress. However, I knew that even now I must obey the law of the wild and stay away from her. The birth of an infant was something which did not involve the male factor of our race.

To my knowledge there are 10 of our kind remaining on this planet. Of our closest relatives, who live in the East, I have thus far learnt nothing – not even if they survived the last great onslaught.

I am leader of our herd; I am responsible for future life. Most do not believe in the coming freedom I predict, as they have not yet learnt to understand the mind of the creature who rules over all.

The distress cries have ceased and the midwives are triumphantly announcing the birth of a son. This child is the key to that freedom I see in time to come and I will be proud to be his sire. I will spend many hours telling him of the glories and sorrows of our past. I will give to him all I have learnt about life and earth so that he, after my death, will continue to lead our kind toward a greater form of existence. As each new day dawns, little by little, my son will develop and will grow to understand the essence of survival.

I have lived for 70 years, having been born in a place known as Southern Africa. It is with great joy I recall my youth, spent wandering free across wide open spaces. It was a completely natural existence, with our lifestyle affected only by the environment and the seasons.

We were a powerful factor of bush-life then, being the largest of all on the land. Often in our quest for sufficient food and moisture we would have to uproot whole roots. Once we reached full-size, we had to kneel before no other creature – only before Great Mother Nature. Now, of course, things are different.

We always lived close to the African waterholes – the great magnets for wildlife. Water means life to our and all other species. We were dominant and unlike the prey creatures our herd always approached boldly, with pride and dignity, and then drank at leisure. We also played in those waterholes and relaxed; they and the sun were the source of our existence.

Our kind are, and always have been, good to our young, who suckle for a long period after birth. In the bush the herd afforded them love, security, and protection. It is against our code of behaviour to allow one of our youngsters to fall victim to foreign elements.

In those days our tusks were of the utmost importance to us. We needed them to gouge off the tough bark of thorntrees and to dig for tubers. Our tusks are sharp and strong and very dangerous weapons. They, however, were one of the causes of our downfall . . . .

The years passed and we began to notice great changes. By the time I had reached the age of 30, our living space had been drastically decreased and the numbers in our herd had been halved.

He, ruler and his steel companions, became the terror of the bush. Many times I found old friends lying dead, their great heads disfigured where their tusks had been removed. Many times I feared for my own life, especially after the burial of my sire.

Then it came – the great onslaught. My acute sense of hearing, my understanding of the secrets of the bush, my previous encounters with the rulers and, above all, my will to live saved me. Never, never will that nightmare be wiped from my memory and never again will I place trust in that race, who possess intelligence equalled by no other breed, but who, nevertheless, have the most to learn about life.

During that time, carcasses of every description were one of the most common sights. Each new day was heralded with a fresh attack and each new day marked the termination of a thousand more precious lives.

Our race had always seemed so grand, so self-sufficient. We had roamed Africa at will until the arrival of ruler. We were then jostled along to make room for him – for the growing of his foods and the construction of his houses.

That destruction was as the last great assault in a battle – bow and arrow, spear and rifle, poison and fire were all combined in one lethal, ruthless force.

Most of our huge physical bodies were reduced to something resembling a bundle of bones with an old rug thrown over them. Naturally, our great spirit never died. It will never be destroyed – it will always be there, symbol of a proud and mighty, yet gentle creature. Spirit is something every creature possesses, yet it is something which is unique to them. It is our driving force, pushing us forward. No – it can never be reduced to a bundle of bones and an old rug.

Days after the massacre the survivors were rounded up and we were placed in one restricted area. Conditions were cramped and tempers flared, but what distressed us most was witnessing the transformation of our once wide open spaces. The remnants of our beautiful bush were destroyed and replaced by the ugliest things imaginable. That which had been our home became the home of our leaders.

I felt no grief upon leaving that area forever. The remaining members of our species were taken to this place in which we now live. We are captives, but are reasonably content as we have had time to settle down. This space which we inhabit resembles our bush-of-old. However, we cannot love it as we did that bush, since it does not belong to us and since much of it was artificially created.

Our child is growing fast. This growth brings closer that longed-for freedom. Our rulers are glad of my son. Cruel and thoughtless as they are, they realize that other species must not be allowed to die out. Their survival depends on us.

In years to come, our offspring will be free. They will be returned to and will inherit the natural wild, once again subject only to the laws of nature. Surely there is that wild somewhere, far away from the ruin the rulers have created. Son, always remember that where there is life, there is hope . . . . I realize that I will never be wild again; I had my time. I must sacrifice now for my offspring. Forevermore, until the day I die, I will remain in these surroundings.

I will drink from a waterhole constructed out of concrete. I will bathe in mud which contains no bacteria. I will eat only the trees and bush laid out for me. My privacy will be infringed upon by the rulers and their machines. The stars in the sky above will often be blotted out or there will be no stars at all. The stump on which I scratch my back will never be wood. I will never experience complete solitude again, but the earth on which I walk will be the earth I have always known.

In times gone by this earth was far richer, far purer. Now, in this transition stage, it is still earth, solid and alive, but is a grimy replica of what it used to be. However, I fear not its disappearance. The ruler is not that foolish. He knows, as we all do, that it must be preserved if future generations are to exist.

I love its feel when I lie against it. I delight in hearing its great heart-throb. It is as a guardian angel over all its creatures of the wild. It imparts strength and transmits to us the need to strive on, forever.

I am delighted to see my son has my own insatiable curiosity. He is always asking questions. He is eager to know what is happening in the world outside our sanctuary. He spends hours standing at the boundaries, hoping for a glimpse of the leaders' ruin. I tell him too of my experiences and of all I saw before I arrived here.

On my journey I had encountered terrifying sights. Millions of rows of squares in which members of the rulers' race lived. They, too, were like captives. Machines dominated the skies, as well as the earth. In places the warm, cheerful sun was almost shut out and was replaced by artificial lights and heat. There was a terrific noise and I had pressed my great ears against my body in order to blot it out. I noticed the rulers who guarded us and cared for us were never happy without sticks of fire, pills, bottles, or machines in their hands.

Two more young have been born – two more steps towards that freedom . . . . Perhaps the world can be repaired or a new one discovered. Understanding will be necessary. I can visualize it; concrete will once more be grass; the water will be fresh again; the stars will become visible; the air will clear and there will be light . . . .

– The Next Generation –

Melissa Rigney (Age 16)
Eastern Hancock High School, Charlottesville, IN, USA

I glanced at the clock. It was only 1:45, and my shulerqua already showed that I had fulfilled my teaching requirements for the day. The shulerqua is a much more effective measure of teaching than the clock used to be. Twenty years ago teachers had a set time to teach, but now the shulerqua records and measures the quality of the teaching instead of the time involved.

The students were waiting patiently, too patiently, for me to dismiss them.

"You are dismissed. Your next test is on the fourteenth day."

The students left.

They were different from my first two groups of students. It wasn't that they didn't get good scores: They always received excellent scores on every test. But, they weren't interested in anything. Their cold eyes of blue, green, and brown just glared at me and absorbed what I was saying. Never did they ask an unusual question or seem interested in a project. Nevertheless, they always knew the answers, and their projects were always complete.

Those thoughts bothered me all the way home. When I reached my destination, I went down the elevator to my underground community complex.

I passed a few acquaintances on the way and nodded to them as I continued. When I reached my section, I went straight to the main terminal. I had been wondering about those students all quarter, and now I was going to check the computer for any abnormalities.

I scanned the possibilities. Maybe they were all victims of some terrible disorder. Maybe they were all aliens. Maybe they were genetic misfits. Whatever it was, I was curious as to why I hadn't been notified.

I typed in all of the students' names. I found out that they were all born in the same complex on 7/13/98. Now, they were all 10 years old and placed in the same learning establishment. I had a feeling that this was more than a coincidence.

Then, I tried to probe further into the data to find out if there were any more similarities. The only answer that I could find was "Top Secret File." I kept trying for hours, but I still couldn't find any more information.

I just simply had to know the truth. My curiosity had been aroused, and I would never be content until I knew why the students were "different."

After a restless night, I went to the headmaster's office.

"Sir, I would like to have a short vacation, I haven't had one for eight quarters now. Do you think that would be possible?" I asked.

"Yes, of course. Will two weeks be sufficient?" he said.

I nodded my head in agreement.

"I would also like to commend you on the excellent quality of your teaching. You certainly deserve a vacation." He complimented.

"Thank you, sir."

So, I was off to the KW computer system in Washington,

D.C. KW stands for knowledge wanted, and I certainly did want that.

I assumed that since I was not informed of this "Top Secret File," I was not supposed to know. Consequently, when the computer requested my name and I.D., I typed in the name and I.D. of a former friend of mine – a senator.

I held my breath while the computer checked my (or rather the senator's) name and I.D.

Then the word "continue" flashed on the screen.

After questioning the computer about the students, I received access to a top secret file entitled "The Next Generation." It contained a plan so fantastic that I found it hard to believe.

The truth was that these students had been genetically produced from secret donors. As soon as they were "born," a computer-like chip was placed into each of their brains. This chip caused the students to feel no emotions. They saw things logically and without feeling. They did what was necessary – nothing more and nothing less. In actuality, they were nothing more than living robots – anthropoids.

I was amazed. I knew that I must report this to the authorities – surely our government wouldn't condone such a thing as this.

I went straight to my senator friend to see what course of action I should take. I told him my story.

"Well, let's go see the rest of my committee," said the senator.

I was very excited. I had done something to help our great nation, to protect the people, to assist the authorities!

When we reached the office, the chairman closed and locked the door.

"This must be very important," I thought.

Then, to my surprise, two men grabbed me and held me in front of the chairman's desk.

"I am afraid that you have committed the high crime of treason," the chairman started. "It is punishable by death. You will be in Death Row for a few hours."

"But what about my right to a fair trial?" I protested. "What about the constitution?"

"The constitution is a farce. It is merely a piece of paper that helped those people so long ago. It is no longer valid. We must carry through with our plan no matter what. Soon, these anthropoids will fulfill all of the people's needs. No longer will there be rebellions and problems. The anthropoids will be able to do what is necessary. What might be unthinkable for us, is possible for them since they have no emotions. The next generation of people will be worry-free. Everything will be taken care of," explained the chairman.

Grimly I asked, "Why don't you just kill me now then?"

My senator friend answered, "We never said that we were actually going to kill you. We can't kill you – it would raise too many questions. You will be on Death Row for a few hours while we prepare the instruments."

As I realized what was going to happen, my face must have reflected the horror that I felt, for then he said, "You should really feel privileged. You will be perfect with no emotion, and after your vacation, you will go back to your teaching job. Of course, you won't remember anything that we don't want you to, so I will say goodbye to you now."

Then, the senators all smiled their mechanical smiles and prepared the laboratory.

CHAPTER FOURTEEN

Please Tend The Garden

Of course, we didn't mean to do it! No animal would deliberately foul its own nest, especially the "thinking animal," homo sapien! Nevertheless, earth, our garden, is being destroyed by pollution, toxic waste, radiation, mining, exploitative gardening, and land development.

The paradox is that the more we innovate to make our planet more commodious, the less habitable it becomes. It seems that we are unable to walk this earth without leaving our footprints, and our trash. One of the young scenario writers in this chapter has captured, in a poetic condensation, the metaphor of our passing:

> She looks down. Her feet have left dry, crushed marks on the grass. It is not as healthy as it looked. In one footprint, a tiny white flower lies, killed by her passing . . . . She weeps for the dead flower, for the weak world and for herself.

> (The Birthday – C. Belling)

We are the thinking animals largely because of our cerebral cortex, that 3½ pound convoluted cauliflower within our skull. This neo (or new) cortex is shared with only a few of our animal brethren and is the most complex brain in all of phylogeny. Perhaps the most uniquely human part of our cortex are the frontal lobes. When we are born, the frontal lobes are "hard wired" already, but they do not begin to manifest their unique abilities until we are about age 12, when we reach what Piaget called "formal operations." This means we become capable of planning for the future and engaging in reflective and abstract thinking. The frontal lobes make these processes possible. They also make worrying possible, a great advantage indeed! As Carl Sagan (1977) put it, "The price we pay for anticipation of the future is anxiety about it. Foretelling disaster is probably not much fun; Pollyanna was much happier than Cassandra. But, the Cassandra components of our nature are necessary to survival" (p. 71).

The second paradox of homo sapiens is that, in spite of the fact that only man possesses the ability to think reflectively, we behave as though we have not been willing to stop and think of our impact upon the garden. Perhaps we do not think of the garden as ours – after all, were we not exiled from it many years ago? The story of the Garden of Eden parallels, in many ways, what anthropologists and brain physiologists have said about the development of our species. According to Sagan, three to four million years go " . . . genus Homo was perfectly interwoven with the other beasts and vegetables" (p. 94). As the noncortex developed, humans became capable of abstract thought and moral judgments. God had specifically forbidden Adam and Eve to possess knowledge of the difference between good and evil. But, the brain developed this ability, and God said " . . . Behold, the man is become as one of us (godlike), to know good and evil; and now, lest he put forth his hand, and take also of the 'Tree of Life,' and eat, and live forever (Genesis 3:22), he must be driven from the Garden" (p. 93). From that time on, we became strangers in our world, able to transcend it with our thoughts, but never again to be fully at home here. Since then, we have struggled with nature, "conquered" nature, and overcome the limitations of nature by our ability to think and plan. John Locke (1975) said, "Beasts abstract not," and as such, they were able to stay in the garden. But, because we alone are able to abstract, we have seized control of both the garden and the beasts. We assumed both were there for our use; many of the beasts are gone forever, and the garden is dying.

The third paradox of our situation is that we adult humans, with fully functioning frontal lobes, should be best at anticipating the outcome of our exploitation and pollution of the environment;

but it is the children who worry – who anticipate that the garden may be lost by the time they become the gardeners. We have considered the children, with their undeveloped frontal lobes, to be notorious for not thinking ahead, living for today, and not fully understanding the serious outcomes of behavior. The scenarios in this chapter point out the irony that it is the adults who are failing to realize our destructive impact on the earth. Many of the writers see threats to the garden as threats to their own creativity. They seem to see the creative forces of nature, as found in the garden, in dynamic interaction with their own creative forces. This perspective comes through clearly in a scenario by 14-year-old Louise Jermyn, of Sawbridge, Herts, England. Here is an excerpt:

> In one corner of the room by the window, I had a small box of earth in which I grew some real food, carrots and herbs. This was strictly forbidden but quite safe because no authorities could ever find out. But there was also no way to cook them. Nevertheless, it was the sheer joy of being able to create something with your own hands by caring for it that compelled me to make this tiny garden.

Perhaps it is us who symbolize Louise Jermyn's "authorities" who are forcing her to entertain her creative urges in secrecy. If this is so, she must despair that we are in charge of tending the garden. Until the gardening becomes her job as tomorrow's adult, she must wait. The children will eventually inherit the earth's garden – what's left of it.

– The Birthday –

C. Belling (Age 17)
Collegiate High School for Girls, Port Elizabeth, RSA

6:28 a.m., 5 August 2010
The blackness parts rapidly and light intrudes. She opens her eyes. As usual, the light is artificial. Sharp and blue-white. It hurts,

but the pain does not enter her consciousness. It merely serves the purpose of awakening her at precisely the right moment.

She lies on her back beside her husband, who is still sleeping soundly. He is only due to awaken in thirty-two minutes' time. By then, she must have prepared his breakfast.

The woman gets up and walks smoothly to the bathroom. She is fully awake now, but she is not really thinking. The routine she follows does not require much thought. Get up, get dressed, make breakfast. Then, after her husband has left for work at 7:28 a.m., she must make the bed and tidy the apartment, and at 8:15 she must leave for work herself. She will arrive at the shop three minutes later, after a walk through long covered corridors, and she will spend the day selling food to younger women who still have children to care for and are thus not required to earn money. She will return home at 5:30 p.m., in time to prepare dinner for her husband who finishes work at six o'clock. They will eat together, and while she washes the dishes he will complete the day's work. A dentist, he has records to keep and cases to consider. They will then retire to bed and sleep. Having already produced and raised two children, a boy and a girl, now both married, they will only sleep.

She follows this same pattern every day. She is happy. She must be, for she is certainly not unhappy. She has all she needs, and is perfectly contented.

This particular morning starts like the rest, except for one rather inconspicuous difference. Today is the anniversary of her birth. She knows because her identification tape has the date, 1965-08-05, imprinted on it, and today is the fifth of August. It is unusual to know the date, but she has kept a careful record of it. In fact, the knowledge is probably unlawful, but she does not worry. Guilt and fear, like pain, are not known to her.

This morning, she is also vaguely aware that what she is doing is unusual when she sits down on her bed instead of making it, and begins counting. She sits there, saying the numbers aloud in the silence of the empty apartment. She is counting years, backward from 2010, using her fingers, until finally she reaches 1965. She gazes down at her hands. They are trembling very slightly.

"Forty-five," she says. "Today I am forty-five years old."

The words seem to solidify before her and their reality suddenly rips into her contentment, shattering it. Forty-five. Concepts she cannot remember ever having considered before suddenly pour into her mind.

Forty-five. Middle-aged. Here I am, halfway through my life. What have I been doing all this time? Questions and doubts and fears grip her. Thinking fills her whole body and in agony she looks about her. She suddenly sees the plastic, windowless room for the first time. She sees the ugliness of the four flat, grey, functional walls. She looks down at herself. Her hands are clinging crab-like to the grey blanket on the bed. She runs into the bathroom. She stands before the mirror. The face staring back at her is one she has never seen before. The eyes are wide with horror, the complacency and emptiness gone from them. Now the mouth is open, screaming. She hears the sound. Her own voice hurling fury at her helplessness, at the years that have wandered past uncounted.

She picks up a heavy bottle and throws it at the face. The mirror shatters, but her reflection is already gone. In the bedroom, she is tearing the sheets from the bed, flinging them across the room.

Later, she sits again on the bed, thinking. She knows she has worked at the shop for 13 years. It is 13 years since she last really thought and now she is desperately trying to recover what her mind has left behind in that time.

Slowly she begins to regain her past. She remembers a world before the one she knows. She remembers a sick Earth, inhabited by people full of hatred and fear, people ruthlessly seeking power and idleness. She remembers the overpopulation and the overcrowding and the tension-breeding wars. She remembers the deterioration of nature's condition, from satisfactory to critical, aggravated by the virulent spread of pollution. Wild animals and plants became rare sights.

She remembers a desperate attempt by a fast-disintegrating World Peace Organization to ensure a future for mankind. A spacecraft, The Tomorrow, was manned by the geniuses of the world, all the people most likely to be useful in rebuilding a ruined world, and, supplied with all they would need for ten years, they orbited the earth safely as planned.

In 1997, there was no peace. The long-imagined nuclear holocaust was imminent. The leaders of the world were waiting, tense, ready to trigger off the weapons made especially to destroy all life on the planet.

One day a small report appeared in a few newspapers, describing the recovery of a spacecraft resembling the Tomorrow from the Pacific Ocean. There was no evidence of human occupants, but a few days later someone reported seeing one of the famous scientists walking along a street in Washington, D.C., and another was seen in Tehran. The appearances were dismissed as hoaxes, for the world was too busy to pay attention to them, and later when the Change came, no one remembered.

She remembers the Change. It was sudden. The leaders of the world powers met and signed a peace agreement. No reason was given, no speeches made. And then, everyone changed. There was no thought of war. There was also no celebration of peace. Everyone became hard-working. Weekends no longer existed, and each person was driven to perform a particular task, repetitively, each day. They erected huge buildings without design, joined them together with corridors, and enclosed the people.

No one thought of recreation, so no one went outside. The war-torn environment was totally ignored by the people, who worked together, mindlessly.

Mindlessly! She stands up, fury filling her. Of course! The minds of these people are no longer their own! They have been taken over, guided by some terrible force. She thinks again of the Tomorrow. The rumoured appearance of the voyagers, the strange behavior of the politicians, and the Change. She begins laughing bitterly. The great plan. Tomorrow. Why shouldn't the

Great Brains take the world for themselves? Why not use us to gain their own power?

She runs from the apartment and hurries along the great, echoing corridors to the Door. She remembers passing it before. It is larger than the apartment doors, and the only one she has never used.

She reaches it and flings it open. Before her stretches the world. Great green plains, bordered by distant purple mountains. Tall trees. Blue sky. The outdoors never looked as beautiful as this before! She is free! Joyous laughter bursts from her, then stops abruptly as she looks again at the idyllic landscape.

It has never looked so beautiful before.

It was NOT that beautiful before!

Thirteen years untouched by man has given the Earth time to recuperate and slowly begin to recover the wild, untouched glory of a far distant time.

She runs out onto the luxuriant grass, all bitterness gone. Whoever they are, they are right! They have saved us! We were killing ourselves and they rescued us.

She looks down. Her feet have left dry, crushed marks on the grass. It is not as healthy as it looked. In one footprint, a tiny white flower lies, killed by her passing. A hard knot of pain forms deep within her, and forces upwards, throbbing, and seeking release behind her eyes. She lies down on the delicate grass and she weeps. In the realization that she must wait, that Earth is not yet ready for man to run free on it again, she weeps for the dead flower, for the weak world, and for herself. For she has not wept for 13 years.

Hours later, she sits up. Her eyes are dry and the pain is gone. She opens the door, and slowly returns along the grey corridor to her apartment, where she begins to make the bed.

She will wait.

– Abraham - His Story –

Julie Horne (Age 15)
North Clayton Senior High School, College Park, GA, USA

Melinda led me down the stairs and into the living area. We came to a door which the seven-year-old opened.

"That's the bathroom," she said. "Everyone will want to see you after you've cleaned up." Then she scampered off.

Still dazed, I stumbled through the door. I leaned my backpack against the wall and rubbed my eyes warily. Even my dreams had not prepared me for everything so fast.

I looked around the room and spotted the soap by the sink. Grinning faintly I amused myself by making it appear in different places around the room. The "powers" I had acquired were still a novelty so I enjoyed playing with them.

Realizing I was wasting time I pulled myself together and began to pull my shaving kit out of my backpack. As I cleaned up I reflected on what had happened to me the last few months.

I had been, and still am, a writer. I had lived in a small cabin in the Rocky Mountains. My cabin was built into the side of a mountain. This, I believe, saved my life.

I had shut myself off from the world to finish a novel. The one T.V. I had was broken and I did not have a newspaper service. The world had been in trouble before I came to my mountain but it was while I was there that it climaxed.

There came a day when I was unable to concentrate on my story. I was very uneasy and I had a terrible feeling that something horrifying was going to happen. Though I tried, I could not shake the feeling. Finally, I sat down to confront what was bothering me.

I saw a troubled world. Children were starving and crime was out of control. Suddenly there were two great flashes of light. They seemed to last forever. The silence was horrible. It was as if millions of voices had cried out and were suddenly silenced.

When the smoke cleared there was little left of the world. It was desolate and barren. Grassless plains held only a handful of survivors.

The terror and senselessness of it jerked me awake. With my heart pounding I realized that the world of destruction was my own. Our whole world was headed for disaster. There was nothing I could do except prepare to wait it out.

I gathered all my possessions and supplies together and stored them in the basement. When I had everything downstairs I knew I was as ready as I could be. I sat down and leaned against the wall, ready to wait forever.

I had stayed in the basement three-and-a-half months when there came a day I knew I must go outside. I climbed the steps and summoned my courage to step outside.

I felt tingly as soon as the morning breezes hit me. Thinking back, I believe it was the small amount of radiation in the air which enabled me to do things I had never done before, such as moving things by just thinking about them. I believe it was also the radiation which gave me a knd of extra-sensory perception.

A little later, I hitched up my backpack and started on my way to anywhere. As I walked I saw that the countryside had changed quite a bit. What had once been the Rockies were mere hills. There was very little vegetation.

I had hiked for many days when I saw a small sign of life. A small flower. I marvelled at its perfect blue petals and green leaves. What I had once taken for granted became a sign of hope. Since it had survived then I could too. I memorized its every detail so I could carry it with me forever.

That night I dreamed of other survivors. Apparently, an entire city had survived. They were just coming back into the world after having lived in a bomb shelter.

The next morning I set off in the direction of the city. Instead of just wandering around, I had a place to go.

One morning, many days later, I paused to catch my breath atop a small hill. As I looked to the north I recognized the ruins of the city.

As I saw my new home from a distance many emotions filled me. I was glad I had survived and found other survivors, but I was sorry that there had been a reason for so few to be left.

As I stood there I actually considered not going to the city. But then I saw a small girl waiting at the edge of a field. Waiting, I realized with a shock, waiting for me. I took a deep breath and started down the hill . . . .

I have lived with the colony for many years now. Our population is about 25. We do not know of any other survivors but we will not give up hope.

Someday, I hope the world will be a better place, but today we live for now. We are a flower of hope in a barren desert. I only hope one day there will be a garden.

– Encounters With Progress –

Merry Clark (Age 16)
Ross Beatty High School, Cassopolis, MI, USA

Date: October 28, 2008
"Dad, there's a man outside who wants to talk to you. Came in a truck that says 'Agri-robotics' on the side, or some strange word like that. Seems like some government guy."

The young boy was just coming in off the fields after a full day of plowing. He and his parents, sister, and two brothers lived in southern Nebraska and had farmed their land for generations. Noah Jasper, the boy's father, had been well aware for quite some time that something such as this was likely to occur. When his exhausted, dust-covered son shuffled in to bring him the news, something seemed to go limp inside of him. His forehead wrinkled into first a puzzled contortion, then became cemented into a worried position. He was a strong-willed man who had developed a certain air of wariness which his life had demanded. He loved the land in its natural state and never stood for injustice – to either nature or people.

Noah approached the man who was wearing a gray suit, sunglasses, and a straight face – not even a wrinkle. As Noah regarded him carefully, the man flashed a smile across the shaded screen of his face and curtly shook Noah's hand. He then flashed his card which declared him a governmental employee.

"Good afternoon. My name is Alan Billings and I have come to introduce you to our brand-new, highly advanced line of planting and harvesting robots. Please step around this way to observe them."

Before Noah had a chance to reply, Mr. Billings was heading for the rear of the incredibly long truck. By the time Noah got there, he was already talking again.

"These are just the operators of the highly technologically modernized harvesting machines that will arrive at a later date. However, I'd like to show you how one of these works now...."

"Wait just a minute, here, hold *on*," Noah interrupted, "I never ordered any of these metallic 'marvels' as you seem to think of them. I don't even have the buying power I'd need to purchase them, I'm not about to let them touch an acre of my land."

Mr. Billings scrowled a bit at this last statement. He knew this man needed to learn quite a few lessons about modernization.

"Sir, the Federal Government has given me strict orders to make sure that every farmer in this state buys his new agricultural machinery. These electronic and mechanical wonders make all other farm equipment absolutely obsolete. They were designed with increased productivity in mind. Therefore, in the long run, you will be able to make up for the cost of your new work force. There is a retraining station near you which will help you change your way of life in such a way that will fully accommodate the robots. If your problem is financial, you may make monthly payments."

Noah was becoming increasingly bewildered and frustrated throughout this mini-speech, voiced monotonously and with no expression whatsoever. He could hardly believe his own government was actually trying to eliminate his, and other farmers' way of life. How could he turn over his lifework to a pack of mindless robots, who can't even care about, let alone *love*, what they are doing? Whether or not a person cares about his work makes a world of difference. Retrained? For what? Noah does not want to be stuck working with robots, in any way. He values his independence.

During Noah's chain of thought Mr. Billings had brought one of the combine operators out and had begun to show Noah which buttons did what. Mr. Billings moved and talked mechanically as he quickly demonstrated what the robot was capable of doing. Is it capable of truly caring for the land? Noah thought. Does a robot have a heart? Can he understand nature? Noah doubted if even Mr. Billings did. He seemed to have spent a little too much time with robots. Noah almost laughed to himself, but the resemblance seemed essentially uncanny. An eerie feeling came over him as he stared at those blank sunglasses.

"Excuse me, Mr. Billings, but would you mind taking off your sunglasses? The sky is quite overcast today, anyway."

"Why?"

"Because I'm about to say something and I need to see your reaction. Most emotion does show in the eyes."

The federal worker shrugged his shoulders and nonchalantly removed his sunglasses. The eyes which emerged from behind the dark shades seemed to have the same blankness the glasses had. This unnerved Noah quite a bit, but nonetheless, he began in earnest.

"Look Billings, I have worked this land for 20 years, using most of my strength to protect it from chemical contamination, which includes herbicides. I've found that I've grown closer to the land, somehow, by putting nothing artificial between me and it. I could never be happy working for someone else. Do you understand?"

He was met by a blank stare, the same look Billings had had on his face throughout the entire episode. He felt as if he was gazing up into the face of automation itself.

"No," stated Billings flatly, "I do not understand. Farmwork is tiresome and often dangerous when done the obsolete way. No one *really* wants to do it, but we must produce food for the growing population. It has soared in recent years. So we have developed this special equipment which will relieve all farmers of their awful burden and produce food more efficiently."

"But I just told you I love this farm – I love bringing food into this world with my *own* two hands. Anything really worth doing takes effort, both physical *and* mental."

"Your government is doing many worthwhile tasks at the push of a button. Your statement does not hold true. We have many plans for this farm, to make it ten times as productive as you, or any amount of human labor could make it."

"Such as?"

"With the incoming robots, building accommodations would have to be made, a few repair shops, storage houses for spare parts, and, of course, a shelter for the robots, would all be necessary. These old barns will have to be replaced with modernized agricultural structures. I will bring back the contract for you to sign that fully explains and describes what will be done. I will also bring you some computerized readouts which show how many farmers have benefited production-wise by updating their robots."

Noah was becoming very upset – he felt a rumbling deep in his soul. His government was taking away his control of his own destiny. His freedom and happiness were on the verge of draining away and the irony of it is that it was one of man's own creations that had pulled the plug. We will soon become their slaves, he thought miserably, building them obsessively in the belief that we can live better, *easier* lives with their "assistance."

The federal worker had donned his sunglasses, and shook Noah's hand. No more was spoken. It seemed there was only one word this man understood: production. Noah stared after him as he drove away, feeling as if he had just been swallowed by a monster and no amount of struggling could set him free.

*　　*　　*

NOTE: The author of this scenario suggests that the solution offered by her scenario might be as follows:

The governmental worker in this scenario had, indeed, been working with robots for much of his life, including his school years. This does affect him in the way that the scenario suggests – he seems to have lost a lot of his sensitivity and expressiveness as well as countless other "human" qualities. Thus, we: National Council of Futurists, would not allow the robot to be anything more than an educational aid – never to entirely take over a class-

room. We would incorporate classes such as "Robots: How they can help and hurt us" into every curriculum of every educational institution. These classes would be made available to the public at large. Literature would also be made available to all – literature containing information as well as various opinions on robots. Robots must never be treated as equal or superior, in *any* way, to humans. There would be many more counselors employed to help us to keep robots in the proper perspective, to make sure people do not become "desensitized" and start to have trouble dealing with humans. Emphasis will be put on what robots *cannot* do, as well as the individuality and independence which only humans can have. We will play up the power of the arts. This should help stem any problems that might occur because of the impact robotics have on life on the planet Earth in the year 2008.

– A Walk To Nowhere –

Catherine Jean Scott (Age 12)
Ellerton Primary School, Three Anchor Bay, RSA

The dry golden sand shifted as the sun moved across the blank void. It had only a few colour changes in it. Everything was blank – expressionless. The sun was like an old man. Everything in the desert was slow – unmoving. The stillness rang in Rozanne's ears. Slowly she picked herself up. Her eyes were tired, smarting from the light of the burning star and the glare from the honeyed sand.

Rozanne was tired – she was weary of trying to explain. Her life so far had been spent trying to explain her fantastic discovery. Earth was dying. She had been dying for a long time. In a month or so the light of life within the earth would be extinguished. Since Rozanne was 18, she had been trying to tell everybody about her fantastic discovery. Now, ten years later, there was very little food and water left. The human race was being eradicated. It was too late now, but maybe ten years ago . . . .

She began to wonder why she was carrying on. What for? She would die with earth anyway. Her calculations showed that the earth was rapidly being pulled towards the sun. Why had

Rozanne left the city? At least there she would have more to eat and drink. Now in this desert she would die of starvation and thirst. What was the use of going on? She would only be going further into an infinite waste – and her already parched throat was allowed only a few drops of the very precious liquid at a time. Would she ever see a gurgling stream? A bubbling brook? Drained, she lifted her feet and began to plod towards – nothingness.

Endless day followed endless day. Rozanne walked as much as was possible, resting when she was tired.

There was a silence so silent that even the heat waves stopped shimmering. The heat hurt Rozanne's burnt-out eyes. She lay down and closed her eyes.

Rozanne couldn't understand why she was doomed to be the last person on earth to die. She had had a perfectly normal childhood, and it was only much later that she discovered that by using numbers she could work out what would happen in the future. When the government heard about Rozanne's gift, they made her make predictive calculations for them. Rozanne resented having to use her gift under conditions of control and command, but as the government allowed her no other form of employment, she couldn't refuse.

How it came about that the earth was being pulled towards the sun Rozanne did not know. She knew only that the earth seemed destined to experience a catastrophic increase of heat and finally disappear inside the sun.

Rozanne stood up. The heat surrounded her, making a hot covering that she wanted to throw off, but the covering melted into her. She felt her insides drying. With a desperate cry she drank. She drank until there was almost nothing left. It was then that she realized that she might actually die before getting to the end of the desert.

Then she saw it! It must have been very tough to survive the heat. At first Rozanne couldn't believe it. But it had to be true! She fell down into the cool peaceful shade of the only surviving tree. She fell into a dreamy monologue and, heat-dazed, addressed the tree.

"When I was younger, dreams of the future began to fill my mind. I had built a dream city in the Karoo."

"Our city would be such a wonderful place that everyone would want to live in it. We chose the Karoo for our new developments because it is so undernourished that there were great doubts as to whether we could ever make it produce any healthy crop of food again. We were going to have all the shops and factories within walking distance, so cars would not be necessary. There would be no racism. It would be a city of peace, love, and understanding. That city of about 1,000 people would be very much in tune with nature. Nature would be all around us. We would be so surrounded with natural beauty that we, in turn, would become more peace-loving and natural. We would fertilize the richer areas of the Karoo until they became rich enough to support trees. These trees would be planted to bring beauty to the city, and to attract rain, so that there would be more water. In the city, everyone would share. Our protein, well, we were going to first move all the cattle and sheep to a more plentiful area, and eat only a few at a time. We would also hunt game and eat it fresh. We would have a more natural existence, so we might actually grow to love and respect the earth more. Our city would truly be a dream paradise."

"Only, my dream became a nightmare. Pollution from the fuel of the new vehicles to take the place of cars was terrible. These new vehicles were even dirtier than cars."

"Society disintegrated. People did not accept their responsibilities. Aggression took over as the dominant emotion. Fighting and civil wars were raging around the world."

"Man's progress heated up the planet with a greenhouse effect, pockmarking the ozone layer. Unseen radiation was making its way into the earth's atmosphere. The all over temperature of our atmosphere increased by 6 degrees C."

"Our scientists were in a desperate hurry to make new fuels and they tried too hard to find new energy sources. Many catastrophic mistakes were made, and people died . . . . "

"The rest of the story is so terrible that I cannot bear to think about it."

Rozanne stayed in the shade for a little longer, and then she struggled up to move on. She would be walking when she died. She would go on walking dead, and only when she arrived at a cool river with fertile banks, would her soul at last rest.

CHAPTER FIFTEEN

This Time They'll All Sing Along

The scenarios selected for this chapter echo the theme of the book. The scenario authors are concerned about tomorrow on the earth, but they are hopeful. They offer visions of people working together in harmony, creating a brighter world. None of the authors are blind to the difficulties involved in creating and maintaining this kind of interdependence and cooperation. They see clearly the need for vigilance and continuous renewal processes, and recognize that this cooperative interaction can be maintained only by mankind exercising creativity, taking risks, exploring new geographical and scientific frontiers, developing new technology, and providing better medical treatment.

It is uncanny that so many of the solutions suggested by the authors in this chapter parallel those offered by leading futurists. An excellent example is futurist Barbara Marx Hubbard's (1983) essay, "The Future of Futurism." She believes, as do our youthful authors, that though threats to human survival are great and increasing every day, human potentials are also growing, and that by combining the best approaches to futurism, we can realize these potentials. She envisions three types of futurism. The first she calls "crisis futurism," and she sees this as essential in analyzing what things we must stop doing and how we can preserve, conserve, rebalance, recycle, renew, and provide for all. The second type is "evolutionary futurism." She views evolutionary futurism as necessary to understanding nature's patterns of transformation, the creation of new systems, and the invention of new capacities in order to envision a positive future. Hubbard believes, however, that both crisis and evolutionary futurism are in deep need of spiritual futurism, the third approach. She suggests that it will be only through the merger of human consciousness with whatever intelligence is creating the universe, only through "the love of each other as integral parts of the same creation, that we can realistically hope to overcome the crisis and actualize our potentials for life ever-evolving" (Hubbard, 1983, p. 57). Like scenario writers Brent Lang, Takuya Ohkubo, and Jim Schafer, Barbara Marx Hubbard believes that work will come to mean the opportunity to create.

Reading through the scenarios in this book, it becomes apparent that children have an amazing grasp of the issues which confront us all; issues which must be dealt with for the future to be a place-in-time where our potentials can be realized. The concern, zeal, and dedication expressed in these scenarios leave no doubt that the children are eager to meet the challenge.

One question still remains unanswered, however. It is a question of process rather than content. You may ask: "What purpose does it serve to ask children from all over the world to create fantasies about the future? Besides clarifying the issues in their minds, are we doing anything more than asking them to worry? Wouldn't it be better to just let them be children, rooted in intuitional and concrete forms of thinking; and to cross that bridge to adulthood when they come to it? Isn't thinking about the future as if we *know* how it will be, a bit delusional, anyway?"

While we pose these questions as straw men, they surely need to be addressed. Parents and educators asking such questions are not those with their heads in the sand, but those who want us to explain how we are helping children by compelling them to think about the future. They worry that we are asking too much of our children; after all, don't children already know too much for their own good these days?

The most obvious answer is that we are helping to prepare the next generations of adults to be informed and not to stumble blindly into the future. But beyond that, we are giving them the opportunity to take active control of their future. When people do not understand something, it turns into a mystery which often becomes fearsome and negative in their minds. Even if we might wish the children would stop concerning themselves with the future, they will not. Given this, we must help them reduce their negative images of the future by understanding its opportunities as well as possible. Through scenario writing, children's future images are symbolized in poetic form. Implicit and unclear dread becomes explicit and more clear. In a discussion of the relationship between poetry and mental health, author Silvano Arieti (1976) advises, "If you experience an unhealthy emotional attitude, express it openly and it will clear up. If you hide it inside yourself it will grow . . . " (p. 149). The reader will note how many scenarios seem to possess the element of poetic catharsis. By representing their fears, as well as their hopes, the children are better able to gain control of their attitudes and channel their energies toward making a difference in the future.

If scenario writing did nothing more than help children become better informed about issues we all face, and clearer about their personal concerns, this would be ample justification for scenario writing as an activity for children. We believe, however, that scenario writing also teaches children to think. Edward de Bono (1983) has said that good thinking is not simply a matter of intelligence; it is a skill to be practiced in challenging situations. Unless we help children practice thinking, their intelligence lies dormant, without a medium for expression. There are several ways in which scenario writing helps children to think, including helping them comprehend their knowledge and apply it in a more or less, true-to-life setting; distinguishing important details from non-essential ones; evaluating current ideas in light of their implications; and helping the children connect their affective and cognitive understandings.

Perhaps most important, scenario writing helps children develop the abstract and planful thinking considered to be the mark of a mature adult. This kind of thinking, considered a function of the brain's frontal lobes (see Chapter 14), is necessary, for humans to mentally transcend their here and now existence and to keep future events from taking them by surprise. Our own generation, which has apparently neglected to refine these skills, is only now beginning to realize that if we had "thought ahead," perhaps the ecological disasters we are facing now could have been avoided. It is clear that the old adage "take things as they come" is insufficient for a world blindly stumbling into its future.

Scenario writing is excellent discipline and training in two modes of planful thinking: One could be called the scientific "if-then" and the other the creaative "as-if" (Presbury, 1984). Through the scientific "if-then," children are able to connect what they know about cause and effect relationships and extrapolate today's events into the future. For instance, from what they know about the availability of fossil-fuels on this planet, the children are able to predict the demise of gasoline powered vehicles and to begin a mental search for logical alternatives. This problem-solving strategy, practiced in scenario writing, teaches them ways to think of answers for many other future problems.

The future is an abstraction. We can never know the future as we know today. Even though children can use what they know of their current experiences to construct scenarios of the future, they are aware of speaking of future events "as-if" they had actually lived these events. Thus, scenario writers are forced into using metaphor in which they must presume that parts of the future will be "something like" today. In their thinking, the children must construct models of tomorrow which look like what they know today, and then alter those models according to their "if-then" predictions.

When a child is asked to make an "exciting story" about the year 2010 in which he or she is the central character, the child constructs a metaphorical model based on now, and alters the model on the basis of "if-then" considerations. But, since the task is an "as-if," the child is then free to decide how it will all turn out. In doing so, it is necessary to find possibilities which "if-then" thinking, which is bound to the facts, cannot do. The child, wishing a happy ending for the story, must create a means by which such an outcome is possible. If our children can do this, they will be able to avert future mistakes in a way never before possible. With such models to toy with, the children are no longer stuck with how it must be, but can now speculate about how it could be. According to Jaynes (1976), such model building is the basis of all scientific breakthroughs.

Scenario writing is many things. It is a way for children to become informed about the world in which they live. It is a way for them to express attitudes about that world. And, it is a way for them to learn to think of ways to make the world better. But scenario writing is also art. Even a casual reading of the stories in this book will reveal the powerful aesthetic capabilities of the children. Some scenarios are touching, while others are inspirational, humorous, or surprisingly clever. All are a medium for creative expression by the children who wrote them. They are all beautiful, each in their own way. Even if they served no other purpose, they are a wonderful way for us to see into the hearts and minds of children. "Spiritual futurism" is the union of the children with the universe – the infinitesimal with the infinite.

– 2010: A Better World –

Brent Lang (Age 14)
Cedar Park High School, Portland, OR, USA

In the future, our world will become a better place to live, because of improvements in medicine and technology. Man will begin to see new horizons by exploring space and the oceans and will learn more about how to use the earth and the sun more efficiently.

First of all, in 2010, the greatest improvement to the world will be in communications. People will be able to communicate by linked computers, telephones, televisions, and other new devices. This will enable people to work at home on computers and converse with other employees at the touch of a button. Improved communications will also totally change how we buy products. Everything will be bought by television computer links, where the products will be displayed and priced for the consumer. Not only shopping, but voting, making bank deposits, and making many other kinds of transactions will be done this way. All of these will cut down the amount of travel to nearly nothing. This will also save time, which can then be spent with families, reducing the divorce rate, and forming closer and stronger family ties. The time might also be used for hobbies, fitness, or sports, producing happy and healthier people. It will also give more time for reading and discovering what has happened in the past, seeing the mistakes made by others, and letting their errors help us to make the right decisions for the future. Less travel will save gasoline, and fewer cars will mean less pollution. This cut in the number of cars will mean that people won't have to fight the traffic each morning, which will keep them in a better overall state of mind. Altogether, lots of improvements in communications will make a big improvement in our lives.

The use of computers is another area which will increase in importance in our lives. The computerization of the earth will cause the disappearance of most of our menial jobs. For example, at a subway station, there will be machines that will accept money, calculate the cost of the journey, dispense the ticket, and give the change. These tickets will automatically open chutes down onto the platform where an automatically driven train will come. Another example is in factories where people work in assembly lines, doing the same job over and over. In the future, all of this will be done by machines. This mechanization will mean that people will no longer have to do these menial, boring jobs.

But, what will these people do? Basically, while computers do boring, repetitive jobs, man will usually use his creativity to expand his world and himself. He will go into the new, exciting fields of space, chemistry, and medicine, or the ocean.

Space will introduce new working environments which will better suit the production of some items. People will be needed to do research to create these new products and also to develop and construct the space modules where they will be located. Lots of people will be needed for space exploration, to seek new lands and people. These discoveries will be very important because observations of other beings, their behavior, and their way of life, may give us ideas of how to live our lives better.

In the medical and chemical fields, lots of work can be done dealing with creating new molecular structures, fighting diseases, preventing birth deformities, and introducing new things such as clones. Also, chemicals for destroying wastes, producing energy, and killing unwanted pests will be developed. These things will help clean up our world and make it a better place to live.

In the oceans, the research that can be done is endless. There are millions of new species of plants and animals that have not yet been investigated or even discovered. The sea will be a great area for planting food, and hatcheries, for mass fish production, can be built to supply great amounts of food to the world. Also, the immense power of the waves, tides, and currents will be very useful when better ways of collecting and transferring this energy are developed. But, as we explore the sea and develop its resources, we need to remember how we ruined the earth, so this doesn't happen again. If we take care of the sea, it will become a very useful area for producing food and our ideal source of energy.

Another area of improvement will be in farming developments and land use efficiencies. This will especially improve the present Third World countries where there are great areas of wasted land. This land will be farmed far more efficiently with the help of irrigation canals, higher volume producing crops, and future developments in fertilizers. Man may also have more control over the weather. This would help in making decisions about planting and harvesting times and in protecting the crops from frost, overheating, drought, or flooding. Food will also be prevented from being wasted by improvements in transportation. By quick freezing or drying the foods first, they will not spoil and it will make the transportation quicker, easier, and less expensive. These methods of farming, which we are only just beginning to understand, will help us to use the earth better.

The use of the sun's energy also has great potential for man in the future. We are only just starting to comprehend the sun's great force and its importance to man. We are already using its power for heating, solar panels, electricity, solar cells, and farming, greenhouses. But the use of the sun's energy won't stop here. In space, where the sun always shines, it can be used for constant growing, propelling space ships, and for collecting energy, which can be brought back and used on earth. The sun is a whole new frontier, which we know very little about now, but which will be very important to man in the future.

In the future people will be more free to take part in activities they enjoy, at a time convenient to them. They will have more interesting and challenging jobs, in new exciting fields. On earth, man will continue to learn how to use his surroundings and enjoy them more and more. While in the oceans and in space, man will have a new horizon, with a new collection of knowledge and experience to be gained. In a way the earth was like a new toy given to a baby with no instructions. At first, when the baby doesn't know how to use the toy and its features properly, the toy seems worthless. But, when the baby learns how to use it, the baby enjoys it very much. In this same way, as man learns to use the earth and its resources during this age of exciting new discoveries and developments, life will be a joy to live.

– The Right Actions At The Right Time –

Ronan O. Caollai (Age 10)
Scoil Naithi Primary School, Dublin, Ireland

2010! Here I am, forty years of age, sitting in my office at the spaceport waiting for my next flight to the moon. I wonder if there will be any vacancies on this flight. I suppose not, seeing that there is such a big demand for such trips. Many people travel in space nowadays – past-times, holidays, and adventures are the motives for most people. That leaves me a very busy man.

This could not have been imagined thirty years ago. People at that time never realized that hovercraft would replace motor-cars. At that time, only the Taoiseach of our country used a helicopter to go on holidays and to meetings. Talking about politicians, many of them seemed to be in power for wrong reasons, they seemed to be interested only in publicity and travel.

"Enter the European Economic Community," they advised the people of Ireland, "and all would be well." People believed them and we joined in 1973. Things did not turn out as promised. Ten years later we had thousands more people unemployed. Factories and other places of employment were closing every day. Shops were full of imported goods, and Irish goods were difficult to obtain.

This seemed very unfair and worse still that people were willing to sit back and do nothing about it. Having discussed this with some of my friends, we decided that we, the youth of Ireland, must try and change the situation.

The older generation had their chance and their say. We formed a political party and set about getting the country out of the Common Market. We succeeded and thanks to our efforts, things are very different today.

Inflation is down and very few people are unemployed. Agriculture and other industries have prospered. We were right. Ireland is now a much better country to live in.

We have special machines for cleaning up polluted rivers. Pollution thirty years ago caused a lot of damage. It killed a lot of our fish and wildlife. We took the right action at the right time. The ill-effects of pollutions are minimized very much now. We have achieved a lot in forty years, but we must keep going or it will all be in vain. We must give the youth a chance to be involved. This is the way to ensure continuity of what we started in our youth.

– Men Worthy Of A New Era –

Kaori Nishizono (Age 17)
Osaka, Japan

The year is 2010. What am I doing at this time? In 1983 when I was completing high school, I had expected to be married and at the height of rearing children at this time. At that time I had thought it would be a valuable life-job to bear and bring up the next generation. I took pride in this.

I did not realize that such pride was about to be taken from us. The population increased each year and there were shortages of food. The number of jobless people was the highest in history. Pollution had reached an intolerable level. The world was faced with an unprecedented crisis. The United Nations reached the conclusion that overpopulation is the cause of all of our problems. It decreed that it was necessary to reform mankind for us to have any future. It resolved that the population must be reduced two-thirds the present level in 50 years.

As a first step, birth control was decreed throughout the world. "The number of children in each home is ideally one at most. Let us think of the happiness of a child newly born." This catch phrase was really effective. When I was growing up it was thought that the ideal number of children in a family was two or three. I thought that were no choice but to have two or three children.

But times changed. They are now going to prohibit having a child in marriage. Test-tube babies, not by natural means, are made by the artificial uterus. One test-tube baby will be supplied to each of the specially selected couples from among applicants.

When I heard the news that this proposition was approved, I felt my back go cold at the same time as I was astonished. I wonder what the government will think.

"We can control the population by doing so, and we can bring up men worthy of the new era."

Men worthy of a new era! What kind of men does it mean? Does it mean perfectly gentle, socially obedient, and colorless men? Even if it gives an advantage for mankind's future, we can never accept such a humiliating system at all.

Whether or not we give birth to a child is our problem and we have rights to decide it. And at the same time we have an obligation to keep these rights.

If we ask the question of the cause of the crisis we are facing today. Isn't the reason that we did as we pleased on the earth without having a natural enemy for a long time? We cannot help falling if human beings are ruined by accepting punishment.

Will it be better for us if we have many parent-child relationships with no blood relation after 20 years from now? Even if the government practices such a life control, will there be true happiness in the future of newborn babies? They must feel something insufficient, even if they are physically and socially satisfied. However, after a while people will not see anything wrong with it.

Now many people are protesting in a loud voice, holding demonstrations, campaigning, and collecting signatures everywhere. I also am going to take part in these campaigns positively to keep the natural rights of mothers as a woman . . . . And for the happiness of my children and newborn children in the future.

– Half A Brain –

Jim Schafer (Age 17)
Mainland Regional High School, Linwood, NJ, USA

March 17, 2010, Government Headquarters Main Computer Terminal, Washington, D.C.

"Hey Joe, why are you here so early?"

"Special assignment for the President, Ken."

"The President! What does she want with us?"

"She wants whatever we have on a Jim Schafer."

"Jim Schafer, who is he?"

"This year is an election year and the President wants to find out who the nameless leader of the people's movement is. The movement is growing and she wants to eliminate him."

"Is the movement that strong?"

"I don't think it has peaked yet, but she fears the people are getting smart. You know what that would mean."

"People having freedom similar to the way it was in the 18th century? I can't see that happening!"

"Maybe. Rumor has it she has the people stirred up just thinking on their own."

"Well, let's run him through the computer."

"I hope we come up negative like the rest."

"Yeah, I'd like to see the guy get a chance to speak his mind!"

(The two run the name through the computer.)

"Holy shit! It's him!"

"Sure looks that way."

"Man, he has kept himself busy. Look at this record. It dates back to his high school days. It says here he went underground about ten years ago. That's why they haven't realized it was him sooner."

"Just read this:"

Personal Report File
Code: Red
Criminalistic Series
Political Disk
Name: James Joseph Schafer
Wanted for: Illegal Political Movements
Treason
Dangerous: Kill on Sight

1980: Head of American Civil Liberties Union. Led many demonstrations against nuclear arms, governmental control, mind control, and illegal actions ignored by government. Won many leadership awards and was active in sports and student government. (Government action team assigned to investigate him.)

1981: Put more power in students hands than any other school in the nation. Action team sent in to control things. Scandal set up to discredit guidance counselor and Schafer. But too much faith invested in him by students. Plan backfires. Recipient of more leadership awards and recognized as the leader of school.

1982: Following tremendous. Schafer starts to touch other schools. South Jersey is governmental nightmare. Fear of losing control of younger generation is widespread. Better conceived scandal is performed and he is arrested on graduation day. Following loses faith and hope temporarily.

1983: Jailed for six months and released with no fear of returning to power. Schafer enters North Carolina University at Chapel Hill. He becomes leader of insignificant Civil Liberties Union. Schafer is watched constantly anyway.

1984: Honors in pre-law program. Rumors spread that he is head of underground people's movement under the cover of his small Civil Liberties Union: nothing can be traced to Schafer.

1985: Continued honors at U.N.C. Interrogated for allegations pertaining to underground movement. Interrogations turn up nothing. Schafer disciplined to break him down. He turns down nomination for president of student body.

1986: Graduates number one in his class and is accepted into Harvard School of Law.

1987: Becomes head of another small Civil Liberties Union. Watched closely for underground ties.

1988: Honors in law program. Schafer turns down nomination for president of Young Republicans. His Liberties Union is inactive and he resigns.

1989: Honors in law program. Fear of regaining power is lost and watch on Schafer is dropped.

1990: Graduated number one in his class and goes into corporate law. Recognized for his new bold, innovative ways in business law.

1991: Recognized as the tops in his field. He wins many cases in the supreme court representing business against the government. Schafer now has very powerful friends. Watch is again commenced.

1992: Schafer begins defending the common people. He is now a national hero. Rumors again begin of a movement but investigation is negative.

1993: Schafer denies he will pursue politics.

1994: Schafer takes sabbatical to Paris to "find himself." Action team reports Schafer is nowhere to be found in Paris. He is spotted speaking to groups all over Europe. Investigation proves he was lecturing on freedom but nothing derogatory is spoken against present administration.

1995: Schafer goes back to law career.

1996: Awarded Bar Association highest honor for star-studded career.

1999: Scandal breaks out. Numerous claims of ties to underground movement surface. Order immediate capture and execution is handed down by president. Search for Schafer begins.

2000: Schafer cannot be found. Underground movement quiet.

PRESIDENTIAL SUMMARY

Schafer must be eliminated. Without his leadership the people's movement will die forever and we shall be secure. If he is not eliminated, the people will rule and we shall perish.

President Helen Gordon

"Wow! That's pretty heavy stuff. He created a real threat! What are you doing! Why are you burning that?"

"He is the people's last chance. He is our last chance. I wish you luck, Jim Schafer."

"Yeah, good luck. But you'll need more than that."

Little did Ken and Joe know, the entire period Schafer had gone underground, he had made amazing breakthroughs in mental telepathy and brain research by inventing the chemical KN-BC, a substance that makes the intuitive half of the brain dominant. By doing so, his tests showed that mental communication increased tremendously and, over an extended period of time, moral values increased in those same individuals. It didn't take long for the people to take to Schafer's idea. His following became so strong that there was no need for the present government to resist. This was the ultimate as far as he was concerned. Before long, the unthinkable was accomplished. A world united under true democratic values. This world was not without conflict, but it was without violence.

– The Year 2010: Good Times –

Takuya Ohkubo (Age 10)
Osaka, Japan

Now, it is the year 2010. Transportation facilities have improved greatly since I was a fourth grader and people are well off. Linear motor cars run on land. There are space stations in the cosmos and space shuttles come and go regularly. Whenever we become ill, science has already developed a cure, even for cancer and Kawasaki disease. When I was a child, many people died of these diseases. Since these and other developments of science make people live longer, there has been overpopulation. This will soon be relieved by the space stations. Many people will begin moving to the space stations from now on.

I had a dream during my childhood. It was that I would become a veterinarian and take care of many animals or devote myself to the study of animal languages. When I was five years old, I read through 20 books which Reatonbirjus wrote about animals. When I entered elementary school, I read dozens of animal books like Seaton's records about animals and Doritol's story. I was crazy about watching TV programs and films about animals like the story about a fox living in the northern part of Japan, cheers for living creatures, the wild kingdom, and Uncle Mutsugoro's tales, etc. Even when I was enjoying playing with my friends, as soon as the time for the TV program came, I would go back home flying and watch it.

I used to take a net and insect cage with me on summer days. I often surprised my mother by catching many kinds of insects and living things. I sometimes forgot myself when I was insect catching and lost track of time. Often, when I did not come home before dark in the evening, my mother would be worried. After I entered elementary school, I got a chicken and fed it. Before five months had passed, she grew awfully big and began laying eggs. After I came home from school every day, it was one of my pleasures to go to the hen house to see whether she had laid an egg. My pleasure at that time lives in my memory even now. I made a pet of this hen and was proud of her.

I made up my mind to major in veterinary medicine at the university. When I went to the university, I became absorbed in the study of animal language until late at night and I sometimes forgot to take a meal. As a result of all of these efforts, I can speak animal languages now and enjoy travelling with animals. In addition, I have invented many medicines for curing the diseases of animals. These medicines have saved the lives of many animals throughout the world. When a letter from someone asks me to cure an animal, I am full of the feeling of wanting to go wherever the animal is and curing it.

There is something else about the year 2010 that delights me. It seems that people throughout the world are beginning to read the textbook I wrote on animal languages many years ago. As a result, many people are promoting the better understanding of animals and the people themselves are getting along better with one another. I think it was really good to actualize these things which I hoped for in my childhood. Now, I live happily, making pets of animals.

The world continues to be peaceful without war. People seem to communicate better with one another, understand one another better, and lead happy lives. People from different countries are studying the migration to Mars and are getting ready to colonize this planet. Thus, science continues to develop and people are well off and peaceful in the year 2010. Now my heart is full of joy when I realize that this human society has resulted from human effort, understanding, communication, and kindness.

*   *   *

NOTE: The above scenario was translated into English by Professor Ryoji Sakai of Aichi-Gakuin University, Aichi, Japan, while he was a visiting scholar at the University of Georgia.

– November 4, 2010: The Matter of Anna Cronin –

Lynn Bongiorno (Age 14)
River Dell Regional Senior High School, Oradell, NJ, USA

". . . and I, Dr. Frank Harris, as board chairman of this Xerox complex number 52613, would like to discuss with you a topic which has already been negotiated with our worthy competitors: IBM and AT&T. I will explain to you the circumstances. In our fast-pulsing technological society, there still exist those few who, for some reason beyond my grasp, naively choose to dwell in those settlements they term a "home." Since the overwhelming majority of the population elects to reside in our inviting establishments, fully equipped with every necessity (enhanced, indeed, by a variety of luxuries), sales agents of these "homes" will soon be insolvent. Upon their unfortunate demise, the inhabitants of the "homes" will be left without a supplier, and will be forced to turn to . . . us. For this reason, our complex supervisors have assigned to us, the medical division, the task of preparing the coming residents physically, mentally, and emotionally for a life within our complex. In turn, I am assigning each of you a specific way to evaluate the "homers." Dr. Lee, as our psychiatrist, your duty is to determine exactly how much stress these misguided and anachronistic people can withstand."

"Of course," consented Dr. Lee.

"You, Dr. Bongiorno."

"Yes, sir?"

"You, as an obstetrician, will have one of the most significant tasks. In conformance with our medical regulations, you will perform an amniocentesis procedure on every pregnant woman of the homes."

"I see no difficulty, sir, since this practice has long been mandatory in order to avoid the unthinkable possibility of a handicapped citizen's entering our world."

"We'll see how readily your patients comply with this requirement. Please return in one week to report progress. Here is a roster of the "homers" you must seek out. Remember, they have not been trained in medical ethics as you were at Harvard."

"No need to worry, Dr. Harris. I'll have the problem under control in no time at all."

Upon reentering her own office, Dr. Bongiorno nonchalantly tossed upon her secretary's desk the roster of pregnant homers. "Set up appointments with each of these ladies within the week."

"Fine, Doctor," came the crisp reply.

An hour passed before the secretary returned with the results of her queries. "Everybody but one has consented, doctor."

"Who is this?"

"One Anna Cronin. In so many words, she has vowed never to set foot in our wonderful complex! How absurd!"

"Indeed. Did she offer any explanation?"

"Oh, yes. She claimed we were a society obsessed with perfection and devoid of human diversity."

"What a witless woman she must be. All right, Sarah, I'll handle this myself. Thank you."

Well, I suppose I'll have to lower myself to a homer's level and actually visit her. The procedure must be done, and evidently this Anna woman will *not* come to us. I'll convince her now, and in two years she'll be begging to stay here; what's more, she'll be grateful for this act of civilized restraint.

After three more days and three more fruitless calls to Anna Cronin, Dr. Bongiorno impatiently called for a car to drive her to the woman's house. To her, the variety in house design reflected untidiness. How could one live in such a disorganized fashion? What a chore it would be, properly conditioning these ignorants!

The noticeably pregnant woman who received Dr. Bongiorno was rather short. Her brown eyes looked serene as she greeted the doctor and glanced briefly at her medical bag.

"You must be Mrs. Cronin," Dr. Bongiorno began tentatively.

"Yes, I am. And who are you?"

"I am Dr. Lynn Bongiorno from the Xerox complex number 52613. I am sure you have received my calls. Evidently you follow some sort of occupation which has prevented you from visiting our hospital facilities. I have, therefore, come myself to perform the amniocentesis procedure here in your own quarters."

"Nothing hinders me from getting to your office, doctor. I am a social worker, and regularly visit the survivors of your assault upon this town. The plain truth is I do not want to venture into such a setting."

"Then would you allow me to enter your home?" asked the doctor.

"I suppose it can't be helped," was the indifferent reply, as Anna showed the doctor into her quaint living room. Her furniture included many old pieces and, as she later explained, other relics for home use which had been handed down from generation to generation. Unseemly photographs from the past hung about the walls.

Dr. Bongiorno was perplexed. "Where is your computer screen? We need it to complete the procedure," she explained, searching the room.

"I wouldn't worry, doctor. Under no circumstances will I submit to amniocentesis."

Impossible! I have strict instructions to screen every pregnant woman for any possible defect in her unborn child. A handicapped infant has no place in our world. Our complex quarters cannot be altered for individual needs. We are better off without such freaks, believe me. Most handicapped persons cannot fend for themselves, much less contribute to society in any productive fashion. Why should we indulge in such burdens?" demanded the doctor.

"They can love us, and we can love them! Has your society deteriorated to the point where love doesn't count anymore?"

Love . . . I seemed to remember that word. My professors at Harvard had demonstrated quite convincingly that this decadent emotion impeded the progress of technology. Past life had suffocated under the pressures of intra-personal relationship. "Well, Mrs. Cronin, I see I am wasting my breath trying to convince you of the necessity of this procedure. There are more sensible women waiting for me up at the complex. In case you should change your mind, you know where to reach me."

The following day, Dr. Bongiorno's video screen directed her to report to Dr. Harris' office.

"So, Dr. Bongiorno, did you find your patients as compliant as you had expected?"

"Oh, yes, Dr. Harris, every woman was quite agreeable, except for one."

"What do you mean 'except for one?'"

"Well, doctor, a Mrs. Anna Cronin was quite vehement in condemning our philosophy. I simply ignored her."

"Such aberrant behavior! Nevertheless, her defiance gives us even more reason to perform amniocentesis, and I am reprimanding you for not fulfilling the task I had assigned. Do not return here without the results of that test! Sally, send in Dr. Lee."

Walking back to her office, Dr. Bongiorno imagined that the eyes of her colleagues were staring at her accusingly. No, she would not approach Mrs. Cronin again and submit to the woman's scorn.

During the following weeks Dr. Bongiorno busied herself with trifling research labs and minor appointments. She was always "too busy" to return Dr. Harris' calls. Finally, however, she could no longer dodge his persistent badgering. She would have to pay that terrible woman a second visit.

Reaching the street, Dr. Bongiorno, again affronted by a variety of housefronts, noted that many cars lined the sides of the road (there must have been at least four!). One man was limping frantically toward Mrs. Cronin's home, the center of much commotion.

"What is going on here?" demanded the doctor.

"Why, dear Anna Cronin has gone into labor! We've all come to help out," explained a teen-ager who spoke with a slight speech impediment.

This outlandish personal cooperation shocked Dr. Bongiorno. But she rushed into the house to play her part as doctor. As she crossed the threshold, several thoughts raced through her mind: What if the child is handicapped? "Get that amniocentesis done, Bongiorno, or you'll pay for it with your job!" Just at that moment, the birth protest of a new-born reverberated throughout the dwelling, as if announcing, "Here I am, world. Make room for me!" Dr. Bongiorno hastened to the bedroom to encounter three excited people: an elderly woman dressed as a nurse, Mrs. Cronin, and her red-faced and vociferous baby boy. The doctor approached the nurse, "How did *you* manage to deliver a child under such primitive conditions?"

No reply acknowledged her curiosity. The nurse merely gaped at the physician, her hands busy with her patients.

"Sondra can't answer you, Doctor Bongiorno: Mrs. Mum was born mute. Luckily she came here just in time to deliver my baby."

Doctor Bongiorno's attention shifted to the bundle held by Mrs. Cronin as if the two were still one. The mother crooned,

"How precious, precious, what a wonderful gift, what a beautiful baby."

Doctor Bongiorno leaned over and peered into the now quiet blanket. She winced at the scarlet birthmark disfiguring one cheek.

"Would you care to hold him, Doctor?" she heard Mrs. Cronin offer.

As if on cue, the baby stretched out its arms, thrusting two small fists into Dr. Bongiorno's face. At this, she tumbled backwards. One arm was observably shorter than the other and seemed capable of only partial movement.

And yet the mother's eyes gleamed with happiness and pride. She touched the impaired limb lightly, lovingly, as she placed the baby in Dr. Bongiorno's arms.

Some wall of resistance within the doctor fell apart. She gathered up the warm little bundle and heard her own words dropping joyfully into the silence of the room: "Oh, what a love," she murmured.

References

Apple, M. W. (1983). Curriculum in the year 2000: Tensions and possibilities. *Phi Delta Kappan, 64,* 321-326.

Arieti, S. (1976). *Creativity: The magical synthesis.* New York: Basic Books.

Barney, G. O. (Project Director) (1983). *The global 2000 report to the president: Entering the twenty-first century.* New York: Penguin Books.

Beasley, W. M. (1985). Microcomputer applications in the education of the gifted. *Dissertation Abstracts International, 45,* 2832A.

Bigner, J. J. (1983). *Human development: A life span approach.* New York: Macmillan.

Bruner, J. S. (1966). *Toward a theory of instruction.* Cambridge: Harvard University Press.

Buchwald, A. (1983, November). Capitol punishment: Put on a happy face. *Washington Post,* page 1.

Burchard, H. (1983, November). A legacy of Jewish art and suffering. *Washington Post,* Weekend, page 41.

Clark, B. (1983). *Growing up gifted* (2nd ed.). Columbus, OH: Merrill.

Collier, A. (1977). *R. D. Laing: The philosophy politics of psychotherapy.* New York: Pantheon Books.

Cornish, E. (1977). *The study of the future.* Washington, DC: World Future Society.

de Bono, E. (1983). The direct teaching of thinking as a skill. *Phi Delta Kappan, 64* (10), 703-708.

Educators for Social Responsibility (1983). *Dialogue: A teaching guide to nuclear issues* and *Perspectives: A teaching guide to concepts of peace.* Cambridge, MA: Author.

Erickson, E. (1950). *Childhood and society.* New York: Norton.

Erickson, E. (1964). *Insight and responsibility.* New York: Norton.

Fishman, C. (1983, November). Unicorn was product of promoter's imagination. *Washington Post,* page Metro B-1.

Flavell, J. H. (1977). *Cognitive development.* Englewood Cliffs, NJ: Prentice-Hall.

Glasser, W. (1969). *Schools without failure.* New York: Harper & Row.

Gordon, W. J. J. (1961). *Synectics.* New York: Harper & Row.

Guralnik, D. B. (Ed.) (1972). *Webster's New World Dictionary of the American Language: Second College Edition.* New York: World Publishing.

Hawkes, G. W. (1983). *What about the children?: The threat of nuclear war and our responsibility to preserve this planet for future generations.* Mooretown, VT: Parents and Teachers for Social Responsibility, Inc.

Henderson, M. (1983). *Coping with loss – A series of training workshops for professionals in the field of death and dying.* Staunton, VA: Full Circle Counseling.

Hubbard, B. M. (1983). The future of futurism: Creating a new synthesis. *The Futurist, 17* (2), 52-58.

Jaynes, J. (1976). *The origin of consciousness in the breakdown of the bicameral mind.* Boston: Houghton Mifflin.

Kahn, H., & Wiener, A. J. (1967). *The year 2000: A framework for speculation on the next thirty-three years.* New York: Macmillan.

Kilpatrick, J. (1981). The coming catastrophe. *Nation's Business, 69* (2), 17.

Kubler-Ross, E. (1975). *Death: The final stage of growth.* Englewood Cliffs, NJ: Prentice-Hall.

Laycock, G. (1973). *Autumn of the eagle.* New York: Charles Scribner's & Sons.

Locke, J. (1975). *An essay in human understanding.* In P. H. Nidditch (Ed.), incomplete, Oxford: Oxford University Press.

Masuda, Y. (1981). *The information society as post-industrial society.* Tokyo, Japan: Institute for the Information Society.

May, R. (1969). *Love and will.* New York: Norton.

Plowman, P. (1979). Futuristic views of gifted. *Gifted Child Education, 1,* 142-155.

Polak, F. L. (1971). *Prognostics.* New York: Elsevier.

Polak, F. L. (1973). *The image of the future.* New York: Elsevier.

Presbury, J. (1984). *Using a token system to teach thinking: Blending behaviorist technique with cognitive theory.* Unpublished paper, James Madison University.

Reston, J., Jr. (1983). Herman Kahn's final vision. *Omni, 5* (12), 68-76.

Richmond Times Dispatch, November 8, 1983, page 4.

Smith, W. (1983). 'Day after' shocks some. *The Red and Black, 91* (34), 1.

Safter, H. T. (1983). A phenomenological case study of highly gifted and creative adolescents. (Doctoral dissertation, University of Georgia). *Dissertation Abstracts International, 44,* 443. (University Microfilms No. 831 4744)

Sagan, C. (1977). *The dragons of Eden: Speculations on the evolution of human intelligence.* New York: Random House.

Shiras, W. H. (1974). In hiding. In B. Bova (Ed.), *The science fiction hall of fame.* Vol. IIB. New York: Avon.

Singer, B. D. (1974). The future focused role image. In A. Toffler (Ed.), *Learning for tomorrow.* New York: Vintage.

Tate, A. (1952). Narcissus as narcissus. In B. Ghiselin (Ed.), *The creative process.* New York: New American Library.

Toffler, A. (1974). *Learning for tomorrow.* New York: Vintage.

Torrance, E. P. (1962). *Guiding creative talent.* Englewood Cliffs, NJ: Prentice-Hall.

Torrance, E. P. (1965). *Mental health and constructive behavior.* Belmont, CA: Wadsworth.

Torrance, E. P. (1971). Stimulation, enjoyment, and originality in dyadic creativity. *Journal of Educational Psychology, 62,* 45-49.

Torrance, E. P. (1975). Sociodrama as a creative problem solving approach to studying the future. *Journal of Creative Behavior, 9,* 182-195.

Torrance, E. P. (1976). Creativity and mental health. In S. Arieti & G. Chrzanowski (Eds.), *New dimensions in psychiatry, Vol. 2.* New York: Basic Books.

Torrance, E. P. (1977). Enriching images of the future. *Gifted Education Newsletter, 3* (4), 3-9.

Torrance, E. P., & Hall, L. K. (1980). Assessing the further reaches of creative potential. *Journal of Creative Behavior, 14,* 1-19.

Torrance, E. P. (1981). Predicting creative achievements of elementary school children (1958-80) – And the teacher who made a difference. *Gifted Child Quarterly, 25,* 55-62.

Torrance, E. P. (1983a). The importance of falling in love with 'something.' *Creative Child and Adult Quarterly, 7,* 72-78.

Torrance, E. P. (1983b). Status of creative women: Past, present, future. *Creative Child and Adult Quarterly, 8,* 135-144.

Verney, P. (1979). *Animals in peril: Man's war against wildlife.* Provo, UT: Brigham Young University.

Vogel, E. F. (1979). *Japan as number one: Lessons for America.* Cambridge, MA: Harvard University Press.

Webster, N. (1978). *Webster's Scholastic Dictionary.* New York: Airmont Publishing.